THE DESCENT
OF WOMEN

by

Frederick Sontag

Other Books by Frederick Sontag

Divine Perfection: Possible Ideas of God, 1962

The Existentialist Prolegomena: To a Future Metaphysics, 1969

The Future of Theology: A Philosophical Basis for Contemporary Protestant Theology, 1969

The Crisis of Faith: A Protestant Witness in Rome

The God of Evil: An Argument from the Existence of the Devil, 1970

God, Why Did You Do That?, 1970

The Problems of Metaphysics, 1970

How Philosophy Shapes Theology: Problems in the Philosophy of Religion, 1971

The American Religious Experience: The Roots, Trends and the Future of American Theology (with John K. Roth), 1972

Love Beyond Pain: Mysticism Within Christianity, 1977

Sun Myung Moon and the Unification Church, 1977

God and America's Future (with John K. Roth), 1977

What can God Do?, 1979

A Kierkegaard Handbook, 1979

The Elements of Philosophy, 1984

The Questions of Philosophy (with John K. Roth), 1988

Emotion: Its Role in Understanding and Decision, 1989

The Return of the Gods: A Philosophical/Theological Reappraisal of the Works of Ernest Becker, 1989.

Uncertain Truth

Wittgenstein and the Mystical

The Acts of the Trinity

Forthcoming

Truth and Imagination: The Universe Within

THE DESCENT OF WOMEN

Frederick Sontag

PARAGON HOUSE
St. Paul, Minnesota

Published in the United States of America by

Paragon House
2700 University Avenue West
St. Paul, Minnesota 55114

Library of Congress Catalog-in-Publication Data

Sontag, Frederick.
    The Descent of Women / Frederick Sontag.
        p. cm.
    Includes bibliographical references, index.
    ISBN 1-55778-719-0 (pbk.)
    1. Feminist theory. 2. Feminism—History 3. Sex role.
I. Title.
HQ1190.S66   1997
305.42'01—dc21
                                      97-19626
                                          CIP

For the Eves, Marys, and, perhaps especially, the Carols of your human history, who have given of themselves for the sake of all of us. We celebrate their collective ascent.

"He has routed the proud of heart, He has pulled down the princes from their thrones and exalted the lowly."

Luke 1: 51-52, The Jerusalem Bible

Acknowledgments

Given the massive amount of literature and the rapid shifts in trends, this book project has been in process for several years. However, this and three other manuscripts were essentially completed during a fruitful sabbatical year, 1991-1992. The first summer was spent at the University of Hawaii and then the academic year as a visiting fellow at Jesus College Cambridge.

That four manuscripts could have come to some form of completion in this time is largely due to the generous hospitality of the Chairman and Department of Philosophy at the University of Hawaii and the Master, Lord Renfrew, and the Fellows of Jesus College, Cambridge.

These two venues proved to be an extraordinarily fruitful setting to bring these projects to completion, and so my thanks must go to these two institutions and their faculties for inviting me to join them for a time.

Since returning home to Claremont from Cambridge, the manuscript has gone through extensive revisions, and for the final preparation of the manuscript for publication, I owe many thanks to my research assistant, Eirik Harris.

Table of Contents

INTRODUCTION

Anyone who wants to write on any aspect of The Feminist Movement in the late Twentieth Century should first read three cover magazine articles all of which, coincidentally as far as anyone knows, came out in September/October of 1993.

As The Movement gained power and prominence, many of its vocal spokespersons (if not every woman) seemed to assume: (1) that all women would unite across every cultural, economic barrier including race and religion, and would find solidarity and power in their new-found identity in sisterhood; (2) that the common identity for all women which would result would be distinguishable from all "male-dominated" cultures that had preceded it; and (3) that by so doing, women, all women, could hope to rise to the fulfillment of heretofore repressed potentials.

Few can doubt that, at least in some societies and in some circles, women have recently risen to new levels of responsibility, prominence, and productivity. Although differences had been emerging until 'difference' itself was said to be a cause for Feminist celebration, the Fall of 1993 still serves as the symbol of a watershed. It is the time when all illusion of unanimity based on sex or gender role disappeared.

Then, is there nothing left to write about "The Feminist Movement" taken as a whole? Certainly there is. The facts of women's recent achievements are too well documented, the inspired debate too prominent, and the fresh perspective given to ancient questions too illuminating.

What this present essay proposes to offer is not a "history of feminism in our time." That would be a massive bibliographical project, as a reading of any publisher's list of new books on or by women would indicate. Certainly the following account does not intend to be a polemic, a "backlash," or a diatribe. What is at stake in the issues which women have raised is too important for them and for all human beings,

but every critical evaluation of recent results is welcome as a step toward a proper perspective.

However, inspired by Darwin's account of our long upward struggle toward dominance in the animal kingdom, our thesis is: That it is time for all of us, male and female alike, of whatever religion or race or culture, to set this important and massive "media revolution" into the context of the human animal's long struggle to improve its lot and to take control of its destiny.

If we assume this approach, Feminism does not lose its distinctiveness. Viewed from either a sex or a gender category, this revolution has shaken too much thinking, altered too many social, political, and family structures, caused so much useful—if at times skewed—debate that its dramatic effects are by now a matter of historical record. But can both sexes, and all in the human-animal kingdom, gain by seeking our ancient common roots, our ancestral "common cause"?

The joy of the Movement now lies in its diversity and in the room for debate that it has opened up, as *Ms.* reports.[1] If so, there can be no monolithic view to which everyone must conform; intellectual heresy is no longer possible in Feminism. Individual women cannot "break ranks," if there is no rigid rank established to begin with. We are back to Socrates and the edification which dialogue offers us about serious issues, but only if we do not expect dogmatic conclusions. Yet Bell Hooks reports, "To me the essence of feminism is opposition to patriarchy and sexist oppression" (p. 35). However, just what these key terms mean lies at the heart of the matter, since 'diversity' and 'debate' have no fixed meanings. Not everyone—in fact perhaps always only a minority—will struggle for a cause, even a just one.

Yet when Bell Hooks says, "What produces a feminist movement is...commitment...to feminist politics" (p. 42), one immediately infers that if "no intellectual agreement, then no movement." A discussion

---

[1] "Let's Get Real About Feminism," *Ms.*, 34-43.

group is edifying, but it cannot be counted on to change much socially. "We are talking about a left, revolutionary movement" (ibid.), she still concludes. But given the agreement to accept dissent, that cannot be assumed to be the feminist "common cause." "Different women define and relate to feminism differently," Wendy Kramer concludes[2] (p. 53). If so, then no single voice can claim to speak for all women if "unease with the term 'feminism' has been a persistent concern in the feminist movement" (p. 56).

If Carol Gilligan's conclusion is accepted, "that women share a different voice and different moral sensibilities" (p. 59), when this is put together with the stress on diversity and the opposition to unified ideology, such a 'different voice' must apply to one woman vs. another and so excludes any unified stand for "all women." Yet Wendy Kramer opposes any movement that encourages people to feel fragile and helpless, and she concludes that "women need a feminist movement that makes them feel strong" (p. 66). However, surely that sentiment applies equally to male and to female, to all individuals in the human race. Such spreading out of "the lessons of feminism" to embrace everyone, regardless of sex or race, may be feminism's "most enduring contribution."

Mother Jones reviewed Women's Study courses and their curriculum[3], and it is clear that diversity, which is so prized by this generation, is entering into Women's Studies. "Diversity is the mantra of both students and professors, but it doesn't apply to political opinions," (p. 4) they stated. Yet the separation of the political and the academic is emerging again. "Students go to college to be academically challenged, not cared for" (p. 49). "There's a huge difference between conceding that education has political elements and intentionally politicizing" (p. 51). "A distinction has to be made between historical interpretation of

---

[2] "Feminism's Identity Crisis," *Atlantic*, Oct. 1993, 51-68.

[3] "Our Minds, Our Selves: Is feminist education limiting her potential?" *Mother Jones*, Sept./Oct. 1993, 45-68.

the past and political reinterpretation" (*ibid.*).

The notion that only women have suffered and only males have subjugated others vastly oversimplifies the complexity of the human drama, its highs and its lows. Such simplification cannot lead to our much needed correction and change. Women have also been protected and venerated, just as some men are compassionate and just. The difference in our time lies in the recent medical control of birth. Pregnancy and its threat subjugated women more than any other single factor, surely, even if it did ease life in certain ways, for example, by offering security in a home. But now those physical bonds have been loosened, and this means that a new relationship between the sexes is possible.

However, we need to trace our history even further than to the Garden of Eden, further even than the history of consciousness, if we are to set ourselves in Darwin's Time. It is a farce to think of early man, seeing beside him a woman with a dozen children in various degrees of health, herself racked by the life-threatening trauma of childbirth, somehow consciously inventing "patriarchy" to subjugate women. It simply was not possible, until very recently in our history, for the majority of women to seek public opportunities on a level with men. This still is not possible for all women, but it is now for many. "The Conspiracy Theory" of male domination is a red herring on the trail to enhanced human rights.

Once upon a time, many advances were either denied to us or were rare and were achieved only by the valiant few. There were heroes, male and female divinities, but they were few and far between. As we humans take the reins of destiny into our hands, first very gradually and then increasingly in recent centuries, we must beware of simple solutions. Where male and female are concerned, few universals hold, except the biological, and even these lines are often blurred. Where political orders are concerned, revolutions may be possible, but we must be cautious of the ever-new tyrannies that too often result. Where sex is concerned, "revolution" is probably an illusory term. Gradual, partial, a never-guaranteed change for all, is more the rule.

Chapter I

Selection in Relation to Sex

A. The Descent of Man

Everyone knows that by "the descent of man" Charles Darwin meant the rise from our lowly origins to our present standing as a sometimes ruling species. This is his account of how over millenniums, we improved our status in the animal kingdom by struggle, pain, and loss and so achieved a measure of intelligent self-direction. Everyone also knows, or should know, that in *The Descent of Man*[4] Darwin includes both sexes. In point of fact, Darwin considers the sexual division of the human race to be a crucial item in our evolution, since not all species are sexually divided as we are. His immense book (475 pp.), which followed *The Origin of Species, The Descent of Man*, carried a subtitle: "*and selection in relation to sex.*" Darwin's 'plot' (to follow Gillian Beer's analysis of his theory's focus)[5] gives sex a wide role in our development "up from slime." Given our intense recent interest in women's "struggle up toward an equal share in the light" it might be instructive to use Darwin's account to try to parallel "The Descent of Women."

Our aim is to see if Darwin's story of our common rise gives us any insight into why both sexes did not rise to equal levels at the same time and under the same conditions, given how important he sees sexual division to be in the roles we achieved within our species. Since our origins go far back beyond our acquisition of intelligence, no conscious forces can have played an early role. If 'patriarchy' arose as a dominant concept or rule in our cultures, it could not have been consciously exercised when humans were "emerging from the swamp." Yet Darwin

---

[4] Charles Darwin, *The Descent of Man* (Princeton: Princeton University Press, 1981). All pages referenced in this chapter are to this edition.
[5] Gillian Beer, *Darwin's Plot* (London: ARK, 1985).

gives sexual selection a major role in the evolution of the human species so that our physiological distinction is a part of our rise. But did it at the same time prevent the equal rise of both sexes?

Beer offers one insight: "In contrast to other species (where the female most commonly holds the power of [sexual] selection), among humankind the male dominates choice. This reversal creates crucial difficulties," she adds with typical British understatement (p. 211). Beer's analysis of Darwin's method of constructing his evolutionary theory is to compare it to the development of the plot in a work of fiction. Her subtitle is "Evolutionary Narratives in Darwin, George Eliot and Nineteenth Century Fiction." After analyzing Darwin's theory formation by comparing it to the fiction in his time with which he was familiar, she goes on to show how his evolutionary theme was picked up by novelists in the time following Darwin.

"Can fiction in return," she asks, "restore to the female the power of selection which, Darwin held, mankind had taken away? And can women writing, shape new future stories?" (p. 218). Since increased choice for all women is a prime goal of our age, understanding how natural selection worked to give her a sometimes second status might help women increase the conscious direction of their own descent.

Furthermore, in a time in which our reigning theories stress so fundamentally the distinction between 'sex' and 'gender' roles, Darwin certainly might help us to see how these were at first linked in our descent, that is, in the ascent into our present hierarchies. His *Descent of Man* not only stresses the role he sees sexual selection to have played in the evolution of our human species, but he is at great pains to try to extrapolate from all this an account of our cultural, intellectual, and moral "rise from the swamp." Darwin's convictions about our lowly origins in no way makes him demean human accomplishments. Our physical progress toward exercising a self-direction of control has led to (although not by some necessary, directed process) our recent and still current leading estate.

Of course, since Darwin sees all evolution as the result of a struggle for survival, it should not really surprise us that he sees women's status developing as one result of this natural struggle, or that we should find women's attempts to improve their status involved in intense struggle yesterday, today and always. Such is the reigning mechanism in our biology, and this natural possessiveness and aggressiveness has in fact led to the much improved status as we have over other animals. So we must not treat the struggle demanded for survival, or for improvement, as all bad, for example, complain about backlash. It is nature's own way. And there is no improvement in the species without it, wasteful and painful and chaotic as it usually is. Beer speaks of the infusion of dread into the process and sees it "as part of the special condition and particular power of women" (p. 221). There are some by-products in women's status due to the operation of sexual selection that gives her a certain power, as well as certain restrictions, in her developed biological role. Such paradoxes are inherent in our evolutionary process, as all Existentialists will be glad to hear.

"Fear is a response to danger, but also to repression" (p. 228), Beer concluded. But there is another side to this biological coin, "Passivity and silence may be means of insurrection..." (p. 229). Women's biological status as 'the second sex' leads to the natural formation of the technique of passive resistance, so much stressed of late for all revolutionary causes. But for women this is, evidently, biologically founded. Yet the way sexual selection operated in our descent at the same time gave women a naturally exalted status, as Beer points out. Woman is the premier representative of the fecundity which has enabled those outside the parkland to endure. We know about Darwin's stress on the necessity for overproduction in the species in order for evolution to take place. This places women's reproductive capacities, so much more crucial in earlier days than today, at the center of our primitive struggle for survival.

If we give an account of 'the origin of species' A.D. (After Darwin), women are central to the whole drama of our rise, and we all know it. Can it be that, as her role as biological reproducer lessens, her central—and correct—role in our struggle to survive as a species is forgotten or understressed in 'advanced societies'? When we speak of evolution, woman is a better symbol than man if we are to gain an understanding of our origins and of how we came to our present status in the physical world alongside the animals.

'Plenitude' is a key Darwinian concept in evolutionary theory. Without fecundity and surplus, there would be no evolution, no descent, that is, no rise. Yet Darwin's attention to this crucial symbolic role for women in our achieved survival carries with it not only a privileged place for women but the dark side of our pressing to limit all of them to this role. Retracing his account, what clues can it offer us for the descent of women, that is, their ascent, to a different role in the human process today?

In sketching this, we need to be aware of Darwin's stress on chance, on struggle, and on pain and suffering. It is part of our evolution which he both accepts and stresses as necessary. For Darwin, neither man nor woman started from some idyllic life or status from which we somehow fell into the bondage of a lower estate. Men could not consciously have held women in bondage to a second status at the start, since there was no intelligence present in our origins. That appeared only late on a scene where instincts had long dominated, just as our developed instincts are still important today, even after the arrival of intelligent thought.

Darwin sees no easy utopias. Irony and paradox come easily into his plot. There can be no single, simple role for women just as there cannot be for men. There can be change in our species—that is his central theme. But this comes not without considerable pain, struggle, and loss. Survival, even improvement in our status, is possible, but it can be neither simple nor easy nor guaranteed against future loss. Without constant effort to ascend, it is all too easy to descend to a former estate.

B. The Origin of Inequality

In their introduction to *The Descent of Man*,[6] John Bonner and Robert May have offered an overview of Darwin's theories on sex and selection, particularly highlighting the knowledge about biological inheritance we possess but which Darwin could not have. What is amazing is their continued recognition of the value to his theories, even granting its outdated portions. Where women are concerned, the Descent is important because he delves into cultural history and development, some of which of course is quite dated and rooted to his time. Yet other suggestions about the role which sex plays in natural selection, and the resultant effect it has on women's status, are still insightful.

Had Darwin read de Beauvoir's *The Second Sex*,[7] he could have

---

[6] See note four above.

[7] De Beauvoir, Simone, *The Second Sex*. Trans. and Ed. H. M. Parshley. (London: Picador Classics, 1988). *The Ethics of Ambiguity*, Trans. B. Frechtman, Citadel Press, Secaucus, NJ, 1980; *Memoirs of a Dutiful Daughter*, Trans. J. Kirkup. Harper and Row, New York, 1959.

Like all important authors, de Beauvior is difficult to pin down precisely. She is J.P. Sartre's long-time friend, like him a novelist, and also a contributor to Existentialist thought. However, her massive volume, *The Second Sex*, is widely regarded as one basis for the form which the contemporary women's movement took after the demise of the women's suffrage movement. However, more than most outspoken feminists might like, de Beauvoir sees women's situation as ambiguous, much like all of life. She uses concepts borrowed from both phenomonology (the Other) and Existentialism (ambiguity) and applies them to her comprehensive study of women's situation. She stresses the need, as Existentialists do, to achieve clarity and understanding, almost more than social action, but women have been forced to occupy a secondary place in relation to men. Women fail to take a place of human dignity as free and independent existents. This is a call which Existentialism gives to all human beings, but de Beauvoir finds it particularly applicable to women. "Equality is not quite her call, since she observes that neither men nor women enjoy working under feminine direction."

A radical she is not, partly because Existentialism calls more for understanding and acceptance than for social revolution. De Beauvoir does think that things are changing, and for the better for women, but this is due more to general social movements than to women's actions, she suggests. Every female is not necessarily a woman. "She must share in that mysterious and threatening reality known as femininity (p. 13)." So there is a "feminine

used that title, in one sense, due to the restricted role which the dominance of men placed women in. But he would have rejected her account in another sense, in that he found feminine birth and fecundity to be metaphors absolutely central to the origin of species as we find them. It is from the female of the species that the plenitude comes which allows for our ascent. Darwin makes the crucial and central role of women quite clear.

---

mystique"; it derives from our uncertainty about femininity. Women must themselves bring about the change from inessential to essential. But women have "no past, no history, no relation of their own (p. 19)." They are often more attached to certain men than they are other women. The two components (male, female) are necessary to one another, but woman is Other. Of course some are pleased with their role. The eternal feminine corresponds to the black soul and the Jewish character. "But women today are in a fair way to dethrone the myth of femininity (p. 32)." De Beauvoir then gives us a long account of the data of biology on the subject (Book I, Pt. I) and the psychoanalytic point of view (Chap. 2). A woman defines herself by dealing with nature in her emotional life. But it is impossible to bring the sexual instinct under a code of regulations. Part II gives an historical review, and, counter to the notions of peacefulness, she finds that "woman has shared in warfare and with no less ferocity and cruelty than man (p. 93)."

"Christian ideology has contributed no little to the oppression of women," she observes (p. 128). But neither did the French Revolution change the lot of women, as expected. "During the Revolution women enjoyed a liberty that was anarchic. But when society underwent reorganization, she was firmly enslaved anew (p. 141)." Part III then examines myths. For woman, man is sex and carnality, but she has never proclaimed it as men have done for women. She treats elaborately the myths of women as they appear in five authors, but she notes that a number of incompatible myths exist (p. 283). Part IV then treats the women's Formative Years, next the Lesbian, the Mother and the married woman, prostitution, and old age. But "women have never constituted a closed and independent society (p. 608)," she concludes.

In Part VI de Beauvoir considers the Narcissist, the women we love, and the mystic. But in the final section, Part VII, she moves "Toward Liberation." Her model is "the independent woman." There always will be difficulties, but the independent woman "has chosen battle rather than resignation (p. 696)." De Beauvoir concludes, "today neither men nor women are satisfied with each other (p. 725)." Instead of wishing to put man in prison, woman endeavors to escape from one. She seeks "to emerge, herself, into the light of transcendence (p. 726)." But as an existentialist, de Beauvoir sees that submission instead "is the temptation of ever existent in the anxiety of liberty (p. 730)." But, "her destiny is not predetermined for all eternity (p. 734)." In the existentialist formula, existence precedes essence.

6

In *The Descent of Man*, Darwin shifts away from strictly biological forces. He wants to study "intelligence as a central feature of adaptive change (Introduction, p. vii)." Physical, physiological sex differentiation was important as we emerged from the swamps and in this the female is crucial. But if we want to understand male-female roles differently, we must see how the dawn of intelligence eventually took over as a deciding factor, for good or for ill. In the recent feminist pressure for gender roles with increased fluidity, Darwin offers support; the general character of the two species changes over time and so is not fixed by nature.[8] Even in the evolutionary process itself, or perhaps particularly in that process, adaptation is crucial to survival. Absolutely fixed sex roles, in our pre-history, in recorded history or now, would inhibit adaptive behavior and thus is a deterrent to both sexes. Our ability to change is crucial to continued survival. To fix either sex in one role is stagnation.

On the other hand, less favorable to feminists' goals for change is Darwin's insistence that modification results from and demands a 'struggle for existence'. Individuals with certain variations may be and probably are favored. Feminist proposals for change should not expect to go unopposed. There is no need to cry 'backlash', since the very law of survival is struggle, which has not been lost as civilizations emerge. Every action spawns its reaction. The process is now the same; it is only subjected to a particular civilized dress and more subtle discourse. Certainly, Darwin's thesis gives the male an original advantage. His theme: Certain traits in the male, and sometimes in the female, make him or her more successful in mating. The result is a

---

[8]   Cynthia Cockburn, *Machinery of Dominance* (Boston: Northeastern University Press, 1988), p. 2, 240.

Research finds women still filling relatively routine occupations. A misunderstanding of technology is partly at fault. There are processes of tremendous powers sustaining the sexual division of labor. Technology is a medium of power, but the author acknowledges women's reluctance to take up technical careers. The book then moves on to outline a detailed study in Britain on the sexual division of labor.

dimorphism between the sexes. (Darwin might have more trouble accounting for gay or lesbian views on the selection of partners.) But Darwin did not begin by either affirming or complaining that inequalities exist. He simply observed. It was a fact that variability existed. It needs explanation, not condemnation.

The Descent begins as a materialistic description, but Darwin wanted to extend it to account for both the rise of cultures and the differences in people and civilizations. Today we might contrast 'gene inheritance' with the inheritance of 'habits'. Darwin did not have our sophisticated knowledge of genes, but the distinction he draws is quite similar. The body of man or woman is a biological structure. But our culture can now move on a new hierarchical level of intelligence. If Darwin felt that "evolutionary biology had nothing to tell us about this higher level" (Introduction, p. xxii), it is also true that the cultural level we achieve is not fixed by the more deterministic operations of natural selection—thus he allows for chance. There are many varying cultures and one constant biology, all of which illustrates the greater cultural patterns open to us by choice. But even these are also threatened by constant struggle and threatened loss.

The Descent focuses on the relation of cultural change to evolutionary change vs. *The Origin* which outlined biological selection. Where male-female is concerned, we might speak of this as 'biological sex' vs. 'gender roles'. But we must realize that Darwin does not divorce the two. Rather, he wants to set cultural patterns on a higher plain; yet at the same time he sees these in relation to a harsh set of sexual characteristics and relationships which are never fully excluded.

For one thing, he portrays what we might call a 'crossover' between the sexes of their characteristics. Virginia Woolf's *Orlando*[9] would not seem to him a complete fantasy. His is a story of subtle

---

[9] Virginia Woolf, *Orlando* (Oxford: Oxford University Press, 1992).

interplay between the sexes, variation in roles. But always a simple, crass, physical feature of attraction is at the core and plays a basic role. We can talk of "genes in the sex chromosomes" being expressed differently in the two sexes, but Darwin was content to see that characteristics could be shared or passed from one sex to another. As sexes, we are inevitably linked together by our descent.[10]

Darwin presents one underlying issue in our evolution which in many ways is still the same: the question of the evolutionary advantage of sex itself. We all know Darwin's central theme: the fittest survives in the struggle; the weakest does not; strong characteristics thus naturally survive and are inherited, leading to the continuance of some species and the loss of others. Sex obviously plays a role in evolutionary selection. Does it advantage one sex over the other? It must, or else it would not be so prominent, both in our biological history and in our cultural evolution. "Is there an evolutionary basis for social organization in animals?" he asks. We know his answer must be "yes". But as we seek today to detach gender roles from sex and to make the two move distinctly, it would pay us to ask if the primary role of sex in our evolutionary history retains such influence in defining cultural roles that we cannot eliminate it.

Darwin states the central theme: "Species are the modified descendants of other species" (p. 1). But in this investigation he wants to ask

---

[10]   J. K. Conway, S. C. Bourque, and J. W. Scott, ed. *Learning About Women: Gender, Politics and Power* (Ann Arbor: University of Michigan Press, 1989).

The word "gender" was conspicuous for its absence in the 60s, but the current stress on the term implicitly rejects the idea that "biology is destiny." However, gender cannot remain narrowly defined. It must include women and men. But there is a tendency to reject what formerly were supported as "liberal ideas" as unsympathetic to current goals. The early women's movement stressed liberal philosophies, but "women have not made the political strides that early advocates of universal suffrage anticipated" (p. x). There is a revolution in child care, but still, for instance, "only a small number of British women will opt for a career in politics" (ibid)

Advances have not resulted in a wholly new political or psychological environment (p. xv). And there are complex social and cultural processes in which the differences between men and women are neither apparent nor clear-cut.

9

how the relationship between the sexes is a descent of the evolutionary process too. This does not at all fix the relationship between the sexes permanently; in fact it does the opposite. The very process by which all things emerge is subject to great variation. And sexual selection not only alters relations between sexes, "It seemed to be highly likely that sexual selection has played an important part in differentiating the races of man" (p. 4). Since we bear in our bodies clear traces of our descent from some lower forms, we know that our structure has not always been the same. Thus, change is characteristic and is the standard way in behavior modification, not fixity. In fact, rigidity in behavior and failure to adapt to change is the classic key to extinction ('Male chauvinists', General Motors, reactionaries of all kinds, take note.)

In our bodily structure, we bear traces of our descent from lower forms. In parallel, all women today bear in their reproductive organs evidence of a time when, of necessity, this was their chief biological function. But it need not be so today, any more so than males must behave in a 'primitive' fashion, once we have 'advanced' to form cultures and morals. Yet our more primitive forms of behavior are still there, always just below a cultured surface, as global-wide slaughter today attests. We are always subject to the instincts of the struggle for survival. This means the constant presence of pain and suffering.

We must work constantly if we are not to regress to that level, since our connection to our primitive origins is still all too direct. Thus, women must move to rise above their still simple biological function, which Darwin admits served them well in surviving in their evolution and so is still important. Birth control, which was a delayed discovery in the emergence of intelligence, allows the biology of sex to be diminished in importance. But it will still be uppermost in many minds governed by instinct, both male and female. We discount the force of the means of our successful biological survival at our own peril of experiencing its powerful, even destructive, reassertion.

Darwin's most important message for feminists who are determined to achieve change away from inherited sex roles: "Man ([i.e., both sexes] is variable in body and in mind; and that variations are induced, either directly or indirectly, by the same general causes, and obey the same general laws, as with lower animals" (p. 135), as the current global savagery which we witness attests. Our cultural idols can easily become savage too, as we know. Yet what Darwin gives to revolutionaries with one hand (the biological basis for variability in body and mind) he takes away with the other (our bodies and our minds are subject to the same laws that govern lower animals). Thus, we forget our kinship with our animal cousins and forbearers at our peril, since our cultures came out of a sometimes terrifying struggle to rise above our biological origins.

Darwin's view is not the phrase "biology is destiny," not at all, since his study convinces him of the immense changes we have already gone through. Our roles were not fixed in advance. Yet he sees contradictions and perils everywhere. Life does not grow without consequent loss. The very process of struggle which brought us here operates still, even if the emergence of intelligence allows us to adapt to change, as few of our animal cousins can. Still, we must be constantly aware both of where our intellectual powers came from and what forces lie beneath them.

Conclusion? Darwin is no romantic about progress, in fact the opposite, "We must remember that progress is no inevitable rule" (p. 277). Evolution has led to civilizations of various kinds; he does not rank them all as equal. But our evolution came out of a struggle in which the fittest survived. Competition was brutal and still can be brutal, even if now we sometimes wear golden gloves.

However, all great theorists have their lapses into inconsistencies. Darwin is so impressed with the spread of Western, that is, largely British, culture that he forgets his own origins and predicts that "At some future period ... the civilized races of man will almost certainly eliminate and replace throughout the world the savage races" (p. 201, "Britannia Rules"). In evolutionary struggle, replacement is possible, but the very basis of the power of our evolution lies almost closer to savage ways than to culture. Darwin might not have been so optimistic had he witnessed the twentieth century as it concludes.

In his optimism over the rise of cultures, he also momentarily forgets the contingency of the whole process, a fact which he has so often stressed in opposition to all necessity and certainty. "If a single link in this chain had never existed, man would not have been exactly what he is now" (p. 213). So if we misstep once in our cultural evolution, all advance can be negated (Achtung, all Feminists). Hegel, it turns out, did not sufficiently appreciate the operation of chaos in biology; all loss does not lead to progress but just as well to regress, not necessarily to synthesize.

Time is irrelevant when the length of our painful ascent reaches beyond history and beyond our comprehension. "History" is a late comer, whose very driving forces are non-historical, just as intelligence emerges from instinct and physical struggle only tentatively but never without retaining the interfering forces of the power that instinct had before consciousness emerged. Human consciousness is not autonomous, and it will lose its power if cut off from biology. The same lessons can be transferred across to women's struggle for change and a greater independence from their biology. This is possible; it may even be desirable, but do not consider it inevitable or able to detach itself entirely from our ancient biological origins or roles.[11]

This account involves Darwin's highly suggestive, if not fully factual, views on the role of 'sexual selection' in adaptive change. As noted earlier, regarding the primary power of the female in sexual selection, which he also notes in other animals, he gives the primary selective role to the male, that is, where humans are concerned. This leads to strengths bred into the male that gives him enhanced survival

---

[11] Carol Christ, *Diving Deep and Surfacing, Women Writers on Spiritual Quest* (Boston: Beacon Press, 1980).

Christ states, "I am seeking to find a voice and style of writing that is passionate, personal, political and scholarly, and reflective" (p. xi). She proposes that we give up our quest to ally ourselves with a transcendent source of power. The goal of the mystical quest is to understand that we are part of the world. "The telling of women's spiritual quest has the power to transform our lives and our relation to the world in which we live" (p. xxiii).

power and thus an edge in dominance, in spite of the central role which Darwin always gives to fecundity. Intelligence, as biologically biases, may modify this, but thought will always find physiological forces just beneath its surface.

Intelligence can now assert itself to become an adaptive force and so achieve a measure of self-direction. However, no necessity governs it, directing it either to succeed or to fail in its intent. It is never totally autonomous or free of physical interference. Sexual selection, he concludes, "appears to have acted as powerfully on man [i.e., on both sexes] as on many other animals" (p. 249). Saint Francis was only speaking a biological fact when he called animals his brothers, but he could still opt out of sexual selection through celibacy. Through achieved intelligence, we can still say today, our most significant determinations come.

The question is how far have we been modified through our sexual selection and still are. Darwin is intently interested in secondary sexual characteristics, some of which we might call gender roles. These are not the physical roles themselves, but he still connects them "with the acts of reproduction" (p. 253). If this is at all correct, we must be careful in claiming any total freedom of gender roles from biological sexual reproduction. Even if this does no longer totally determine us now, it is a force of ancient power still to be reckoned with.

This is so primarily because sexual reproduction is—and was—a force in our ascent. Thus, if women wish to ascend, for example, descend further from our non-human origins, this is quite possible. But the power of sexual reproduction can never be ignored, primarily because its power is still ever present, as every celibate monk or priest or nun knows. Tabloid journals would have less fun with our public figures if our leaders could rise above their reproductive attractions and claim immunity, like the diplomat's immunity from local laws. The very forces which account for our ascent to such religious or political heights in itself denies us exemption from the power of sex. Thus, our constant 'sex scandals' are not likely to cease.

Here is Darwin's vies of the origins of inequality between the sexes: "Sexual selection must have come into action, for the males have acquired their present structure, not in being better fitted to survive in the struggle for existence, but from having transmitted this advantage to their male offspring alone" (p. 257). We leave to geneticists to assess the literal corrections of Darwin's conclusion. Still, his insight into the origins of dimorphism between the sexes is enlightening. His is a more physical story than the average account of the origin of patriarchy,[12] but quite probably he has touched a more basic factor.

In support of the feminist's agenda for change, note that he specifically denies that men are in any sense 'better' fitted to survive. He feels that he must always give a powerful importance to female fecundity, since it is the stuff of our progress and must be acknowledged to be so by all males. Culture's mores do tend to overlay the primary importance of women's reproductive role. But this can never lie far beneath our consciousness, really, not even for the most sophisticated cultures, as the popular play, "Dangerous Liaisons," portrays so graphically.

Although on Darwin's account "Male dominance" is sexually based, it can also be consciously exercised and thus may be consciously modified—within the limits of biology. Men "know what they are about and consciously exert their mental and bodily powers" (p. 258). So of course do women. But sexual selection has given men some biological advantages for dominance. This is his thesis. This is Darwin's plot. However, when we try consciously to alter this dominance by the use of "mental and bodily powers," we must not forget that both our intellect and our consciousness do not float free in full self-control. These powers are still biologically derived and so are subject to the same power struggles that brought us forth on these continents as a new species, to paraphrase Lincoln.

---

[12] See Gerda Lerner, *The Creation of the Patriarchy* (New York: Oxford University Press, 1986).

"Sexual selection has played an important part in the history of the organic world" (p. 259). We are "blowing on the wind" if we deny its still potent, if subliminal, power. Camelot can exist "for one brief hour," whether in California, in St. Petersburg or in Washington. Yet it is haunted, if not faulted, by the power of sexual selection constantly working at odds with noble ideology. Still, The Feminist Camelot can be brought to exist, even if precariously.

Sexual selection does not act with the overbearing power and the necessity of a Hegelian rational dialectic. It "acts in a less rigorous manner than natural selection" (p. 278). Parents and priests can urge the young to control their sex drives and not be completely unrealistic in doing so. Priors can administer oaths of celibacy to monks and not consider their exhortations to be an impossible reversal of nature. Sex need not rule us uncontrolled. Remember that Darwin had placed a strong element of chance and contingency in even the process of natural selection.

Our biology allows us a flexibility derived from the very process by which we have been formed as a species, but not if we deny the power of the selective process or the key role which sexual selection once did occupy and still may. Our sex roles are far from fixed. In fact, the opposite. Their very origins indicate their instability. In the *Genesis* account, Adam was born male, Eve female. But this was not due to the fixity and definiteness of our distant swampy origins. Definite roles were achieved; they are not original.

Darwin actually sees great flexibility as possible in our sexual roles. We might call these gender roles, but in fact Darwin would probably be reluctant to distance gender too far from sex, given the power of our biological origins. Still, "one sex may lose characteristics proper to it, and may thus come to resemble to a certain extent the opposite sex" (p. 284). Again, Virginia Woolf's *Orlando* is as much fact as fantasy. These variations are of course possible, since our evolution depends on variations for its advance. Anyone who argues for fixed sex roles determined either by culture or by biology does not know where he or she has come from, biologically. Fixity is a comparatively temporary achievement, one which is always under challenge since it was not original. Even God, if admitted to this process, did not fix our roles from eternity, since they did not exist from eternity but emerged. This fact tells us nothing of God's intent, or of what our realized cultural intent should be. It does tell us that nothing is fixed beyond change, that survival of any structure of species is precarious, is always under challenge and depends on adaptive struggle. Biological roles are made not born.

Women plotting change or men who resist it—both must be aware of the subtlety and complexity of the web of forces they challenge, the ever present Pandora's Box of sex. "Sexual selection is in itself an extremely complex affair, depending as it does on ardor in love, courage and the rivalry of males, and in power of perception, taste, and the will of the female" (p. 296). Note that Darwin does not give all the power or all the rights to either sex. Our origin is an immensely tangled affair stretching beyond our comprehension, as once we said God did. So when we seek to alter sexual relationships, we are not dealing only with cultural fashion but with elemental and fierce forces in our unseeable past now transmitted finally to our present, however much our cultural and intellectual pride causes us to deny our origins. Our intellect and will are powerful, but only if we are cautious in our suggestions and sensitive to the forces at play upon and within us.

We are not alone. "The law of the battle for the possession of the female appears to prevail throughout the whole great class of mammals" (p. 312). "Our brother/sister porpoise," Saint Francis might say. We too often tragically overlook our animal kinship in our mutual struggle. Saint Francis achieved a 'high culture', which is possible, and he divorced himself from the fierce and violent aspects of his brother animals. But we are foolish if we do not realize his as a rare and fragile achievement. Every novice master in a monastery knows full well that the would-be monk did not leave off sex with his civilian clothes. It is easier to tonsure the head than to control the passions.

Thus, we may moderate the "battle for possession of the female," outlaw slavery, concubines, and invoke prison sentences even for 'date rape'. But we should not pretend that the battle does not still go on. "The law of the battle had prevailed with men during the early stages of his development" (p. 324). We might paraphrase this and say: "You can take the boy out of the swamp but you can't take the swamp out of the boy or girl"—completely, that is. But of course, you can try.

When Darwin says, that "the strongest and boldest of men have succeeded best in the general struggle for life" (p. 325), this need not be interpreted to be true strictly according to sex and biology. Nor in our day need we confine it to males. Darwin knew that women have exercised vast powers and still do; he stressed the biological necessity for this. But he did feel that the drift of sexual selection had first given males the advantage of acquired strength. This can be revised, selection's course altered. But we know our origins and the means by which we arrived here and the fact that, among the many species who were lost, "we alone survived to tell the tale," as Job's servants reported to him. For Darwin this dictates that "the strongest and boldest" are most likely to succeed. Emerging from their 'nursery confinement', if women want different rules to govern success now, they should study the mechanism for the origin of species and the avenues by which the Ascent of Man—and now woman—is made possible and not rely simply on a wish to oppose ineliminateable forces.[13] Darwin is unequivocal about the superior status of his sex, "though the contest of rival males, and partly through natural selection ... man has ultimately become superior to women" (p. 328). Chauvinist as this sounds, it is of course confirmed by the feminist revisionist analysis of history, although they may attribute less to simple sex. Still, for Darwin the very forces which placed males in this position may be altered, but because the forces that brought this

---

[13] See Carol Christ, and Judith Plaskow, *Weaving the Visions* (San Francisco: Harper and Row, 1989).

preference about are far from inevitable, even though natural. However, far from Naomi Wolf, the author of *The Beauty Myth*[14] who recommends that we ignore the pressures of 'beauty' pressed upon us, Darwin sees the attractiveness of beauty as so elemental and so powerful that no change is possible if we ignore its power everywhere present, since it had so much to do with bringing us to where we are. He is not, however, culturally provincial; "We see how widely the different races ... differ in their taste for the beautiful" (p. 350). It is one thing to recognize that ideas of beauty vary culturally, quite another to deny their multiple powers.

Beauty rests on the enhancement of physical endowments. "Man admires and often tries to exaggerate whatever characters nature may have given him" (p. 351). Women are not different from their opposite sex. And each sex responds to the other, or to its own, as far as assessing beauty goes. Difference does not mean that beauty is not real, only that it has been made various, which adds to our interest and intrigue. However, although sexual selection still operates and beauties still attract, we are fortunately free from some, but not all, of their primitive power. "Whatever influence sexual selection may have had in providing the differences between the races of man," Darwin admits, "this influence would have been much more powerful at a very remote period than at the present day" (p. 368). But if we think we have escaped primitive selective powers entirely, we live in fantasy. True, since we are no longer so deeply bound, we may now hope to exert a conscious direction into the complex play of our still powerful inheritance.

Darwin is fortunately modest in the assertion of his theories. Although properly proud of British culture, unlike Hegel, he does not claim that all history has reached its climax in his time in Cambridge. Nor does he argue that his logic is inexorable; dogmatic he is not, insightful he is. Philosophy was born in its denial of a claim to possess

---

[14] Naomi Wolf, *The Beauty Myth* (London: Vintage Press, 1990).

'wisdom'; it is simply the search which its followers are now in love with. Darwin is a philosopher in his love of understanding and in his claims of non-finality. "Many of the views which have been advanced," he concludes, "are highly speculative, and some no doubt will prove erroneous" (p. 385).

'Fact' is not determinative. If that which we must understand lies in such obscurity, beyond even what we call the past, and if it contains an element of the unknown, theory cannot—ought not to—assume dogmatic form. What we call past is accessible only to the imagination, never directly as final fact. Women today, in pursuing advancement for their sex, cannot detach the present from the powerfully distant forces which brought us all here. Thus, all proposals concerning change in sex roles or gender roles must be tentative.[15]

Dogmatism in theory or assertion, where sexes or species are concerned, shows a lack of appreciation of our distant origin and of the uncertainties which did and still do govern our struggle for survival and advance. Paraphrasing Kierkegaard's continued presence, "It is not so long since you were in an unconscious, desperate struggle to detach yourself from your origins." And in this advance much was lost and only a little survived. In the struggle from our origins "many are called, but few are chosen." Religious seers merely reflect the aristocracy of biology.

Only vain humans, ones who are unaware of, unappreciative of, the precariousness of their origins, could assume a dogmatic pose in an effort to overcome uncertainty by pretense. Certainly a deity would know the breathtaking story of human evolution and could perhaps express concern. However, no evolutionary divinity could demand rigid beliefs, which are so inappropriate to either a divine or a human status. Feminine theorists should be cautious of the Marxist certainty of theoretical truth

---

[15] Compare Sulamith Firestone's radical proposal in *The Dialectic of Sex* (New York: Bantam Books, 1970).

as they work for their sex's descent toward new roles that raise them above their originating struggle. Men accomplished this, unknowingly, by sexual selection. Women may now select by conscious intelligence.

Whatever may prove outmoded in his suggestions, as happens in the course of our evolutionary sequence, Darwin is convinced that the program of descent stands fixed. "The great principle of evolution stands up clear and firm" (p. 385). Women in their quest should be guided by this. In the struggle of existence, the fittest survive. Omit the struggle and the species (also the sex?) declines. Having achieved a level of intelligent direction the struggle need not, but may still, be vicious. This should be expected and not be an occasion for surprise when it reappears. We know the means by which the human species has been raised to its present state, but even evolution is not inflexible, perhaps especially evolutionary progress. There may be other "perhaps undiscovered" means by which man or woman can be raised, for example, birth control, education, and advanced medicine. Nature was of necessity "raw in tooth and claw"; conscious civilization can now moderate but not eliminate this. We may change our future by means of adaptation, if we do not ignore our physical base.

Just as a belief in our moral accomplishment rests on no certainty, so it is impossible to maintain that belief in God "is innate or instructive in man" (p. 394). Instincts abound and they are our salvation, but none are directed to God. God is not fixedly there for us to discover. Divinity must evolve in relationship to us, since that is the mode and means of our rise and probably of our existence. God becomes the law of life, but this is 'life' as we have now come to understand it. Darwin's myth of origin is more challenging than *Genesis*, more fitting to a scientifically oriented humanity. God need not, but still may be believed to, have designed the means of our origin and descent. Yet this could not have been in its exact detail and specific outcome, since the variability in the evolutionary process itself rules that out as contradictory.

Women, insofar as they avoid dogmatism and antagonism toward men who did not design the process of selection but only illustrate it, can now descend as man has done before them. 'Descend' is actually a better term for women's new estate than 'ascend,' since evolutionary status requires constant awareness of our species' still painful evolution, our struggle up toward intelligible light.

C. "Advancement Is A Most Intricate Problem"

'Simple solutions' where sexual relations are involved can only depend on ignorance or avoidance of our complex, precarious evolution. We have advanced, like other animals, through a struggle for existence, consequent on our rapid multiplication. This 'wasted' surplus does not speak of the use of 'most economical' means but rather of a process involving great loss. No idyllic conditions were given to us first. Such were constructed years later, with skill and with difficulty if at all, and certainly not as permanent, beyond alteration or loss—as every morning newspaper now makes crystal clear. This uncertain struggle allows future change, but not easily. If we are to advance still higher we "must remain subject to a severe struggle" (p. 405). The walls of Jericho may come tumbling down for our entry, but not by the mere blast of trumpets. Severe struggle remains the means of all advance and, unfortunately, of all destruction.

This offers us no egalitarian democracy of uniform accomplishments. Yet the attempt is open to all, or should be, who wish to accept the challenges and commit to struggle. "We bear in our bodies the indelible stamp of our lowly origins," Darwin repeats again and again. Hubris is fatal for one so lowly born, no matter how high he or she may reach. Our accomplishments as a species are real and the more spectacular, given where we all began, how far we had to go and how hidden this past remained for so long beyond our sight.

Darwin cannot, of course, be sure about the plot he has uncovered in our human drama, but it is an exciting tale, as full of terror as it is of glory. And that same sense of terror and destruction is still near at hand, reminding us every night how uncertain our position is. Woman's advancement, once we have—after so long—discovered our origins, her descent away from an inhibiting origin, is now made possible. This advantage was once said to be excluded by an unchanging God, which we now realize to be the product of a human unawareness of our contingent condition and a consequent human urge to enforce certainty. Women can, at last, advance, but cautiously and only by addressing "our most intricate problem."

Any theory of a universal male conspiracy to subjugate women and hold them from their rightful place is too simple to be really helpful,[16] and it ignores the powerful physical forces working through us. Laws, customs were enacted, have been enforced, to keep women in a secondary status. But even Beauvoir's account of why women are 'the second sex'[17] does not go back nearly far enough into our origins. All that affects us is not in our conscious life or available in our history. (Freud's account is far too simple, too limited in time, too confident and too optimistic.)

Since we deal with forces not visible to us in their effect, speculation not certainty is the only necessity. What lies open to us in consciousness is a bubble on the surface. Jung spoke of our 'collective unconscious', which probably does affect us. But our collective struggle, before humanity even formed a separate species, may be even more explanatory of our present condition. We are both in the world and of the world. Women are still the source of future generations in this continuous struggle. They bear both the advantages and the unfortunate restrictions of this fact. But Darwin is not at all telling women that their future is fated. *Genesis* condemns women to suffer childbirth due to sin, although we must not forget that Adam is her co-conspirator and is ejected from Eden with equal anger. *Descent* offers women—and all of us—options, once the long climb to consciousness and intelligent direction is accomplished. "We

---

[16] See note 7 above.
[17] See note 7 above.

have suffered enough already just to get here," Adam and Eve might have said to Yahweh in response to his anger over eating a mere apple. After all, to get even within range of the tree of knowledge, we human animals had to climb through ages and physical threats almost too much for even God's imagination. In fact, the 'infinity' and 'omniscience' often attributed to divinity is now translated to mean that only a God of vast scope could possibly encompass the pain and struggle and terror which the new species went through to become nearly human. It was far from easy to arrive at Eden's gate, only to be driven out again for making a claim to a partial knowledge which was so long in coming to us.

Looking back over immediately past centuries, ignoring for a moment the abyss of time which lies before that, we can see now why we mistakenly thought of our advancement, after the advent of Modern thought, could now be less horrendous than our origins and adventures had been up to that time. Science had dawned, mathematics explained, the Enlightenment come, democracies proclaimed, education opened, universal human rights expanded, even authoritarian churches challenged by men and women who thought God gave them independence and the right to interpret religious documents for themselves. This is 'heady' stuff for one who came up from slime.

Suddenly, it all seemed worth the struggle it took to emerge from those long (not simply Medieval) Dark Ages. The human animal so long in production could become the Superman; Neitzsche had proclaimed it so. Marx challenged all oppressed to arise. Christianity and all religions in one way or another had spoken out with an offer to relieve human suffering. Now we know that our suffering had begun long before we could even have been conscious of it. But the Copernican revolution had come; we could now relieve our own suffering and then advance.

This Modern Project all made vast sense, and much of it proved true beyond our primitive imagination. Why, then, did general human advancement not follow so automatically as projected? How could

Marxist proposals for the suffering masses prove so illusory and even turn and become the cause of massive slaughter? How could an enlightened era witness some of history's most cruel holocausts, when the Age of Man (and, soon Women) had been proclaimed? Democracy had been instituted, constitutions forced over monarchs, medicine advanced to defy death's harvest, space explored in ways none of our early ancestors could have thought—if they could think of it at all—possible. "Where did we go wrong?" The picture we dreamed of for our self-controlled future can hardly be faulted. We had followed Nirvana or a Christian Heaven for centuries. Why should we object if now knowledge had been placed in our hands such that it allows us to bring the Kingdom of Heaven on Earth under our own power and guidance?

But we had forgotten our lowly origins, and we thought we had made ourselves into gods. Of course, our Modern leaders thought this intellectual and cultural hubris was justified, not excessive. We may have begun so low, but now we had recently risen so high. How could anyone deny us the fruits of such a horrendous struggle? Once we thought our race had only started at Eden's exit gate, "East of Eden." The Greeks, of course, and others had thought our world and our human course had been set out from eternity. But then we gave time a starting date, voided eternal worlds, and Augustine wrote us an optimistic account of God's plan, securely delivering us to Heaven's Gate, or at least those of us elected to deserve God's grace.

If we now return, not only to no fixed time span of relatively short duration, if we open up ages beyond what the Greeks could imagine, if we explore a time before life as we know it; and if we see non-human primitive forms of life emerge and "struggle upward toward the light." Our new metaphors and symbolic account of the human plight makes Plato's story of prisoners in a cave seem like child's play. We did not begin watching shadows on a wall and then turn to seek their source. In our beginnings, we could not even clearly distinguish light from dark.

As Darwin frequently reminds us, we bear the evidence of our origins in our bodies still. But since he himself is a child of Modern thought, he did not stress fully enough that our minds and wills still bear an even closer resemblance to our primitive, non-human origins than do our bodies. "You can raise a mind up out of this slime, but you can't take the slime out of the mind." We originally had to perfect the art of struggle and survival or else we would not have arrived at this point. Darwin stresses the importance of instinct in our evolution. Why should those predatory qualities, those that give us dominance over our primitive competition, now be abandoned? Could they be washed away by Christian baptism or Zen Enlightenment? Predatory instincts still haunt our Enlightened goals; the terror that characterized our pre-conscious years no Freud can rationalize. "Advancement is a most intricate problem"—and is still quite subject to loss.

Was this miscalculation about the limitation of our powers due to 'Western bias' that now-under-attack notion of the superiority, or at least the privileged, accomplishments of Western Civilization? Not really, since Eastern, or Asian, or middle-Eastern, or any thought you care to name was equally unconscious of our 'really-primitive' origins B.D. (Before Darwin). Western 'superiority-consciousness' undoubtedly overstressed its advance from the primitive cultures it freely subjugated (although the sport of conquering others was not at all a Western invention; it was the very means of our evolution and is not easily set aside by any culture).

However, no culture B.D. really sensed how close all cultures, all races, all religions still are to our pre-human origins. True, Western Modern thought was sure it could escape from its very-recent origins and stressed that its descent was from the earlier amazing flowering of human insight that stemmed from the Greek city states. But the fact is that, until our evolution was clearly delineated, no one could understand either just how far we had come or how far we really had yet to go. Modern confidence made the distance yet to go to our 'final advance-ment', to our human coming-of-age, seem close to hand, much too close.

Has the recent rebirth of the earlier successful women's movement made these miscalculations any more clear to us? Only if we set the Feminist Agenda[18] in the context of Darwin's Ascent. That is, when we see the forces of sexual selection operating within the evolutionary process of natural selection, then coupled with the importance of fecundity and birth abundance for survival, the female of all species assumes primary importance, even if in the case of humans male sexual selection gave them a short-term advantage.

Now, as intelligence emerges to challenge simple biological advantage, women see the possible reversal of their long time disadvantaged role. But we must set this energetic, basically optimistic, even revolutionary feminist agenda back into the context of the origin of all species.[19] Moved away from Utopian Western self-confidence in a

---

[18] See Barbara Sinclair Deckard, *Our Women's Movement*, (New York: Harper and Row, 1993).

In textbook fashion Deckard sets out a great many primary texts and facts that form a background for the women's movement. She lists negative sayings that have been used to stereotype women, so that if one wants to understand "sexism" as it is used pejoratively, the material is set out here. She defines "sexism" as the premise that "women are inferior to man" (p. 11), which is then used to maintain the power of the dominant group. She admits that this is based on the assumptions that all women are alike, but this raises the question of whether all men have equally believed this as well.

A wealth of material is set forth on psychological theories, on the family, the exploitation of women, the law. Then in Part II, she moves in history from early societies to the rise of women's struggle for equality, and then chronicles the success of women's suffrage and the factors which gave rise to the "New struggle for Liberation." Deckard ends with an accounting of current issues, outlining a wide spectrum of theories of women's liberation. Noting the diversity, she ends by saying, "women, even movement women, are not yet all sisters" (p. 469). Her book offers a wealth of material for an overview of the Feminist Movement.

[19] I. Cebara, and M. C. Bingemer, *Mary: Mother of God, Mother of the Poor*, trans. P. Berryman (Maryknoll, NY: Oubis Books, 1989).

Two Brazilian theologians have given us a restatement of the role of Mary in the Roman Catholic tradition from the perspective of Latin American Liberation Theology. They see Mary as the "ally of the oppressed, faithful to the struggle of the poor" (p. xi). They propose "a Marian theology whose starting point is women and Latin America" (ibid). They feel that much Mariology has been "Platonic" in origin, leading to a deep separation

radical conquest over Nature, the terror and suffering and constant challenge of survival shows us that women's advancement, like all advancement, is neither simple nor easy nor irreversible. Instead it is always precarious, under challenge, "a most intricate problem."

Viewed in Darwinian retrospect, it is not so long at all since we were all, male and female human beings, sub-human, unconscious, under total instinctual control, fighting to survive. For the majority, this was a losing battle. How we few survived and emerged as human is not a dialectic Hegel could chart, nor is it "the best of all possible worlds," a human comedy Leibniz could turn into a smash hit for Broadway or Paris. "Tell it to the extinct species in Peoria," we reply, since in Illinois they are all too familiar, as they are in Bangkok or Pretoria, with the elemental survival instincts that still drive man—and woman—to attack.

We can and do control these instincts at times. But the veneer of civilized manners is all too thin, and what lies beneath appears all too often to make us either too comfortable or too optimistic. We can advance—we have "come a long way, baby"—we can go on further, men and women. But we cannot do it without raising the opposition, that instinctive response that comes when any existing way of life is challenged. Those who have achieved an exalted plane of existence, move even unconsciously, to protect it from loss, for example, primary change. Thus biology doth make conservatives of many.

Old Yalies can still wave a white handkerchief and sing sentimentally, "For God, for country, and for Yale," except that the divinity coordinate with our evolutionary ascent (and there can be one) created no easy or certain path for us. Racial harmony can exist, but its existence is constantly fragile. Reading Darwin's *Origin* is enough to make us all

---

between men and women. They want to overcome hierarchical frameworks. God's transcendence is to be manifested in God's creation (they do not say how); spirit-matter dualism is to be overcome. Mary becomes "the divine in the female expression of the human" (p. 11). Tracing the history of Mariology, the authors seek a new statement for today.

long to start over again in *Genesis'* Eden. We could easily give up apples if we had not had to struggle so hard and so long even to get started. Eve would have chosen submissiveness, as would Satan, if any God had informed them of their origin, and how really long the fall would be if they challenged the Garden's rules. Yahweh did not play fair; the odds looked favorable to Eve, which they were not. Now today, we can, women can, challenge our present imperfect systems, demand equality, aspire to our place in the sun. But we must do so knowing how few make it through to Olympic competition, realizing how vast the number of starters were in this human race. We can, we have succeeded—a very few of us. We can rise, at least some of us, to a new level. But we still bear the vestiges of our sub-human origins in our mind and in our instincts for self-preservation. Every advance creates a challenge and a threat. Someone loses whenever others survive and advance.

D. The Descent of God

The concept of "the descent of God" is usually connected with the Christian notion of the 'incarnation', or with what Russian theologians sometimes call the 'man-God' problem. The notion of the occasional presence of divinity among us is, of course, not absent in other religions, notably the Muslim's belief in their prophet's direct revelation or the Hindu belief in the incarnations of various gods. However, for whatever reasons, some do consider Jesus to be God's representative, or even God's actual presence, among us. In the era A.D., 'descent' must now mean 'ascent', as it does the coming down of divinity. No God involved in such a long, arduous process as biological evolution could have any pressing need to make a sudden appearance. And in fact the loss of the sense of God's presence, if not the actual death of God in recent times, is due just as much to the intellectual revolution implied in evolutionary concepts as to any human 'coming of age', as was sometimes argued by the Enlightenment. Our whole time frame has now been radically revised, including our idea of time itself. Augustine's sense of history is too simplistic[20] and in fact it even excludes God, if evolution is our pathway to ascent.

If human beings have descended from non-human predecessors, how can a divinity be related to such a radical time concept? Surely it will not be the God of any of the Modern Philosophers, possibly slightly exempting Hobbes and Hume. 'Nature', since it is not fixed and eternal in its construct, does not refer to a God existing out of time. All knowledge is not only temporal but radically temporal, and any God outside of and untouched by the evolutionary plan could not relate to it.

Of course, a divinity need not be subordinate to it, nor need we feel romantic about our progress in order to feel that God, too, evolves "in the right direction." Process Theology, really 'Progress' Theology, was unfortunately not born out of Darwin's evolutionary process but more out of Modern optimism. For these theologians, Darwin is too close to the evil of massive destruction, chance and chaos. There is not, there cannot be, any assurance from watching even our own present process, let alone our pre-history, that all will turn out for the better, that all of value will be preserved. Such notions of God's 'all-will-be-made-right' goodness takes on the aspect of an unlikely, not even a likely, tale A.D., after Darwin.

Is God in A.D., then, excluded from any religion that takes nature's evolution seriously? Not necessarily. And as Darwin points out, although we could not count on the emergence of human intelligence and a 'higher morality' as a necessity, it did appear, and we must not discount it. But the uses to which our acquired intelligence is put, and the ways in which any moral code can be ignored or held privately in contempt, not to mention the painful awareness of our original and our present links to that too-long brutal waste—all this conspires to keep any honest man or woman from too easily projecting a happy ending. That can neither be

---

[20] *The City of God.* Trans. Walsh and Honau (Washington, DC: Catholic University Press of America, 3 vols. 1954).

based on what intelligence currently sees nor on what our best moral qualities might hope for. Evolutionary biology does not, it cannot, tell us that right will triumph, virtue be rewarded, and that "all's right in Heaven and with God"—even if it is not so now on Earth after our human emergence. "Peace on Earth, goodwill toward man" can be sung as a hymn, as a devout wish, but our origins and our still close connections to terror make it no certainty.

If Modern philosophers and theologians did not predict how radically the rise of the science they celebrated would disrupt their congenial concepts of God, can no concept of divinity be derived from our biological heritage? Those Gods which do not project both a certainty and a fixity in knowledge and a history acted out by script—they could come close, and there have been such. However, chief among the predecessors to the evolutionary sensitive theologian comes the long line of mystics.[21]

Oddly, Anselm really thought God was greater than could even be conceived, not the being that which none creator can be conceived. He almost seems to have been intentionally misunderstood, since the simple version of his 'ontological' argument seemed to place God at reason's apex, just as Hegel later did. But a divinity greater than our conceptions casts us into uncertainty and into an endless quest. Dionysus and Eckhart assert this boldly, while Anselm does it subtly, so subtly that his major point is often overlooked. Darwin, like Nicholas Cusanus, leads us into a 'learned ignorance'. We know more after reading *The Origin*, but at the same time it exposes our unerasable ignorance.

If in our era A.D. a divinity cannot be the God of Modern Rationalism, least of all Descartes' clear and distinct idea, what could a divinity be like that would descend to us in our own evolution? Jung suggested one in his *Answer to Job*,[22] that God first evidenced a primitively cruel

---

[21] See Mary E. Giles, *The Feminine Mystic* (New York: Crossroad, 1982).

[22] Jung, *Answer to Job*, trans. R. F. C. Hull (New York: Meridian Books, Inc., 1960).

morality in dealing with Job but then repented and later became incarnate in Jesus as divinity's atonement for allowing an undeserved suffering to be imposed upon Job. Yet Jung's notion of a divinity who does not realize and control the results of its actions are incompatible with recent cosmologies outlined by theoretical physicists. The God that emerges there, if one does, must possess massive intelligence far beyond our evolved human plane. God cannot in any literal sense be subject to the terrors, the loss, and the uncertainties of the evolutionary movement, since it has not, as Theilhard de Chardin optimistically thought, always clearly been directed toward some omega point. Human reason cannot have been intended as the final arbiter to all questions of divine outcome, powerful as it has become at times, since it is also destructive and too often uncorrectably biased.

The God of evolutionary descent can be claimed to have been present in Jesus, or in Buddha or in Mohammed or in Joseph Smith, since the system is loose enough, open enough, unpredictable enough, to allow for all these possibilities. On the other hand, Moderns rejected miraculous divine appearances, because they thought that these destroyed the projected neatness and finality of rationalist's schemes. If we do not exercise full control, as evolutionary biology assures us that we do not, events that come from outside our control should be no more disturbing than the daily inconsistencies and uncertainties and human willfulness with which we constantly deal. God need not be thought to be evil or as having intended our destruction vs. growth. But the needless waste in our world and in our behavior becomes less mystery than we need to try to discount, if human recorded time appears only after the long struggle of evolutionary time. We entered that fierce struggle, we sought human survival, and we did survive. Thus, it is not at all odd that struggles for survival still break out and plague our Utopian plans.

What about the promises of Jesus or the predictions of Mohammed or the Jews' long expected Messiah? Can a God of descent be found to be at all supportive of these visions, or claimed to be in a position to deliver any one of their expectations? Can Buddhism, Zen or otherwise, be true or fruitful if biological evolution is the framework within which it must be set? Since our natural history has no absolute fixity, we should reject terms which do not reflect much of the sense of our history's progress and not a progressive rational dialectic; and since the present day is not exactly cut off from its origins, we may be a lot lower than the angels, not just a little.

Yet there is also room for any divinity to move in ways that will destroy logical neatness, since no such thing exists in strict fact—but only in theories, which we construct. Our theories of evolution, none of them (however many may be proposed) can predict a peaceful outcome as a simple consequence of the way in which Nature was formed and is still being formed. Fixity of evolutionary theory as an absolute truth is an impossibility, due to our distance from its beginning, plus the late arrival on the scene of intelligence and human inquiry.

Evolutionary theory is a 'quite likely tale' (to expand Plato's notion in his account of our world's origin), but it cannot assume dogmatic command and rule out other notions. Powerful as we have become, such finality is not placed within our grasp, if we now project a descent of God. Descent, of course, in Darwin's usage means how we emerged from lowly, less than human, origins to develop the use of intelligence. In God's case, or for any divinity, it would mean how that force deals with evolutionary powers to bend them to command. Hyden pictures God having the world spring into being "on his command." For evolution's God, that is a little rash and a little too sudden a means for the creation of creatures. But the descent of God may still occur, matching our understanding of humanity's arrival up from slime. It can evidence itself in divinity's various forms of later descent or appearance.

As Feminist Theology developed,[23] their focus has come back upon

---

[23] Sallie McFague, *Models of God* (Fortress Press, 1987).

In this book, McFague goes beyond her suggestion of a model for God as 'friend', because she rejects what she calls 'imperialistic imagery' of God as opposed to life. She wants to add the image of God as lover and mother, together with the world as God's body.

She says that what she can say with assurance about the Christian faith is very little. She believes past models for God have been oppressive and are outmoded. She wants to end with the Christian faith as destabilizing, inclusive, non-hierarchical vision of fulfillment for all. Relationship and interdependence, change and transformation, these are the categories for theology for our day. The play of chance and necessity replaces determinism.

The relationship between God and the world needs to be unified and interdependent. Traditional language, McFague claims, does not "address the contemporary situation" (p. 45). Liberation theology which is her perspective, is "a new way of being in the world free of all hierarchies" (p. 48). Salvation must be a social, political, economic reality in history. It is the task of all human beings working in concert with the loving power of God. The entire universe is expressive of God's very being. The universe is the self-expression of God, God's incarnation. Unlike the God who is king, the God who suffers with the world cannot wipe out evil. "Sin is the refusal to be the eyes, the consciousness, of the cosmos" (p. 27).

As mother to the world, McFague insists, God mothers each and all. The resurrection promise is the presence of God in the body of our world. Male metaphors, she admits, are natural for God, but when she includes mother, she also wants to remind us that "God is beyond male and female" (p. 99). The relationship between lovers is the deepest human relationship, so it should be a central metaphor for modeling the God-world relationship. It is a love that finds goodness and beauty in the world and desires to be united with it. God needs the world. We must understand God as needing us, which implies that God needs us to save the world. "Salvation is the unification of the beloved world with its lover, God" (p. 135). "Since there is no evil power comparable to God, God is in some sense responsible for the worst that happens in the cosmos" (p. 141). We participate in our own salvation.

"Metaphorical theology is in the business of reforming and revolutionizing society" (p. 135), she concludes. "God as friend asks us, as adults, to become associated in that work" (p. 165). To be friends with God is the most astounding possibility. McFague admits that less has been said about divine transcendence, but she has concentrated on the immanent rather than transcendental models. What one needs most to become aware of, and to appraise, is her view of what is possible today and what are unacceptable as views of God. She does not quite make out why the tradition she rejects is no longer acceptable.

Sallie MaFague, *Metaphorical Theology* (SCM Press).

McFague describes her perspective as feminist, "skeptical, relativistic, prophetic, and iconoclastic" (p. x). (She will not assert more than the evidence supports, she reports, but of course everything depends on what one counts as 'evidence'). Our age is secular and McFague thinks we should conform to it. She rejects biblical language as 'boring and repetitious', which certainly would seem to represent a special intellectual view, not a very common one. She rejects 'sacramentalism', but no evidence seems to be offered other than her claim that it is gone. Obviously, she takes as given a 'Modernist' perspective and the evolution of thought. She offers us a 'metaphorical' theology which begins with Jesus' parables. To that point her proposal has little to do with feminism, except perhaps the stress

God. To say this may sound strange, since theology's task has always been to "speak about God"—insofar as this is thought possible. But when the Modern Era shifted the emphasis to anthropology, even religiously interested persons often became shy in speaking about God. As the ease and confidence about the obviousness of God to all faded away, the theoreticians were less sure about their ground in describing God. Many retreated into silence, not the mystic's alive and inspired silence which comes from the awe inspired by their task, but a silence more induced by a creeping agnosticism.

Why, then, 'modern' as they claimed to be in most of their philosophical premises, would feminists focus so quickly on God as they sought to develop a theology? Because for centuries 'God' has served as the intellectual focus, the lynch pin in our world-views, even if divinity sometimes did this negatively as in the agnostic rejection of God. Positively or negatively, God as a concept has always played a crucial role—or one might substitute 'the transcendent' for non-theistic religions, or 'the sacred' as opposed to a crass secularism. Feminist theologians immediately sensed that the reconception of God, that once traditional theological task, must be revived as a focus if it was to be changed.[24]

---

on 'personal', 'relational categories', which feminists often stress.

McFague adopts a process and relational metaphysics, as if it were an obvious preferred form for theology. She rejects the notion that models depict objects and insists that they are concerned only to picture modes or patterns of relationships (p. 134). At this point her metaphysics should appear questionable, since it again assumes the epistemology as being universal and restricted by our time, where there is little evidence of its universality or the necessity for the 20th Century thinkers all to adopt that view.

McFague wants to stress the metaphor of God as 'friend'. She admits that evil is a major problem for many post-enlightenment theologies, but the comfortable image of God as a friend in itself surely makes little sense of the long suffering of women or how a God who created sexual inequality can be called a 'friend'. She wants the root metaphors of Christianity to be "against all hierarchies" (p. 161), but the irony is that she must deal with a God who created a world open to hierarchies.

[24] See Rosemary Radford Ruether, *Sexism and God-Talk* (Boston: Beacon Press, 1983).

Considering now "the descent of God," if we put Feminist proposals in this focus, how do they appear? First, of course, we know that Feminists have attacked the 'male' image of God and the patriarchal structure of most religions. Considered in our era A.D., this is an odd notion, since the evolutionary process depends vitally on the female of the species. Although Darwin thought, rightly or wrongly, that males had been given some advantage by sexual selection in the human species, the primary driving force of the evolutionary descent is fecundity, overabundance or birth of every type, a quality Darwin associates as primarily female.

Is it possible that it is the Modern humanistic hubris, with Prometheus as its symbol, that stressed males as those who had stolen the divine fire, *knowledge*, for themselves and that religious traditions before the Modern era were in fact less 'male dominant' in their concept of divinity? Certainly Jesus and Buddha both stress what might be called 'feminine' qualities. In any case, any God who accepts evolution as an instrument of creation is at least bisexual and probably female biased.

For instance, Feminist theologians have suggested 'mother', 'lover', and 'friend' as images for God.[25] Female fecundity is central for Darwin and does not need to be re-stressed. 'Friendship' is a much later human development, and unless overly romanticized it must be set within the basic frame of the struggle for survival as the primary force in creation. 'Lover' might seem to reintroduce 'sexuality' into divinity, but the God who is forced to 'descend' to us has used sexual reproduction as a primary means.

God must be continually reconceived; Feminist theologians are right, since ironically the stressed characteristics which make divinity real for one time do not necessarily hold for another. In fact, any fixed notion may block our access to the divine. In our time After Darwin, the

---

[25]   See Note 18 above. And Virginia Rames Mollenkott, *Godding,* (New York: Crossroad, 1988).

mechanism of evolution, whether as conceived by Darwin or by 'revisionist' scientists, must be taken as the primary metaphor of Nature, and thus also for any divinity who is compatible with it. Lover and friend are far less obvious, that is, if we watch and visualize Nature's descent or the explosion of our universe or black holes. God is 'unnatural', unless conceived first of all to incorporate nature's primal force. Beyond that, the special qualities which any religion's tradition discerns may be added.

Following the Modern Era's treatment of God as clear and obvious and sweetly disposed to create optimum conditions for our life (odd, Darwin never speaks about "the best of all possible worlds," only of the terror-filled struggle to produce this one), there has been a tendency to claim the merger of all religions as being compatible, and out of all these to devise a 'God' who is, behind many masks, basically one for all. Like the difficulty of reconciling the God of Descent with the Rationalist creator of the best of all possible worlds, it is difficult if not impossible to render any diversity compatible in one divinity, the even wild variety and hostility, of one religious tradition toward another, particularly its competitors. You could claim 'cultural evolution', that this has been true but that now all religions can live together in enlightened harmony. Still Hegel's predictions not withstanding, there is little evidence for the reconciliation, or for the merger, of various religions, even if their warfare can be moderated.

The diversity and conflict we see may really indicate that there is one God who merely has many names.[26] However, considering the origins of our species and the origin of the great variety of religions paralleling each other, plus the vast outpouring of nature which so impressed Darwin, it seems much more likely that any divine center must be quite diverse in its nature and so capable of speaking with many voices. The diversity of languages introduced at the Tower of Babel reflects the

---

[26] John Hick, *God Has Many Names* (London: Macmillian, 1980).

complex and not fully consistent voices which a God of Descent has used. Of course, since universes come together and do not always fly apart into discord, the voices of any such divinity must circle around some controlling core. But nothing about this says that it was intended that we should translate all these into one common, consistent divine discourse. Biologists can classify the variety of species. But considering the multiplicity necessary for their emergence, we do not find all to have a single common denominator such that it reduces all complexity, any more than the human species can be given one mode of description.

The God who Descends, then, can be given many names, but not because we have made diversity out of that which in fact is a unitary core. Rather, the variety of ways in which divinities have been conceived[27] indicates our sensitivity to the diversity which is at the center of Nature's evolution and of any divine life associated with it as well. Varieties of religions are needed in order to reflect a superfecundant deity, although they (religions or deities) can never be one, just as all species cannot be reduced to one.

The God who produces by massive abundance cannot have had unity as its governing quality. That characteristic was projected, by Neo-Platonists and others,[28] into divinity by human wishful thinking. Just as the origin of species was characterized by proliferation, so God exceeds any single concept. Just as Darwin places evolution's beginnings beyond historical time and beyond our final description, so the Descent of God created an unerasable diversity within religious consciousness.[29] And we must choose between these by using the will and the intelligence which our process of origin has finally given us. We must not claim that all is unified and made consistent for us. The Descent of Man and Women parallels the Descent of God. Our task of producing and sustaining some

---

[27] See Karen Armstrong, *A History of God* (New York. Ballantine Books, 1993).

[28] Plotius, *The Annead*, trans. Charles Branford MacKenna, 2 vols. (Boston, no date).

[29] See William James, *The Varieties of Religious Experience* (New York: The Modern Library, 1902). Note "varieties," not unity.

37

degree of order is alike in both cases, just the same for the human as for the divine.

E. The Ascent of Man and Woman

If we set the context of the descent of man, originating as it first did in an agonizing struggle up from the non-human and then moving against human competitors, if we can trace how human rights, freedom, and self-determination were finally won for man, then we can hope to see more clearly how this can be accomplished for women. What pitfalls lie in women's path if they assume that men simply 'walked into' or inherited a directive position over all of nature and over women too? If self-determinism must be achieved, how can women parallel this advance, following the lead of a few men who pioneered it for them?

We misperceive our problem, for both men and for women, if we act as if *Genesis* gave us a literal account, as if the reins of power and control were simply given to man at his outset. 'Patriarchy' was not given. The author of *Genesis* paints sin and human self-destruction as breaking out even in the opening scene of the human drama. But to see our task as to overcome this defect is different from realizing that our problem is to struggle up from below the primitive, a long, arduous journey before Eden is even achievable.

We may be able to reconcile *Genesis* with an evolutionary perspective more easily if we make it clear that both men and women share equally in the responsibility for their inherited conditions. Antonia Fraser[30] makes it plain that it is wrong to see women as the originator of

---

[30] Antonia Fraser, *The Warrior Queens* (New York: Alfred A. Knopf, 1989).

As Antionia Fraser puts it: "The paradox" of the women who have led their nations in war is a major consideration for current feminist theory. True, quoting Gibbon in *The Decline and Fall of the Roman Empire*, these women are "a singular exception," since under conditions they would have been deemed incapable of "the smallest employment." Yet since we do not want to stereotype women, a limitation which the Movement has fought against, we must consider the exceptions as well as the generalized notions about femininity, and ask if any gender role, including these normally assigned to men, is closed to women.

sin and that in fact to do so contradicts the notion of a patriarchy. Superior power means superior or, at the very least, equal responsibility. She Quotes Emilia Laniar in *The Weaker Vessel:*

But surely Adam cannot be excused
Her fault though great, yet he is as much to blame;

Fraser begins the tale of Badicea, "a gallant – and a savage – story." Was she cruel and destructive? In any case, the noteworthiness is the "remarkable excitement" the arrival of a Warrior Queen causes; "beyond the ability of a mere male to arouse," in spite of the fact that woman has for ages been considered physically inferior to man. Clearly matriarchal societies may, but not necessarily always, lack aggressiveness. She quotes Lynn Segal's *Is the Future Female?*: "I accept that women are gentler at the moment," but, "if they had the same amount of power as men, they wouldn't be more virtuous."

Thus, the concept of the Warrior Queen cuts across not only man's view of woman's traditional weakness but also woman's view of her own ordained role as peacemaker. The Warrior Queen is one who combines both elements of rule and martial leadership, although Fraser admits the United States has not known one yet. But perhaps this will change with the advent of militant feminism.

War has become, Fraser finds, the fiery process which has guaranteed some women passage into the realm of honorary men. Boccaccio had said: In order to govern, it is not necessary to be a man, but to have courage. So "courage" must be a trait acquirable both by men and by women. The Warrior Queen, when she emerges, comes with a mingled sense of awe, horror and ecstasy, not quite the way the nineteenth century pictured great women. Goddesses have recently received renewed interest, but Fraser points out that they too were both clamorous and ferocious. Some are cunning, imperious, and lustful. Cleopatra was not only strong-minded but ambitious to have her own empire. Isis was the queen of war.

The Warrior Queen is a symbol of sexual freedom as well as female independence. Thus Gandhi had Gurga and Kali, the rulers of fertility and destruction, hovering about her, but she benefitted from Hindu traditions of powerful women in religion, literature and history. So we know that all cultures have not sought to portray women as weak. That is a particular gender role of a particular time, not something inherently feminine.

Thus we owe a great deal to Antonia Fraser for correcting a one-sided view of the feminine which portrays them as weak and inherently peaceful. Thus, *Warrior Queens* are a possible gender role too, although not every woman may aspire to become one. Yet we learn that we must not be hasty to take some recent or present gender role, which may seem to be "eternally feminine," and lock all women into it. The range of roles which women have occupied is wide and varied and overlaps the male at many points. Women have had, and can have, a wide variety of gender models to copy, even if some recent ones seemed to us to be fixed.

> What weakness offered strength might have refused;
> Being Lord of all, the greater was his shame.

And it is not at all clear that the author of *Genesis* ever intended to say that man was superior as a sex.

In the mythical account, Eve was created as man's co-worker, as the one much needed and without whom Adam could neither exist nor continue God's creative work. This account brings the parallel to *The Origin of Species* closer to *Genesis,* because we realize that the sexes are co-dependent, 'correlative'; they rise and fall together, each implicated in the success or failure, future or extinction, of the other and of the species. As Aristotle tells us, they are 'correlative', defined only in relationship to each other, neither independently. Their lives, their species, their very self-understanding, lie intertwined. In like manner, W.E.B. du Bois tells us that black and white are irrevocably intertwined in the United States.[31] So today in the attempt of women to redefine themselves, their present role or their potential roles in order to compete with men on every level, we should first review man's rise from a lowly estate and see what women can learn from that of profit. Darwin offers us the account of the emergence of intelligence, which once achieved then allows us to make conscious modification in our present estate.

By following the Origin of Man, we learn several things: (1) There could have been no conscious move of male dominance "in the beginning," to borrow *Genesis'* opening line (which fits very well), since there was no original consciousness. We males could not have begun by plotting superiority, since we were as yet not conscious of our own existence; (2) If the course of our descent gave males an advantage due to their sex, either as Darwin makes this out in his account of sexual 'selection' or by other means, this is not unalterable, once conscious cultural redirection appears. However, whether this will be for good or

---

[31] W. E. B. du Bois, *The Soul of Black Folk* (New York: Washington Square Press, 1970).

for ill is quite another matter. The factors most important in tracing the Descent of Woman toward her future, are (3) fecundity, over-abundance, and change—these are the early mechanisms which dominated our origin as a species. Thus, (4) 'male' was not one thing "in the beginning" and neither was 'female'. Diversity, not unity, is the medium of our descent from lower states. No single definition of species or sex over time is possible—or even desirable, since multiplicity is more important to us than unity.[32]

Unities do form, particularly as species gain definition, but these are neither unalterable nor originally given. They may be culturally, or even morally, imposed, as Darwin or others account for this. But any unitary restriction placed on our roles is artificially imposed and actually worked against nature's mode of development and progress. Cultures achieve a fixity which is necessary for their stability, but we live in illusion if we do not see, as reflected from our origins, a vast complexity and profusion, all of which breeds a strong competition for survival.

The quality of terror involved in all of this, which still survives at the edge of our consciousness and is reported to us every day, leads us to make frantic efforts to impose limits; this is not because Nature has placed them there in some unalterable form, fixed from some imaginary eternity. Rather, it is just because we need stability to offset our panic over the lack of fixity, which any insight into our origin and the mechanisms for survival—and the current outbreaks of chaos—has induced in us.

Moreover, we must go further and contrast our physiological evolution with our culture, even spiritual, evolution. In this case, realizing and accepting The Descent of God becomes our best model. Had divinity in fact been fixed in nature from eternity, immune to time's inevitable change, we would not witness our mode of descent as we inquire into the origin of our species. God's involvement in this vast

---

[32] See "50 Ways to be a Feminist," *Ms.* Vol. V, No. 1, Special Edition, (1994): 33-64.

struggle with chaos (which, however, is surely successful in God's case, thus reflecting divinity's 'perfection'), the random qualities and the chance aspects in our descent as they are reflected in God—all this rules out fixity in our nature. But more importantly, (5) it distinguishes our biological descent into somewhat distinct sexes from our cultural or our spiritual evolution. In that important realm, the opposition and distinction of sex differential almost disappears—or they can.

As Antonio Fraser remarks, in the soul there is neither he or she.[33] True, because of this lack of distinctiveness and rigidity of form, humans have as they struggle ironically focused on outward, physiological qualities as weapons to be used against any challenge to our attained special status. Thus, our cultural commonality as human beings is blocked out by a too-simple reference to sex roles. In the struggle to sustain our precarious status, which cannot be 'God -given' in the older sense of that word, we instinctively seek to carry forward any natural advantage we have gained. Sex has at least temporarily (i.e., perhaps for recorded history) offered males some physical advantage, which they can use to claim that they have survived as 'the fittest'. However, once consciousness and cultures have arrived and been created, physical advantage need no longer dominate—although violence always lies in wait.

In their evolutionary struggle, women had to wait a much longer time than men for their cultural release, since their sexual role as bearers of the future of the race gave them the traditional role of fecund source. This is crucial biologically, but it is reckoned to be less primary once males perfected some rough technologies and conscious governance. Women could then also experience their ascent toward self-governance, and so explore the non-sexed nature of 'soul' vs. 'body'.

This is an important distinction which feminists must maintain in their ascent to equality, since physiological status alone does not yield it.

---

[33] See note 30 above.

'Soul' was heretofore more limited in religion and culture as in politics. However, our means of descent from vast heterodoxy tells us that it is self-defeating for women to try to define any essence for themselves as sex derived, since our non-sexed cultural qualities and potentials are what it is now time for them—for us all—to explore in greater range.

All things may be gendered, as some feminists have argued in support of their quest for recognition.[34] But we must be very careful not to connect this too closely to biological sex. True, males if they have evolved with a privileged status over women, whether as Darwin describes it or by other means, have sought to establish this advantage as firmly biologically based. But women fall into the trap set by male deception if they appropriate the same route and try to tie their "claim to virtue and talent" to a biological base. True, males often tried to link the subordinate status of women to female biological inferiority. But since men were wrong in this, both as regards to their own status and their own origin, women build their castle equally on a bed of sand, as men have, if they do not detach talent and accomplishments from any biological status.

Antonia Fraser notes that the desire for children in marriage, as many as possible, as quickly as possible, was universal. But we need to underline 'was', in opposition to males who have often claimed that characteristic to be fixed. The biology of our descent did in a sense 'fix'

---

[34] Judith Butler, *Gender Trouble* (London and New York: Routledge, 1990). Anne Fausto-Sterling, *Myths of Gender* (New York: Basic Books, 1985). Linda Kauffman, ed., *Gender and Theory* (Oxford and New York: Basic Blackwell, 1989). Peggy L. Day, ed., *Gender and Difference in Ancient Israel* (Minneapolis: Fortress Press, 1989).

Gender must be addressed when discussing biblical texts, the editor states. If biblical text "falsifies" women's experience, "the biblical text does not have the authority of authentic revelation" (p. 2). The claim is that the texts reflect predominantly male experience. Feminist theologians "have claimed female experience as a yardstick of theological truth" (Ibid). "The skills of cooperation and negotiation are survival skills that women have honed through long years of being in a subordinate status" (p. 9). The strong female presence in the biblical text has been muted, and the authors of these essays seek to rectify that.

that role on women, since plenitude was the rule of survival. But intelligence, although it took centuries to refine (not so long a period in evolutionary time, after all), the female of our species could finally detach herself from that much of biology, control productivity, and divert energy into other channels. Again male and female had to work in concert, since males had to pioneer production of our kind, thus protecting our survival—a necessity which some people still see as linked to our survival. Yet human abundance itself was connected to our lack of fixity and our ability to adapt to new circumstances.

The brighter side of women's basis for claiming her sex's ability to adapt to new changes and the lack of any necessity to be bound to earlier conditions, that very fact which enabled both sexes to reach our present state together, has its darker side. If we claim that there is no necessity for any individual or species to be bound to any stage of development, and if we stress adaptability to new conditions as our great achievement, we also know that there is nothing fixed or necessary about any advance we can achieve that keeps us from regressing again. In such a metaphysical universe, God's imposed necessity of nature drops away too. As men achieved democratic self-determination in some societies that are no longer of necessity bound to kings or to tribal laws, it was too easy for Darwin to suppose in a time of freedom "that the dark days of repression will never come again" (p. 464). So women who argue that their sexual role is flexible and can be further advanced must realize that that very fact also makes every improvement subject to possible loss in the continued struggle for survival.

In "Darwin's world" a certain amount of terror, violence and completion "comes with the territory." Thus, for women who seek to eliminate competition may be to induce a slide toward decline. On the other hand, following Darwin's *Descent,* we know that the arrival of intelligence and morality means that we may consciously modify our estate, for good or for ill. For instance, the terror of male physical dominance, once it was achieved, seemed natural. But now it may be controlled, if it is suppressed by conscious decision and rule. Laws may replace instinct, or at least seek to keep it under control.

However, the protected status which was created for women to shield them from the brute forces of struggle, that restriction will be loosened too as women reject the special protections demanded by motherhood. Once reproducing the human race is rejected as their fixed biological status, they enter into the advantages—and into the disadvantages—of open competition.

Chapter II

Women Are Not Alone

A. Sexual Prejudice

The necessary early distortion in some of the recent forms of the Women's Movement ('Feminism' in the early phase), one which we now need to correct, is to set the emphasis on women back into the human context. At the start, they rightly stressed 'women' solely and completely and the supposed unity of all that gender. This correction of mine is not entirely a 'male' suggestion.[35] Dedicated separatists are few and always will be, and they should be encouraged in order to promote the spirit of dissent.[36] However, the majority of women want

---

[35] See Judith Nies, *Seven Women* (New York: Penguin Books, 1978).

[36] Mary Daly, *Pure Lust: Elemental Feminist Philosophy* (Boston: Beacon Press, 1984).

Mary Daly wants a knowing that is intuitive/immediate. Thus, "our quest implies constant Creation" (p. xi). She seeks to escape old ways of knowing. "Essential female lust is intense longing/craving for the cosmic concrescence that is creation" (p. 3). Her premise is that "by releasing words we can release ourselves." She wants to break the obstacles that block the flow of Female Force. Sometimes, Daly feels, female creativity is misdirected into misplaced rage against other women. Daly wants to develop a feminist philosophy that gets to elemental being. Lusty women will, of course, speak in symbols.

Mary Daly, *Gynecology: The Metaethics of Radical Feminism* (Boston: Beacon Press, 1978).

Mary Daly "completes" her pilgrimage with this volume. Beginning with an aim to reform the Roman church's practices regarding women, she moved on to decide that Christianity, all men and all institutions, were beyond reform. Now she recreates discourse in an attempt to break the hold of forms of the past. Its focus is "beyond Christianity," since male images cannot be removed from God, and the basic premise of her radical posture is that *all* male referential speech must go. She wants to establish an "Other" way of thinking/speaking."

It is "an invitation to the Wild Witch in all women who long to spin" (p. xv). Radical feminism is the "journey of women becoming" (p. 1). It is an extremist book, she admits.

to be in the mainstream and to affect the world. The early thrust of Feminism was to re-study history,[37] to find in our society and in our literary/intellectual life an under-stressed, under-examined role of women and the contributions they have in fact made. But in most cases, in literature, in philosophy, in science, the ultimate aim is to take this redrawn "Women's History" and to use it as a base to

---

And radical feminism is not reconciliation with the father" (p. 39). Seeing through the controlling (male) myths is the beginning of living; the basic problem which must be corrected is that "the words/expressions of female spirit are roped, twisted, tortured, dismembered" (p. 93). Thus, the need for entirely new ways of thinking, expressing. In the attempt to murder the Goddess, "the deed can be revoked by re-invoking the Goddess (p. iii) spinsters spining out the self's own integrity can span the splits in consciousness.

[37] Bonnie S. Anderson and Judith P. Zingger, *A History of Their Own*, 2 vols. (New York: Harper and Row, 1988).

The feminist complaint is one of "the almost total absence of women from the pages of history books" (p. xiii). Literally, of course, this is not quite true. There have been famous women, but the generals, writers, scientists, etc., have been predominantly male. What have ordinary women done, our two authors ask, as history unfolded? Until recently, all women were defined by their relationship to men. What would history be like if men were seen through the eyes of women and ordered by the values they define?

Our authors divide their examination of European women into those of cities, walled towns, courts, etc. They try to focus on the lives of ordinary women. But much as they hoped for it, they discovered no era in our historical past in which women dominated, no women's Renaissance. In fact, women's opportunities actually declined in the Enlightenment, relative to men's. They conclude quoting the German feminist, Louise Otto-Peters, "women will be forgotten if they forget to think about themselves." Yet they say, "it is not necessary to believe myths of a feminist Golden Age in order to plan for parity in the future," quoting anthropologist Kathleen Gough (p. xxiii, vol. I).

Women were in history, but just not many in numbers. "Catherine the Great, Empress of Russia, personified the absolute monarch for her contemporaries and for subsequent generations" (p. 3, vol. II). The world of the courts offered opportunities. But, for those less wellborn, as our authors conclude, "the vast majority found satisfaction in their lives, whatever the limitations" (p. 6, vol. II). Women were central in many protests, including the French Revolution. Thus, women were not absent from the pages of history, just not always in key roles in the same numbers as men. Childbearing made that impossible until recent years, but we do need a more complete record of women's varied history, one which these volumes offer.

Rosemary Radford Ruether and Rosemary Skinner Keller ed., *Women and Religion in America*, vols. 1-3 (San Francisco: Harper and Row, 1981-86).

critique present society and its customs. The aim was to use it as evidence, as a wedge to demand greater access, greater recognition, now. That goal, of course, was made clear. But is there a 'next phase' which is not yet so clearly seen?[38]

This early feminist program to turn history 'upside down' may be a "necessary first distortion," one needed to establish "Women's Pride" (like "Black is Beautiful"). But in the end any separate treatment of women is distorting and ultimately self-defeating to the cause of women's future. We must take every stress on women's roles, both past and present, and set them back into the context of the human family. As we do this our first question is: How were men treated at the time of history in question? What was the society which women now reexamine like, and was it equally repressive for the majority of men as it was for women? Granted that those who survived pressure and attained prominence were in greater proportion men, can the status of women be better understood, even more easily corrected now, if we see that the conditions we argue against and want to change were on the whole the general condition of non-liberal societies and not in every case the result of simple male hostility and a repression of "women only?" To what extent was the condition of women we now so deplore a condition of that society as a whole, men *and* women?

Consider one example: John Cornwell writes about his investigation of young women who have had visions of the Virgin Mary, the great attention they attract, but also of the hostility that often comes from priestly authorities. In exploring why the priests might be so negative regarding a known religious phenomena, he says, "The investigation into the religious paranormal were projected substitutes for the clergy's unconscious inclinations to doubt and apostasy, their

---

[38] See preface.

deep fear and hatred of women."[39] Thus, if we separate out simply the female history of persecution, we could focus on the last part of his suggestion. It may be the male "fear and hatred of women," which makes so many priests hostile to the young women's visions, is one more instance of the phallic prejudice, as he suggests. But if we accept this, true as it may be to some extent, we miss the wider significance of the phenomena and skew our understanding.

How so? If those who are professionally involved in religion have doubts about their faith which they fear to show openly, then miraculous visions threaten the security of their faith and their official position just because this highlights their doubts. Thus, those who are insecure in their position and in their convictions turn hostility toward *anyone* favored with ecstatic experiences. In the case of the appearances of the Virgin, the recipients were often women (and children too), so that hostility to women adds itself in. But, we will not understand the human situation if we isolate the "women's issue" and do not see it in the wider context of its connection to the question of doubt being challenged by certainty. Women are not alone in this. Anyone, any sex or race, could provide that challenge and provoke the same reaction.

In every issue regarding women, which is so much the object of exclusive focus these days, we must take any account of repression and set it back into the whole cultural/historical scene if we really wish to understand it. Women have recently taken center stage as the focus of many issues, and rightly so. But if we let our attention narrow, we may miss the other factors that contribute to the recorded injustices. And if we allow this, such as in the case of the priests' self doubts, we cannot advance the problem or its solution, because in fact the causes are more complex than simple sexual prejudice. Granted, such probably is present. But if we consider sex bias exclusively, any

---

[39] John Cornwell, *Powers of Darkness, Powers of Light* (London: Viking, 1991), 96.

promise for fair treatment of women will be meaningless, just because factors other than sex still promote prejudice.

Consider the hostility which women claim they face as they enter the workforce and the professions in greater numbers. It is an established fact that lower economic strata whites in the Southern United States evidenced deeper racial prejudice as slavery was abolished than did affluent, plantation owning whites, those who did not compete with blacks in the cheap labor market. Thus, to say of blacks or of women that either race or sex prejudice alone holds them back economically may miss what may be the more potent economic factor: Hate springs up toward anyone, of any race or sex, who challenges us in our economic or social position. As prejudice, it may be given racial or sexual expression, but we will misread the complexity unless we see that economic or social position might be *the*, or at least also one, major cause.

In what sense, then, is the hostility toward women, for example, sexual prejudice, simply based on sex? The answer is: probably very seldom. Thus, to attribute all unfair discrimination to this factor is to miss "the human tragedy." We focus on outer characteristics which are easy to identify. We falsely attribute all discrimination to physical characteristics which may be only a cover for less tangible factors. These may conceal, or at least make us less conscious of, the real source of the hostility. If so, we can do all we want with generous statements and new laws against sexual discrimination (not that these are bad), but we risk treating the surface and not the root cause of inter-human hostility. Is the individual woman brighter, more talented, more hardworking than the male with whom she competes? If so, without even being conscious of it, he may respond with slurs on her sex, just as another revives racial or religious hatred when under pressure. Males give the same response to the man who challenges them, but we don't think to call it a sex-based prejudice.

Jews know this phenomenon well, because they often succeeded in the cultures that allowed them to employ their talents. But when times get tight economically, or when politics turns violent, even well-accepted Jews know that racial hatreds often re-emerge, all the more difficult to deal with because their source is ultimately not racial but simple human envy. Successful Jews have often been 'assimilated' into the culture by all outward standards. Whenever, then, we appraise the situation of women in any society or time, we must set this within the wider human problems of the era. Specifically, we must determine: How did men fare as a whole? What problems did males face as individuals, and how might this help explain what we find out about how women were treated? Were there difficulties which all human beings in that time faced, socially and politically? And how is the solution to "the women question" tied to the solution of "the human question"?

But of course, there are many other senses in which it is true to say that women are not now, and perhaps never have been, alone. The issue just pointed out is that for intellectual, historical accurate understanding, the situation of women must always be placed alongside that of men in the human context. But as mothers, as objects of love and attraction, women have always been in good—and sometimes bad—company. Many is the woman famed in history, in literature, whose life was made full by a love affair. Many have found their desired context in their children, for good or for ill. But more than that, it always has been the case that men, and societies in general, recognized that the world could not run, or be accurately represented, without the power of women—granted that the primary role was assumed to be Motherhood. If in fact in biography, in social history, in the individual lives of the multitude, women have never been alone or been considered alone, how then can one claim the 'exclusion' of women?

Reviewing human history, the only senses in which it can be found that women seemed alone or excluded are in the seats of power. It cannot be denied that women were "the second sex," or "the weaker vessel," not in their importance to human life but as to their prominence in public role. Queens there have always been;[40] goddesses have always had their roles;[41] strong women have always dominated weak men and over-powered complacent children. True, public roles were still largely occupied by males. Nevertheless, we should not take this to indicate an absence of a strong sense of women's presence. If today some women desire more public, more socially powerful roles, this new goal should not blind us to "the real presence" of women in previous periods of history, even if that status or presence is not desired today.

We must note another irony in the modern feminist quest for public equality, even though we have noted their private positions of influence all along. That is, just because some now are able, thanks to modern medicine, to rise above the dictates of the birth cycle and to seek almost any role which formerly was male dominated, does this mean that all women will seek prominence, even if it is now open to them? And if there are women who do not seek the limelight, or who find the reigns of power not something they want to pay the price to obtain, then these women are not alone either, because in fact a majority of men have always sought a quiet role and even found it satisfying. Those women who now seek the public spotlight, in other

---

[40]   See Antonia Fraser, chapter I, note 30.

[41]   Elizabeth Dreyer, *Passionate Women: Two Medieval Mystics* (New York: Paulist Press, 1989).

The author wants to single out the emotion of love, particularly in its passionate expression, but she does not have sex in mind. Rather she examines the role of passion in the writings of two medieval women. They do use erotic language, but one is subdued (Hildegard) while Bernard's mystical accounts overflow with intense erotic language and imagery (p. 25).

However, the second woman considered, Hadewijch, was not a nun but the member of a popular movement, a representative of "love mysticism." In contrast to Hildegard, her writing has an intense erotic tone. The "mystical union God is lived here on earth as a love relationship" (p. 51). But it is not enjoyed without costs. All considered and against popular assumption, "the reader is struck by the freedom and spontaneity of expression in the literature" (p. 72).

than its classical focus on their noble mothering or their beauty, must recognize that they join not 'all males' but only a minority in the human kingdom who want public prominence or who are willing to struggle for it.

Somewhat ironically, the women who now seek entrance to the seats of power and to the courts of public praise may be more alone in their pursuit than the women who stay, with the vast majority of men, in a less public spotlight where women need not be alone. To star, or to seek to conquer in the intellectual, political, or economic world is in most cases inevitably to be alone. You are in competition, and this breeds an air of isolation, since one cannot succeed, whether male or female, without ousting someone else from the top spot, the center of public attention, while catering to the dispenser of the privileges connected to success and power. Men have not all banded together to seek the top of every ladder. The majority have always been with the women who have not sought prominence.

How then shall we evaluate the goals of recent feminist campaigns?[42] They often began with an idealistic call for sisterhood, the togetherness of all women. And like other revolutionary groups, moments of solidarity were genuinely experienced. Yet when you

---

[42] Barbara Sinclair Deckard, *The Women's Movement. Political, Socioeconomic, and Psychological Issues* (New York: Harper and Row, 1983).

Anyone interested in the recent feminist movement should stop and review the earlier history of the women's movement. This book attempts "to synthesize the old knowledge with the new" (p. xi). The author undertakes "a survey of the status of women from primitive societies through the nineteenth century" (ibid). One issue discussed is why the movement died after 1920. In the contemporary women's movement, the author identifies "three major ideological positions" (p. xii).

The book begins with a review of sexual stereotypes and questions the underlying assumption that all women are alike. All attempts to find an identity reveals many sex differences to be more apparent than real. Under pressure, some previously all-male preserves have been breached. The book brings together an amazing amount of data and identifies three major ideological positions: moderate or women's rights feminists, the radical feminists, and the social feminists (p. 449).

remember that women's suffrage fought for the vote and legal equality but did not see much need to alter women's role in the family, you begin to realize that recent feminist's goals have really been aimed at the top, that is, to be recognized as classic novelists, as active scientists, to occupy political office. At first glance there is no reason to challenge their desire to have half the Nobel prizes, half the seats in the U.S. Senate, half the Bishop's offices in every church, half the Board memberships and Presidencies of every corporation. But in this quest for greater public presence, they enter the competitive realm of "the male minority" too.

Everyone cannot be a college professor, law partner, politically elected official, exhibited artist or film director. If women are now more free than ever before to "go for it," if the sexual prejudices which were perhaps too long held over from their past preoccupation with birth can be reduced, their goals are within reach—for some, but only for a very few. And if the accomplishments of any woman do not receive the recognition which she or her sisters feel due, "male prejudice" may need to be considered and overcome. At the same time we have to examine how any individual, how any male, gets public recognition, and then worry about the selection process that leaves the work of many, both male and female, unrecognized. Males who exclude other males can be accused of prejudice, but hardly of sex prejudice.

So if not every male makes it to the top of every profession or finds his books on best seller lists but only the few, will the removal of sex-based prejudice really eliminate all the 'prejudice' (read standards of evaluation) to which the work of those who seek recognition are subjected? Hardly. Women are not alone in their struggle to allow their talents to find a recognized outlet. Men have been trying for centuries and only a small minority have ever succeeded. For the male to tend his family, his sheep, his crop; for the woman to gain appreciation for her home, her family, even her religious compassion—all this is relatively, or at least not publicly competitive, easy for both male and female. But everyone does not qualify for top recognition, else the world would not show such conflict. However, the gate is wide and the path is broad for those who seek a lesser satisfaction and only a private reward from life (see chapter VII - E).

Some women may cheer on those "who go for broke." Males bask in the reflected glory of male sports stars too and gain a certain sense of satisfaction from a stellar performance, if this reflected glory is not spoiled by envy. But as women seek social, political, and economic equality under the law, just as men only recently in human history struggled to achieve this too, some of their sex will cheer them on and be happy over the success of the few. But all women will not, could not, seek "the chief seats in the synagogue." And if corruption or brutality become instruments used by women for their success, such women may find themselves, in their climb, just as alone as are the men at the top in bearing the retribution of enemies or the destructive power of envy.

Women are alone neither in being virtuous nor in being infamous. With the resurgence of feminist concerns, much has been said to stress the virtues of women. In truth, 'woman' as the model of virtue has been idealized many times. Although this adulation may be given a new slant,[43] we know that in fact the idealized model of woman in

---

[43]   Carol Gilligan, *In A Different Voice* (Cambridge, MA and London: Harvard University Press, 1982).

Professor Gilligan's book has received wide attention and it should. When talking about morality, do women's voices have a distinct sound? Of course many people and groups, racial and otherwise, speak differently about morality. But if women can be identified as a class, we need to know that. However, the different voice Gilligan describes "is characterized not by gender but by theme" (p. 2). Thus, it may not be as much sex related as due to gender training, in which case it is variable by education and is not fixed.

Gilligan's subjects were students, so we know a highly selective factor is operating. High school dropouts might speak with a different voice. Still, the theme she traces has inherent interest. The feminine personality defines itself in relation to and in connection with other people, more so than the masculine personality, it is suggested. However, we know this is a function of adopted gender roles, not something rigidly fixed by sex, and thus it is subject to change and variation in different eras.

However, can this book about men and women and the differences between them be universalized? Or is it about certain gender types in certain eras, which might be quite changeable by education and varying cultural patterns?

"'Males' gender identity is threatened by intimacy while feminine gender identity is threatened by separation," we are told (p. 8). But that of course depends upon the gender role adopted, a factor which is subject to change. What would the results have been like, we must ask, had Professor Gilligan used ghetto blacks and Tongan women as her subjects. How restricted are her results by the initial sample she selected, and could this study be expanded to apply to all women universally?

Some time ago Piaget had discovered that a legal sense "is far less developed in little girls than in boys" (p.10). But did Piaget study the daughters of women who were partners in major law firms? Does girls' play tend to develop "empathy and sensitivity," as Gilligan suggested, or would this be true of only certain girls in certain cultural situations and certain gender roles? Would it be true, for instance, of Chinese women during the Cultural Revolution?

Sex roles are "one of the most important determinants of human behavior," Gilligan quotes David McClelland (p. 14). But how do and can sex roles vary? If women 'feared success' as Matina Horner found in 1972, do they still today and must all women do so? Gilligan discovers "a more contextual mode of judgment and a different moral understanding" (p. 22), in her sample. But is this universal for all women, and is it universally connected to sex, or does this vary by gender role? Just how representative of their sex are twenty-five Cambridge women?

Do all women have "a non-hierarchical vision of human connection" (p. 62), as is suggested, or only a certain sample? Do all women attempt to "solve moral problems in such a way that no one is hurt" (p. 71), or are there some women who are as vicious as a mafia chieftain? One characteristic Gilligan finds is that "identity is defined in a context of relationships and judged by a standard of responsibility and care (p. 160). But again we must ask: Is this for a small group of Harvard women or for all women universally as defined by their sex? "An ethic of care" is seen to be women's special province. But again, for all women universally, or for a few defined by a particular gender role, one which in itself may be quite variable?

There is no reason to question the fact that the 25 college women Professor Gilligan studied did speak with the 'different voice' she outlines. The remaining questions are two: (1) What does this tell us about 'all women' worldwide? but, the even more basic issue is: (2) has she simply articulated a 'gender voice' that is fully changeable with different education and culture and not something indigenous to all women as members of the female species? Put in another way, would Gilligan's twenty-five highly selected women have spoken in this voice if they had been differently trained? or, if circumstances forced them

57

the past has come primarily from men. It was never the case that all men put all women down. For centuries men saw in women those virtues which their society either did not allow males to exhibit or which they saw as a needed compliment to their own talents, for example, the protective mother vs. the aggressive warrior; laboring in mines or on the land or on ship vs. caring for a home. The problem with these past idealizations of women, as feminists point out, is that they can be used as an excuse to confine women to those stereotypical gender roles, whereas the new press is to open other gender roles which before were closed.

But for any virtue you can name, women have not been alone. Men can exemplify them or women can fail to express them too. Virtue, then, is where you find it, just as infamy is. If men have held larger numbers of public power roles, their infamies are also more devastating, more noticeable, for example, torture, oppression, and slaughter. But if these negativities are a byproduct of power, women will be capable of exhibiting infamy too and will be not alone in this. This has been true privately; with sharing the public stage it may now become overt. Thus, the mixture should become greater as barriers are broken down, and one will not be able to judge either virtue or infamy simply by sex linkage. And because women are not alone in

---

into, say, desperate situations, would they still report as they did? What relation does this study bear to a sample of twenty-five black slave women, or women from the slums of Manila, or from the refugee camps in Cambodia?

We need also to ask if the same voice could be found in men, provided the sample were well chosen. Would Professor Gilligan do a contrast study of twenty-five men from the Boston Gay Student Union and compare the results with twenty-five women from the Lesbian Coalition? And almost more important than these matters: How might the 'voices' of the women she interviewed change if they were successful in achieving power? Did Margaret Thatcher and Indira Ghandi speak in that voice when they were students in Sommerville College at Oxford and then change their voice when they came to power? We need to know this in order to judge whether this 'different voice' Gilligan has uncovered is simply a stage, an intellectual affectation, one which can be shed when power roles between the sexes are reversed.

this, one cannot judge them in independence from the men with whom they interact and challenge.

One irony—but in the long run hopeful—result of "The Feminist Challenge" is that women can no longer be as easily judged in any way that is solely based on their sex. They have always been part and parcel of the human scene, but as a result of feminist stress on 'women's history', women were singled out for attention as a sex in their existing and in their past gender roles. Yet as this stress and special attention achieves its purpose of breaking down exclusive gender roles, the irony is that women become less separate, less identifiable by sex, except for lesbian or other exclusively women's groups.[44] The result of demanding evaluation not on the basis of sex, of opposing all sex discrimination, is that increasingly women must be judged only in the context of both men and women. Thus, so far as the elimination of sex discrimination is successful, women must be judged only on the basis of ability and performance—as we all ought to be too.

Thus, women on the lower end of any scale will in that sense share more with 'marginalized' men than with "women at the top." This is similar to the dilemma of the black woman who finds that she may identify more with poor black males than with affluent white women. What happens is that, increasingly, race, class, education, talent, even religion must come back into play in structuring human relationships, rather than our giving singular attention to women as a sex. In this sense women are still female by sex, which is a meaningful and important fact, but they do not stand alone. Women

---

[44] Carol Christ, *Diving Deep and Surfacing. Women Writers on Spiritual Quest* (Boston: Beacon Press, 1980).

Christ states: "I am seeking to find a voice and style of writing that is passionate, personal, political and scholarly, and reflective" (p. xi). She proposes that we give up our quest to ally ourselves with a transcendent source of power. The goal of the mystical quest is to understand that we are part of the world. "The telling of women's spiritual quest has the power to transform our lives and our relation to the world in which we live" (p. xxiii).

are not alone, not so much in that all women stand together as that they locate their place in any society by any number of norms, as their male brothers do too, and then they find themselves judged either fairly or unfairly.

B. Becket's Women

The contemporary women's movement has cast many things in a new light. It casts old problems in new forms. Anouilh's play, *Becket*,[45] has been a classic since it was first performed in London in 1961. T.S. Eliot's *Murder in the Cathedral* is another version of this famous and traditional struggle between God and country, friendship and honor, love and sacrifice. But thirty years later, it is illuminating to study the way Becket portrayed women. We cannot simply say that this represents Anouilh's view; he tells it like it was in England and France in that time. War fought by horses and foot soldiers quite naturally gives men the dominant position. Becket's women are either slaves or treated as personal property; they are portrayed either as accepting love and favor or as forced to conceal their hatred.

We should not be too indignant about "women's lower role" as Anouilh portrays it. We should celebrate how far she has come and ask ourselves: What made the change possible; what opened a different order to us now? To understand this we must not single out his portrayal of women and complain that they were 'suppressed', which many (but not all) were. First, we must study the life of men at that time, the average powerless man, and see in what way "women were not alone." That is, how did their status mirror the condition of most of people who were powerless to control their destiny? A few kings, nobles, warriors were in control. The vast majority of all men or women accepted their destiny or died.

---

[45] Jean Anouilh, *Becket*, trans. L. Hill (London: Methuen, 1961). All page references are to this volume.

What 'rights' did women have? Few men had any rights, except what birth or superior strength gave them. To change this, you first had to establish the authority of law and then the rights of man. Religion, of course, was one way out for both men and women, and this may account for the wide popularity of religious orders before the spread of democracy. But except for Popes and Bishops, the religious life meant giving up any claim to temporal power. Only in a "civil society" can we press for equality for women, but not when most men are unequal and unrecognized as individuals. Further, even after Kings had their power taken away as democratic states appeared, women still had to wait for medicine to release them from the arduous necessity of childbirth before any change in status became possible.

Did both Henry and Becket treat women as their possessions? Yes, but they treated all they could capture as theirs. Did they explore and then conquer? Yes, if they could. What else would it have seemed 'right' for you to do in that day, given the alternative of being a conquered people, which is the undertone in Anouilh's play. To the conquerors belonged the spoils. Who denied that? How could they think differently? In the Hebrew scriptures Yahweh operates on that rule quite a bit of the time. He just promises to help the Israelites if they will obey his commandments—but his 'help' means to slaughter their enemies, oft times.

"The Saxon's only birthright was slaughter," Becket says (p. 9). In such a situation, it would be foolish to talk of "women's rights." How were "human rights" first to be established and won? That question comes first. In at least that sense men were 'first.' For until men succeeded in establishing the right to freedom for all, women had no chance. The king calls the poor peasant he encounters a 'dog', and the man cringes, silent with his hate. Until the male peasant can stop trembling like a cornered animal in the king's presence, there is no thought of women's release. The king reports that "the populace must live in fear; it's essential" (p. 24). That includes both men and women. So nothing can be done until fear of the ruler no longer dominates the majority, just as it is clear that the masses in many places still live in fear today. Burma must throw off the general reign of terror before women can rise.

"No man is worth a horse!" exclaimed the king (p. 31). If so, how can women establish their true worth until men can first establish theirs? "One can't change one's nature," adds the king (p. 33). All men at his time were thought to be fixed by nature just as much as women were. It is not that all men were always free and only women not. "You belong to a conquered race too," says Becket's mistress to him in order to taunt him. But this should remind us that the vast majority of men for centuries lived as someone's captives. And many still do, even if fear has been released. Race was an issue then and now. Becket says, "If you were only of my race, how simple everything would be" (p. 39). Race separates man from man, that is the first barrier—sex is second. Where kings and despots reign, *all* others belong to de Beauvoir's "second sex."

If we act as if sex were the only factor dividing us from each other, as if it were the only weapon of subjugation, we vastly oversimplify "the human bondage" and may fail in our attempt to liberate each other. Where, we need to ask, does sex come in the rank ordering of factors used to keep us all in bondage? And the answer is, at least not in first place. Let women throw off every trace of being "the second sex" and they would still have to ask, "What prevents us from being free? Individual freedom may be a rare commodity, one which is only slightly sex linked." That sex has been used to repress, all that is too true. But the issue is: if now we are released from all sex discrimination, are all human problems in each individual woman's control?

The king's barons say, "When you meet the enemy on the battle field, do you ask yourself questions, 'like a pair of women'? No, you just fall to and fight" (p. 41). And so it was and still is often so. In this case, we first have to hold war and hatred in check so that the privilege of asking questions is established and can become an alternate way to solve human problems. When this 'civilized level' is accomplished, then women can emerge with their questions, as they have of late. Otherwise the world tends toward butchery, as Becket observed and as still is so often the case. It is not true that all advance in human rights is the creation of Western Civilization. But we do have to ask where we might be without Greece, Rome and the cultural and political struggles of Europe, not to mention our religious tradition.

God plumbs "the hidden depths of poor men's puny frames as carefully as those of kings. And sees beneath these outward differences...the same pride, the same vanity, the same petty, complacent preoccupation with oneself," Becket reports (p. 94). Cannot the same thing be said about both men and women? What do we conclude, then? That we have to work, always, constantly, to remove, or at least to lessen, the external barriers that divide us and hold all back. But when we have lowered each barrier, sex perhaps more recently for purely medical reasons, the preoccupation with oneself is as common a failing of women as of men. It infects all we try to accomplish, whether our leaders are men or women.

We distort our problem if we make out the poor and women to be the source of all virtue. Virtue and vice, it may be, are connected to no single outward, observable sign, easy as it would be if they were. If sex has been used to "put women down," as it has, overcoming that prejudice of physiology, like the prejudice of race, does not guarantee that all who formerly were suppressed will now become the fountainhead of virtue and accomplishment. The sources of our humanism, as well as of our powers to destroy one another, are still there, and they actually operate more insidiously when not connected to observable characteristics. "Becket's women" have a long way to go to achieve the status that many women have today, but the majority of Becket's men had to suffer and die for their own cause first, in order to open the door to the possibility for a "new deal" for all oppressed groups.

C. The Women's Movement Rests on Difference

"The catch-twenty-two" situation of the Women's Movement in its recent re-emergence perhaps lies in its assertion of the necessity for full equality now. In pressing for this, they have of necessity argued for the virtues of their sex in order to offset the negative assignment of deficiency asserted by some males in an effort to fend off challenge from new competition. As Deborah Rhode puts this paradox, "The women's movement rests on the difference it seeks to challenge" (p. 1).[46] Feminism seeks a unity among all of its sex in order to challenge the confinement to any fixity of role. But this can only be a valid argument if no fixity binds the sex and all rigidity has been imposed upon it from outside, except reproduction which is now made voluntary. Feminists often assume a universally shared

---

[46] Deborah L. Rhode, *Theoretical Perspectives on Sexual Difference* (New Haven and London: Yale University Press, 1990).

The issue of "sexual difference," the editor argues, is central to the American women's movement, and this set of essays does a fine job of bringing one up-to-date on the movement, particularly its diversity. The paradox: The women's movement rests on the difference it seeks to challenge (p. 1). Feminism assumes a shared experience, but the issue is complicated by the diversity of those experiences. Can you acknowledge differences without amplifying them? Some even want to "dislodge" difference, to challenge its centrality as a principle.

As one example of the challenge to the supposed benefit of "difference," women's participation did not purify politics as gaining the vote was predicted to do. Partly due to these observed results, feminist theory has expressed growing ambivalence about the capacities of theory. Post-modernism has been influential in this tendency, but can the "deconstruction" of theory serve as a basis for the feminist desire to construct a social vision? "Yet how can feminists rally around the concept of Women once they deny that any such category exists?" (p. 8). "The emphasis is on understanding the complexity that really exists when we speak of gender," the concluding essay remarks (p. 260). This is a remarkable collection.

experience, but that is also exactly what they seek to challenge. Yet any evolutionary climb is built on the adaptability, not the fixity, of any species, male or female (see chapter I).

Can you assert 'difference' as the basis for your demand for change? For instance, some feminist theorists have been attracted to "post-modernism"[47] as a mode of thought precisely because it challenges the fixity of 'essence'. Then, can you call for all of one sex to rally around the concept of 'women' when you have just celebrated the fact that no such fixed categories exist but that all categories are artificially constructed? Yet Rhode notes ironically, "Without the category of women, the feminist project founders," (p. 15) —at least in fixing any agreed goals solely based on sex. She concludes, "Feminists are caught in the dilemma of simultaneously demanding and scorning equality with men" (p. 253). If they claim any privileged status, they are by that very claim restricting their freedom for the change they demand as their evolutionary right.

The graphs of our human progress do not ascend in a straight line, perhaps not even in a logical dialectical line which is rationally detected and comprehensible. Much as Moderns do not like to hear it, whether they are male or female, a cyclical model is perhaps worth bearing in mind. However, given Darwin's account of our origins, we know that advance, self-control, artistic-creative life is possible, but it is just as difficult to sustain as it is to achieve. It is always based on struggle and loss and, without exception it depends on cooperation between the sexes. It is, of course, no contradiction for Darwin to see competition, even warfare, between the sexes as still operative too, never completely eliminated, but as our primitive origin still operative. All forms of human liberation are involved in the complex balance of loss and competition, terror and achieved peace, of which the liberation of women is only one example. We did not create

---

[47]   Annie Dillard, *An American Childhood* (New York: Harper and Row, 1987).

ourselves; we cannot eliminate our primitive inheritance.

Of course, women can abandon any claim to protected status and point to their higher death rate in childbirth as evidence of the suffering they wish to escape and for which they demand reparation now, long after their lengthy confinement. But we need to note one oversight if women are singled out.

Men shared all the other physical miseries of women, those induced by poverty and disease, and they still do to the extent that these have not been eliminated. Even more important, we must add into the formula for women's compensation that men had "the additional privilege of dying on the battlefields, sometimes in massive assaults involving massive suffering" (p. 467). Now as women enter warfare, will it be improved or eliminated by their sex-linked peaceful nature? Rhode notes: "Women's participation did not purify politics" (p. 6). Antonio Fraser's *Warrior Queens*,[48] and the recently powerful prominent women political leaders, seem to bear this out. The fact is that we cannot count on all women working together in unison to offer us a peaceful world.

If, then, women must claim the same biological lineage as men, inheriting lately the same potential for individual advantage which men have held for some time by claiming it as the birthright of their sex, women must accept the struggle which gave men for so long an advantage and brought them out ahead, as well as the lack of conformity by sex. All men did not become fierce warriors or harsh leaders or even make full use of the temporary advantage which their sex offered them. Some did and turned to impose a limited status on women, claiming this as a fixed biological necessity.

As we discovered in uncovering our means of 'descent', we know that this cannot be true; fixity is the result of struggle beginning from non-fixed chaos; "heroes are made not born" by sex. It is sexual

---

[48] See Antonia Fraser, chapter I, note 30.

limitation that at long last women (at least some, never all) can and want to throw off. But when they do this, they enter into open competition. In this struggle to rise, some in both sexes are weak and will not survive. Once freed biologically, women can compete to survive—if they want to.

In examining Mary Ritter Beard and her early struggle for women[49] Ann Lane finds her an "intransigent feminist," as outspoken and as strong as any male. But she is also against intransigent feminists who claim all men to be demoniac or oppressive. In contrast, she found that women often in fact "thrived in the academic world as she knew it." It was for Mary Beard a matter of entering into the competition without apology. This is not to say that non-necessary barriers and handicaps have not been placed in your way, for males as well as females. But tracing one's origins tells us that survival depends upon struggle and that many will be eliminated,

---

[49] Ann Lane, *Mary Ritter Beard:A Sourcebook* (Boston: Northeastern University Press, 1988).

When one reads that Mary Beard published *Women as a Force in History* in 1946 one should reconsider what is meant when it is said that women have been left out of history. Here is a prominent woman historian's important piece on women in history. Her thesis was that women "have always been a very real, although unrecognized, force in society." Thus, perhaps it is not so much that women have not been there in history so that we need to reevaluate their importance. Beard did not think that women had been oppressed. She thought they had been active, assertive and competent contributors (p. 1). But power in large quantities, that they did not possess. So if one looks in major power areas, one finds women less evident.

Beard did not see any special value in "female culture," but she was militant in her call for equality. She denied that she had a career; Mary Beard had a calling. She wanted an encyclopedia of women to widen "the knowledge of women in history" (p. 44). Modern society actually reduced the power of women, she felt. If women had only stopped and looked at their past, "they would have realized the strength and power they had throughout all of human history" (p. 57). She battled the anti-women as well as the militant feminists. Where there were ruling classes, women in the ruling class exercised enormous power. Slaves suffered not as women but as slaves. Democracy poses certain problems for women, but Mary Beard rejected any notion that women had been oppressed in mass throughout history.

even ruthlessly, unless we can establish standards for "justice and fairness" outside those of strength. This is our conscious addition to an otherwise often terrifying natural competition. But we are well advised not to deny the evolutionary need to struggle for survival. It is our common biological inheritance. In that sense sex is a secondary factor.

Is it true that the women's movement must, as it appears in a new incarnation, rest on a claim to 'difference'? And if this is ironically linked to the very fixity of species which women want to escape (and which Darwin argues cannot have existed in our origins), what is our means of exit from this dilemma and thus for promoting women's advance? First, it depends on outlining the ascent of man from a biologically imposed role toward the self-control of developed talent, political democracy, and moral standards. Next, we must model female ascent on the same plan, explaining the lag in descent due to evolutionary fixity and a biological need for fecundity and overproduction.

Now, conscious direction having led to our biological control of sexual relations, we can argue against any intellectual difference between individuals due to the sex alone. We point out humanity's crowning glory of achieving even partial control over our destiny, not automatically or for everyone, but by struggle and at least for the strong-in-spirit. Some men have tried to hold this spirit of ethical fairness in trust for all, and now this crown can be fully shared by woman—or it can be if she will abandon all claims to simple sexual virtue or privilege.

Women may first want to, need to, identify with all of their sex, seeking a biological identity. But that will prove not to be an adequate basis for equality of opportunity. Next they must, as many of their role models have before them, identify with all who suffer and seek relief. "Becket's women" were considered to be male possessions, sometimes lovingly (we must not forget that as we move to reject all sexual uniformity) and sometimes not. But few men in Becket's time had any feeling of individual worth or freedom either. We seek the identity of a group as the basis for our struggle to advance (which is our biological inheritance). But as these bonds of uniformity by sex prove more restrictive than helpful, and even often become the basis for new repressions, we must seek some human 'common cause' and unite with the best that the human species can produce, morally and creatively. We must struggle with our urge to exist, to define our own descent, our precarious but possible human freedom.

D. Can a Hatred for 'Patriarchy' Produce a Better Society for Women?

"It is lunacy to suppose that appeals to class hatred could produce a society transformed for the better" (p. 33).
—Frederick Copleston in *Russian Religious Philosophy*.[50]

"We must do more than free ourselves; We must embark on the path of healing - and revolutions do not heal" (p. 177).
—Aleksandr Solzhennitsyn in *East and West*.[51]

The Modern Feminist Movement is a 'revolutionary' activity, insofar as it aims at a radical reconstruction of society.[52] In that sense,

---

[50]   Frederick Copleston, *Russian Religious Philosophy* (Notre Dame: University of Notre Dame, 1988).
[51]   Aleksandr Solzhennitsyn, *East and West* (New York: Harper & Row, 1980).
[52]   Mary Daly, *The Church of the Second Sex With a New Feminist PostChristian Introduction* (New York: Harper and Row, 1968).
This reissue of Mary Daly's 1968 book is a fascinating document of contrasts. Her new introduction, written not ten years later, claims that we cannot even recognize the person who was the author. She has changed from 'radical Catholic' to PostChristian feminist. She had hoped to reform Christianity but found it beyond hope. Of course, one must recognize that Mary Daly primarily equates 'Christianity' with the Roman church. She had struggled

it is 'Modern' because 'revolution' as a theory and as an aim is relatively recent in human history. Improvement, change in the human condition? Yes. Classical, even Medieval views, allowed that. Most religions can be viewed as offers of release to the person or even as the giving of 'new life'. But an important change arrived when 'revolution' became a reigning ideology, the thought that societies and human nature could be fundamentally altered by our own power with the use of insightful theory.

Optimism over this new possibility can be seen as one of the major setbacks to religious belief, particularly among intellectuals converted to various proposals for radical change, from Freudian

---

because she was fired from Jesuit Boston College (although restored after a long battle), but she does not consider other forms of Christianity, such as the Society of Friends.

She no longer seeks equality in the church, which the original book did, but "began dreaming new dreams of a women's revolution" (p. 14). Sexism was inherent in the symbol system of Christianity itself, she found, and so it must be abandoned. The idea of 'equality' in a patriarchical system she hoped for originally was doomed. Marriage is oppressive itself, she concludes. She now experiences the growth of New Amazon Culture, not a reform of the old. If God is male, she concludes then that male is God. "Today we are creating feminist theory out of women's experience" (p. 41). Christianity "is the inevitable enemy of human progress" (p. 46), her new conclusion concludes.

Mary Daly, *Wickedary of the English Language* (Boston: Beacon Press, 1987).

It fits perfectly with Mary Daly's increasing radical posture that she should 'conjure' (as she says) a new dictionary. Any inherited structure is contaminated and must be dismantled. But the more difficult task is to create a new language free of male taint. She wants to use the image of the 'weaver' (as Plato did) for women, and in this case it means to be a weaver of words. But it is a 'wickedary' because it is beyond patriarchical 'good' and 'evil'. Nietzsche wanted to go beyond good and evil and Daly does too for quite different reasons. Like birds, Daly wants her new words to be winged.

This is designed to help wicked women to stray and stay off the tracks of trained responses and traditional expectations (p. xix). Women must learn to trust their own sense of direction and timing. Words must be freed from the cages and persons of patriarchical patterns. We are to "unveil and release the powerful witch within ourselves," she says (p. 7). Spelling, grammar and pronunciation must be challenged. "Words and women reclaim our own Nations" (p. 43).

See also: Zillah R. Einstein, *The Radical Future of Liberal Feminism* (Boston: Northeastern University Press, 1986).

analysis, to Marxism, to Nietzsche's Superman. Kings, even com-
moners, need no longer build chapels and churches everywhere they
reside. The power for change, they were sure, had shifted its locus. It
was natural that feminism in its recent incarnation should take a lead
from revolutionary theory, since it wanted not only equal rights but
a fundamental social restructuring.[53]

When the worldwide Women's Movement lists its agenda, it must
be admitted that at least in certain countries great strides have been
made in opening new avenues for women.[54] What remains to be done
to improve women's opportunities is a matter of debate and of
deciding which political organization needed to accomplish further
goals in a wide variety of cultures. But in assessing what has been
accomplished, in dealing with what some call the 'backlash'[55] against
feminists' accomplishments, it might be wise to consider the link

---

[53]   Andrea Dworkin, *Women Hating* (New York: E.P. Dutton, 1974).

"This book is an action, a political action where revolution is the goal," Dworkin
begins. She wants to restructure community forms and human consciousness. There is a
commitment to end male dominance. Once women understand oppression, they begin to
articulate a politically conscious feminism. In doing this, "the destruction of the middle-class
lifestyle is crucial to the development of decent community forms" (p. 22). The culture
predetermines who we are, how we behave, and that is what must be opposed. She wants to
abandon the opposition of man and woman. The words 'male' and 'female' "are used only
because as yet there are no others" (p. 176). The object is cultural transformation,
communities "where androgyny is the operative premise" (p. 193).

[54]   Jessie Bernard, *The Female World from a Global Perspective* (Bloomingston,
Indiana University Press, 1987).

In recent Feminist writings, almost everyone has agreed that 'women' cannot be
defined solely from white, western, privileged experience. The search is for the global, and
Bernard attempts just this. Cultural imperialism in feminism is to be avoided. Yet she makes
no claim to expect a 'global female solidarity'. But almost everywhere, women spend a great
deal of their lives bearing and rearing children. As a sociologist, what Bernard has done is
to examine and collect a great many statistics on women's lives around the globe.
Everywhere women's labor is different from man's. Women have difficulty achieving
equitable integration with the male world, but it is "only slightly less difficult to achieve it
within the female world" (p. 109). Yet due to increased communication and networking, she
predicts "A Decade for Women." "The female world now in process is new" (p. 187).

[55]   Susan Faludi, *Backlash* (London: Chatto and Windus, 1991).

with 'revolutionary' doctrine in the light of recent events. If the breakup of the U.S.S.R. and the admitted terror and human destruction involved offers any instruction, it might be what Copleston argues: That the hatred of a class cannot produce a transformation of society but rather its eventual disintegration.

Revolutions may be necessary, but in themselves they do not produce healing, Solzhennitsyn reminds us. The French revolution and its rein of terror offers, of course, another classical example. Thus, we have to ask: If feminism builds its agenda in any way on a hatred of 'patriarchy' and thus of men, can this lead to the society they want? And further, where wounds have been admittedly deep, is healing more important than vengeance? How can the Women's Movement both veer away from attacking men as a whole and find its own formula for healing the long standing wrongs? The hatred of any group, class, race, or sex as such seems inevitably to lead to further trouble, not to bring reconciliation and a new community of understanding.

Why? Because good and evil are not easy to pin down and do not attach to any group as universally applicable, not even to 'capitalists'. If both evil and good can only be individually attached, why then do rational people ever argue for the good or the evil of any group as such? Because individual assessment is exceedingly difficult, and even individuals offer a mixture of motives which are often hard to sort out.

It would be so much easier if all women were virtuous and all males corrupt. Our love of good, and our hatred of evil, seems to need a clear focus, a target. But if we are wrong in seeing this as attached to one group, then to base any revolutionary proposals on such a premise, for example, against the proletariat, against patriarchy, is to move the proposal for beneficial change toward self-destruction. This is because its target is over simplified. Frustration over unanticipated complexity begets rage, begets destruction.

The notion that all men have suppressed all women, or that all women have always offered support to other women and been the bearers of peace while men as a group breed discrimination. This scenario vastly over-simplifies the complexity of the human situation. It strikes out in general denunciation, when individual appraisal is what is required. Individual men have been peaceful, for example, Jesus and George Fox. Individual women have been hostile and destructive. Certain general characteristics of groups may be discernible and definable at times, but these tend to shift and so form a poor basis for absolute allegation, whether of good or of evil. They so distort the target for revolutionary change that its misjudgments often lead to unleashing a terror that destroys.

The same problem plagues any group hatred, of course, Blacks against White, Catholic against Protestant, Jew against Gentile. The notion that the world splits so easily into good and evil makes nonsense out of the agony of human relationships. Of course, how to deal with this complexity raises the question of adopting "a little bit of Christianity"—or Buddhism, or any conciliatory doctrine for that matter whether Quaker or Baha'i. Groups have been warring against groups, seeking to destroy their supposed enemy, without any knowledge of the guilt or innocence, virtue or vice, of those toward whom guns are aimed and violence unleashed. The notion that one achieves one's independence and his or her fulfillment by destroying one's 'long traditional' enemies— this is an ancient theory, one that still breaks out again all over the world.

Against these holocausts, against the sacrifices of mass victims, stands Jesus' almost plaintive advice: Love one's enemies, forgive your persecutors. Of course, we know that this did not work in Jesus' case. He was crucified. His judges were urged on by mobs who could not have known much about him. The suppression of the Jews, the power of Rome that contained them, all remained in place after Jesus was gone. So on a 'practical' level, Jesus' advice seems little useful.

And also not much practiced. As I say, "Jesus came preaching love and forgiveness and Christians have been fighting about it ever since." Jew or Muslim, Christian or Hindu, the record of each, at least as far as their use of violence to destroy their 'enemies' is concerned, is a dark record with perhaps individual bright spots, for example, St. Francis and Mother Theresa.

Does this mean that feminists, looking at the dismal record and the impracticality of preaching forgiveness, while facing the massive power structures which suppress and resist change—that they must seek power and gain unity for their cause by promoting hatred of a fictional enemy, for example, patriarchy ('fictional' because all men have never united against all women)? No, if the record of groups preaching peace has not been all that peaceful, there is still a negative lesson to be learned: revolutions do not succeed based on the hatred of any group, and the necessary healing in a society is never accomplished by the harshness of revolutions unless a period of reconciliation follows. Of course there is a 'backlash' to any movement, since all cannot unite behind any cause. Human nature is diverse and its roots never uniform. But the more important question is: After our 'high' in tasting blood and power, upon what basis can a new society be built? Is forgiveness and the absence of hatred a necessity?

Underlying this is the other question: Just how much does human nature yield to being reshaped? We know that individuals are subject to radical change, to conversion experiences whether religious or theoretical. But can whole masses of peoples be reshaped on command?—that is the burning issue of the era of revolution. We know that masses can be forced to outward conformity by military might and the use of terror. But whenever that is removed, as happened in the breakup behind the Iron Curtain, do we not find the same human foibles, the same follies, the same indecisiveness, instead of reshaped masses?

That is: insofar as the supposed unanimity of a liberating group begins to splinter, the probable unconscious reaction is to wish to silence all opposition, even if it is only a dissent in theory. We try to bring any who disagree with us into enforced conformity of thought. The closest parallel for "politically correct thinking" in recent times is the Chinese Cultural Revolution. Marxism had won the revolution; Mao was in power, but the total transformation of a vast society seemed to slip from their grasp. The only recourse was to try to silence all dissent, bring all into a thought-conformity, when the reality was that the supposed ideological uniformity had never been there.

Revolutionary movements cannot tolerate democracies or individual freedom of dissent. These political notions of the Enlightenment do not support conformist transformation projects. Far from it. Yet the forces that suppress individual fulfillment are still very much alive. And if they are not opposed, our freedom remains threatened, our ideal goals thwarted. A "razor's edge" must be navigated, but revolutions are usually too blatant in their contrasts of black and white to accept subtle oppositions and so establish a new "Bill of Rights" for all. But take care; use caution; avoid blanket condemnation, so that the change, the revolution in society, does not slip into an illusory, and thus destructive, hatred of any group or representative person as such.

E. "Despite Every Priest in Prague"

Anthony Trollope is lucky that he isn't writing today. If he had trouble in getting his work established in his own day, and if it took him over a century to earn his place in Westminster Abbey as a classic author, he would face a storm of criticism today for violating more recently devised taboos. In *Nina Balatka*[56] he depicts the

---

[56] Anthony Trollope, *Nina Balatka, Linda Tressely* (New York: Oxford University Press, 1991).

struggle of Jew and Christian lovers to overcome the prejudices of race and religion. That much might earn him credit in today's 'open society', but the manner in which he does this could cause protests and demonstrations on any college or university campus. "He indulges in racial stereotypes!," it would be claimed. And so he does, as must every author, else the world could not be written down. The protest comes, "But he portrays women as weak and dependent on men!" And so he does and so they often are. Anthony Trollope would have as much trouble getting an honorary degree at Wellesley College today as Barbara Bush did.

How 'offensive' is his portrait of the Jews in Prague? Not very; Shakespeare was less kind. But in this love affair, Trollope portrays Nina's Jewish lover as torn between love and money. Successful business man that he is, he lets his "sharp business sense" trap him into accusing his Christian fiancee of deceit. True, Jews live in a segregated section of Prague, but the portrayal of their religious life is in fact flattering. The Jewish hero of his story is portrayed as sharp, intellectual, not easy-going. He lets his 'business sense' blot out the emotion of his romantic attachment. Trollope uses "Jew" as a term of reprobation, as it probably was so used in Prague.

Why, then, if his picture is not harsh, could there be any objection to his portrayal of the Jew's sharp and successful business sense? Probably it was just so. Because any persecuted group should only be favorably represented, or so it seems. Or at least they must be depicted as they now would like to be, even if in fact the noted characteristics were once true but have changed.

Yet Trollope could probably survive this attack by claiming that he was "telling it like it was," in spite of anyone's wishes today that it was not so. Still, he would not be free from protest. It is his depiction of Nina Balatka that will have the radical feminists burning his books in the streets. She is silent, inward, dependent, romantically carried away by the mere presence of her lover (there is no hint of pre-marital sex). She swoons at his sight and declares the whole delight of her life is to be in his presence. She is, alas, "male dependent."

Of course, she has a stronger side. Distrusted by her lover, accused of deceit when his "business sense" overcomes his passion, she turns him away and goes off determined to commit suicide by throwing herself off the central bridge. In an ironic touch, the Jewish woman who loves the same man rescues her, befriends her, and is painted as the most compassionate human being in the novel. It is she who overcomes outward barriers of prejudice, and even her own desires for the same man. As we might say, she displays every 'Christian' virtue so lacking in the professional Christians who are all around Nina. It is a touching reversal of roles and an important commentary on the way individuals are caught in the rigid, formal positions of opposed religions. But Trollope's story tells us how at least one person breaks through to compassion and human sympathy.

Thanks to this self-sacrificing intervention, the lovers are united. Misunderstandings are overcome, and they ride off into the sunset (in Frank Capra, Hollywood style). They leave prejudiced Prague behind to begin a new life in a new land (only for Trollope this is Nuernberg not Los Angeles). The one who sets her own love aside and lets compassion work against her own interest, which would be to see her competitor defeated, such sacrifice mirrors Jesus' (another Jew) own sacrifice. But this time the hero is a woman. Romeo and Juliet is not replayed. Stubborn and vicious prejudice does not this time lead to violence. The sacrifice is made *for* the lovers but not *by* them. Can Jew and Catholic alike be satisfied with Trollope's depiction of the role of religion in this near tragedy? True, the priest whose wrath Nina feared did not prove as censorious as she imagined. True, her Jewish lover's father was strict in his orthodox beliefs and practices but was quietly kind and generous.

At the height of Nina's greatest anguish, as the drama nears its climax, she turns to God in sheer fear. But she says she is sure God will not feel as totally blasphemed by her love of a Jew as her Christian family has been. She concludes "He [God] could save her f He would, despite every priest in Prague" (p.185). Surely this is a piece of irony equal to Trollope's casting Nina's Jewish rival in the role of a sacrificing savior for the Christian apostate. The formalities of the Church and its militant believers are lined up against Nina's love for a Jew. But she gets a glimpse that God might stand outside the barriers of religious prejudice and self-righteousness and have some compassion for the individual. God could be forgiving, even if priests and 'Christians' are not.

Thus, Trollope gives us a vivid story of people caught in the struggle between religion and race, just as Romeo and Juliet were caught between the hatred of one family for another. Religious rigidity is contrasted to the loving passion of individuals whose relationship transcends such inconsiderate confines. True, Trollope's portrayal of religious narrowness should cause pastors and priests, even popes and bishops, to protest in Saint Peter's Square that they have been badly stereotyped. And so they have; but again the issue is: Do some deserve it? Even if overdrawn by literary license, is it after all unfortunately all too true? For public consumption, organized religion preaches its message of compassion and salvation. In its officialdom, in its translations into the prejudices and the fears of its followers, it often tears people apart—all the while some individuals outside its hierarchies may practice its professed saving compassion.

Like Humpty Dumpty fallen off the wall, "all the priests in Prague" could not put Nina Balatka back together again. Her Christian priest was not full of denunciations, but neither was he helpful in her distress. But a Jew saved the Christian while all the priests in Prague were silent. Trollope may or may not have intended to preach a religious moral in his story. Yet surely it portrays the damage that religious rigidity can inflict and how religion too often stands against compassion for those who suffer, even those who suffer from the distortions of its own doctrine.

Trollope's is not an anti-religious diatribe; far from it. He focuses more on human prejudices and harm than on its institutional forms. "The human people" are the ones caught in-between the tribal warfare of religious institutions. But as in every major religion's gospel story, it is the people who overcome the prejudice that had been first instilled in them and then played upon by others for selfish purposes. They rise to this height by their human compassion. In such a struggle, women are never alone. They stand together with every person of compassion, whether male or female, of any race or religion.

Chapter III

Feminist Philosophy

A. Is There a Distinctive Feminist Philosophy?[57]

It is crucial to decide whether there is "a feminist philosophy"—or philosophies.[58] Why? Because nothing new can be claimed

---

[57] Ironically, "American Feminist Philosophy" developed somewhat in isolation from Continental thought and was not completely coordinated with British philosophy either. Why? In the case of England, Feminist thought there developed in complete accordance with philosophy authored by men, often following their lead. But Early American Feminist philosophers ere so intent on distancing themselves from men, that they often strove for complete independence from the past.

Continental Feminist philosophers were so much integrated into the thought of male philosophers that it would be impossible to separate their thought from its male influence. Kristeva and Iragaray are major French thinkers. Yet hardly an Early American Feminist traces her heritage to them, since they reflect so closely French thought without hostility (vs. Christ, Daly, Downing, Firestone, Friedan, Lerner, etc.).

However, as the Introduction and Postscript report, the major contemporary movement in Feminist Thought is to internationalize it away from its white, middle-class origin in America, and anti-male orientation, and also to show the pluralism within correct Feminist approaches, rather than to assert doctrinal uniformity.

[58]   Josephine Donovan, *Feminist Theory: The Intellectual Traditions of American Feminism* (New York: Continuum, 1990).

Josephine Donovan has done everyone a favor by documenting so clearly the history and the options of feminist theory. In any movement, there is a tendency to take the latest theory as the obviously "right one." By pointing out the evolution in feminist theory and its connections to various well-known intellectual movements, Donovan lets us see the variety of grounding ideologies open to feminists. She points out that "there was little really new in what these 'radicals' had to say. Much as it had been said, repeatedly, over a century before" (p. xii). Thus, "feminism" is really part of larger intellectual movements. It has appropriated theories for its own ends, but it did not necessarily originate each one.

In the eighteenth century Mary Wallstoncroft demanded the same "natural rights" for women as for men. Thus, the "women's rights" movement came out of "liberal Enlightenment" views, only later extended to women. The Enlightenment had identified "nationalism" with the public sphere and women with the private sphere, each of which was to be treated differently. So the case for women, that they too were covered by Enlightenment goals, had to be made. Proper education is the key to equality. Critical reason is the means by which

for women, other than medical advance and thus biological release, unless we can also mark out something distinctive in thought. Of course, there are women writing philosophy who have individual viewpoints, as could or perhaps should be true for any philosopher. Women now enter that ancient profession in greater numbers then in the past, as is true of a number of fields. Biology, of course, is the key factor to consider first,[59] since that, more then anything else, clearly separates women from men in the field.

But do we want to claim that intellectual thought has a unique sex linkage? In 'ethics', of course, one has the issue of motherhood and how that function raises questions for women which it may not for

women may arise. The obvious implication of this line of reasoning is that men and women are essentially the same, although they have been treated differently. "Intellect is not sexed" (p. 16), declares Gimke, which puts the rights movement on a different plane from some later theories which want to assert the uniqueness of women.

Beginning from the early "rights movement," Donovan traces the movement to Existentialism with Simone de Beauvoir, then to the connection to Marx and Freud, and finally to "radical feminism." What emerges with crystal clarity is the appropriation by feminists of other theories which are helpful to them, then applying these to the specifics of the women's situation. In no case can it be said that women initiated these theories, although in each case they are responsible for modification and application. On reflection, this makes it hard to support separatists movements by women on other than practical grounds, since feminists' theories share so much in common with wilder intellectual traditions. It is also hard to see all previous theories labeled as "male theories" since: (1) they vary so much; and (2) women identify with and use so much theory originated by various men.

Stemming from radical feminist theory, which recently has been more prominent, Donovan sees a "new feminist moral vision" emerging. This is a broader vision than one simply seeing women's rights. However, insofar as these goals envision utopian societies, they cannot claim originality but rather are coordinate with a long utopian, visionary tradition which have already helped to transform society. What is new is the stress on the claim that women's consciousness is different from men's, which goes against the grain of the earlier argument for women's rights based on the essential identity of women and men (p. 173). Virginia Woolf saw women as "custodians of a feminist value system" (p. 183). However, the irony here is that this argument leads us to an essential difference between men and women, an identification of sex and gender roles, a situation from which women have sought to escape.

[59]   Sandra Harding, *The Science Question in Feminism* (Ithaca and London: Cornell University Press, 1986).

men. At the other end of the spectrum, in 'logic' it seems much harder to claim any special perspective for women. In political theory, again, childbearing and the burden of rearing children might make certain issues more important for women. Yet that is not the same as to say that there is something distinctively 'feminine' that is unique to women in the thought about these problems. Certainly the rise of the Feminist movement itself has caused us to see many neglected issues as more important, or at least to see them in a new light.

Philosophy has changed many times during its history. As today it shifts focus once again, there is no reason not to say that the rise of women writers in much greater numbers has altered the context in which we all, or at least some, do philosophy. But to say this is quite different from claiming that there is something singularly characteristic about women's thinking that distinguishes it from that of all men. Of course, we first have to note that, in spite of all the claims of 'patriarchy' and of male dominance, true as this might have been socially or politically, it staggers the mind to try to find any way in which all men have thought alike philosophically. So the question of 'feminist philosophy' would seem to depend, at least in part, on whether there is any such thing as 'male philosophy'.[60]

---

[60] Mary Field Belenky, Blyth McVicker Clinchy, Nancy Rule Goldberger, Jill Mattuck Tarule, *Women's Ways of Knowing* (New York: Basic books, 1986).

Josephine Donovan, *Feminist Theory: The Intellectual Traditions of American Feminism* (New York: Continuum, 1990).

Women will remain 'illiterate' without a knowledge of feminist theory, Donovan states. There is little new in what radical feminists state, she feels. "Feminists have reinvented the wheel a number of times" (p. xii). Eighteenth century feminists hoped women would be entitled to the same natural rights as men. But in the 17th and 18th centuries, the assumption that women belonged in the home was nearly universal. Liberal feminists shared these Enlightenment views. Intellect is not sexed, they argued.

However, the recent argument that women are different from men contradicts the liberal belief that all people are fundamentally similar and capable of objective reasoning. Liberal feminism and cultural feminism occasionally clash, and more recent feminist theory has tended toward cultural feminism. In addition, there are the revolutionary theories derived largely from Marxism. Existentialism also comments on women, but it has not been popular.

This is not to take away from the distinctive qualities of any given woman philosopher's thought. It is simply to point out that the characteristics of the theories can no more be claimed to be 'feminine' as a universal mode of thought than a man can claim distinction as a philosopher merely by being male. Yet the impact of the increasing numbers of women who are teaching and writing in philosophy is undeniable. Of itself it causes all philosophers to rethink both the function and the meaning of 'philosophy'—which has always been the philosopher's perennial question.

'Logic' has a common meaning, in addition to its technical meaning as symbolic logic. There is the question of whether women in philosophy wish to enter logic professionally even as a critic; this

---

Donovan now sees a new feminist moral version emerging.

Mary Briody Mahowald, ed., *Philosophy of Woman* (Indianapolis: Hackett Publishing Company, 1983).

Andrea Nye, *Feminist Theory and the Philosophies of Man* (London and New York: Routledge, 1989).

Alan Soble, ed., *Philosophy of Sex* (Totowa, New Jersey: Rowman and Allanheld, 1980).

Dale Spender, ed., *Feminist Theorists* (New York: Pantheon Books, 1983).

This review of 81 feminine theorists from the 17th century to the present demonstrates the complexity of 'feminism'. In their theories and in their lives, they varied enormously. What unites them is that each found in her experience some reason to challenge the position assigned to women, a fact which also joins them to their male revolutionary counterparts.

Education became a focus for most of them, because the oppression of women had been connected to the idea, held by men and women alike, that women had no need for higher education. Yet these women all see that need. In recovering the history of feminist theory, Miriam Brody cautions us to be wary not to superimpose upon it ideas which are current to our historical condition. For instance, during World War I, all women were not inherently opposed to war, as some feminists have tended to argue recently.

Nor do these 81 feminists at all agree that women are in possession of special moral attributes. Theories can be used to oppress; theories can be used to liberate. Theories by nature cause us to diverge rather than to converge, a fact true as much for women as for men. Three centuries of feminists theories have provided rich detail and stimulating ideas but little agreement, except the need to work for human liberation and freedom of expression.

is the response Andrea Nye has given.[61] However, there is also a sense in feminist theory that it has a 'logic' of its own which we need to come to understand. Since feminist theory was begun or revived in this second half of the twentieth century, its 'logic' is perhaps its 'metaphysics'. That is, we ask: What assumptions are involved in feminist theory and its critique of history and of previous philosophies? It is important to learn the way of its arguments in order to understand the basis of the current protest. It is quite possible that most who listen to or who read the feminist critics hear the surface and do not really grasp the 'logic' of its background.

Is there, then, some special form to the argument that feminist theorists use which we and they could understand? In responding to this question, we should first note the premise almost always articulated which is that (1) they begin with women's experience and then (2) support the full liberation of women and their openness to all activities and professions in our cultural/professional life. Until the

---

[61] Andrea Nye, *Words of Power: A Feminist Reading of the History of Logic* (New York: Routledge, 1990).

Professor Nye concedes that she is not a logician, and she documents her struggles to deal with logic. She starts by questioning the common premise that logic "is not a feminine subject" (p. 2). However, what Nye does from there on is to outline the underlying assumptions in the history of logic, its 'metaphysics', which ends, she believes, with Frege's total emptying of content and formalizing logic by making it equatable to mathematics. Logicians have continually denied the connection of logic to the lives and culture of its developers. Thus, the formalization of logic completes the divorce of logic from its content and its originators' lives.

Nye stops short of 'feminizing' logic, but she wants to set it in a cultural context and to 'humanize' it. Logic began with Parmenides, she reports, as akin to poetry. However, Nye charts the continuous movement away from this connection toward a lack of all connection to the vagueness of life. But she states: "There can be no feminist logic that exposes masculine logic as sexist or authoritarian" (p. 175). Nevertheless, women must plunge into the arena of discussion and demand the right to speak (p. 178) There is an escape from the 'logical dilemma' which she recommends: attending, listening, understanding (p. 183), recognizing our common humanity (p. 184). All that seems odd in this account is Nye's failure to refer to Hegel's cultural, dialectical logic, and also Existentialism and Pragmatism, which argued for the human context of all thought over a century ago.

basic logic of this argument is understood, and next appraised as to its implications and its meanings, feminist logic will always escape us and our response will fall short.

B. Feminism and Theory

Does the feminist desired revolution in human relations depend on a uniformity in theory, or even on any theory at all, for its success? From Hegel to Marx to the Frankfurt School and Freud, theory has been shown to be as 'irrational', as potentially repressive as it is liberating. Totalitarianism rests on theory too. Then, can there be one right, rational theory that is not at the same time repressive? That is a hard case to prove, one yet to be made out.

Some feminists began by stressing 'sisterhood' and wanted all women to join together in their common cause. Yet to insist on achieving unity in theory, or group identity, could, ironically, result in greater division. Any advocated, singular theory can be used to repress dissent. If feminists believe in the long-fought-for right of dissent and the protection of minority opinion, that right must be applied within the movement itself (see Preface). It is quite easy to outline the practical issues: the right to vote, equal economic opportunity, education, and so forth. But to insist that all women must unite around one theory will have the effect of causing extensive arguments over theory, rather than bringing about the desired social change. Feminism needs theory, as all movements advocating change do, but we also need to avoid theory's divisive and repressive potential as being destructive of a desirable goal.

Philosophical assumptions must be at work in the very definition of 'feminism'. The critique one gives of society depends on the philosophical basis one adopts, and no philosophy is either natural or obvious. If new utopian societies are envisaged, either as inhabited by women alone or as based on 'women's values', we must ask what assumptions are necessary in our philosophy that makes us think that utopias can be created, not merely postulated ideally. Plato offered a model Republic, but it is clear that he did not think it could exist in fact, whatever value it might have as an ideal.

All important concepts, philosophers have long argued, are multiple in meaning and need a careful sorting out. 'Feminism', like truth, beauty and justice is a case in point. There is no single, obvious agreement as to what 'feminism' does mean or how it ought to be defined.[62] Its various definitions may be finite and not indefinitely numerous. Still, without philosophical analysis, we cannot be sure what 'feminism' means, or might mean, when it is appealed to. Thus, feminism depends for its force upon establishing some particular view as acceptable. Philosophical analysis, then, shapes what feminism can mean. 'Philosophy' represents that basic questioning of assumptions and terms which must or at least should—take place first, before campaigns are mounted on the basis of any theory.

Have today's women, then, simply rediscovered Aristotle's discipline of 'metaphysics'? That Greek philosopher said that most thinkers assume their premises and then simply argue from them, instead of working backward and questioning their basic assumptions. Aristotle felt that we needed a 'science', a discipline, which turns back and inquires into these assumed first principles. This inquiry he called 'metaphysics'.

Feminist philosophers today question the assumptions of most earlier philosophers, particularly if they exhibit bias against women. Many do not like Cartesian epistemology. But this simply means that they act as metaphysicians and call into question the basic assumptions of that, or of any, view. Male philosophers have engaged in this same basic questioning too, but often it takes a momentous event to cause us to begin such inquiry, which is exactly what 'the women's movement' has brought about.

---

[62] See "50 Ways to be a Feminist," chapter I, note 32.

Perhaps, then, 'Feminism' is simply the latest in the crucial events in western (or eastern or any) thought that causes us to look critically at assumptions in our theories which we have too long taken for granted. Marxism and Existentialism have done this for us by challenging Hegel, just as the 'new physics' has too. And now the question of 'Feminism' has caused the same reflection on assumptions we have long taken for granted. Whether from Marxist revolutionaries or from feminist radicals,[63] philosophers should always consider those movements or groups who challenge us. They cause us to turn to and question assumptions which we have taken for granted.

Feminists often claim that women have been neglected or excluded in recorded history. Therefore, we need to check the basic postulates of current or traditional thought and ask, "Have we made

---

[63]   Charnie Guettel, *Marxism and Feminism* (Toronto: The Women's Press, 1974). Angela Davis, *Women, Race, and Class* (New York: Vintage Books, 1983).

Angela Davis received popular attention when she was denied tenure at U.C.L.A. because she taught, and espoused, Marxist theory. As a serious philosopher, she has turned her attention to the special issues of women and race. Being black, she gives first attention to the special situation of the female slave. Understanding the enslaved black women can shed light upon women's current battle for emancipation, she claims. If the white mother is confined to home and family and seeks escape, the slave woman was a full-time worker first and incidentally a wife, mother and homemaker. Under slave conditions, the oppression of women was identical to the oppression of men, a notion little stated in current feminist protests. In contrast to white women, "the ideological exaltation of motherhood...did not extend to slaves" (p. 7). The slave system did not allow black men to assert male supremacy.

There was no 'feminine mystique.' Black women did hard labor. They were required to be as 'masculine' as men. The hierarchical sex role industrial capitalism forced on white women was contradicted by slavery. Black women were not debased by the domestic functions.

Egalitarianism characterized black social relations, and women often defended men against the demeaning slave system. Black women resisted slavery with a passion equal to men's. Leaning on Marxist categories, Davis asserts, "Sexual inequality as we know it today did not exist before the advent of private property" (p. 224). Women did not enter early into the Communist movement in the United States, but Davis gives an impressive account of women and race as it effects feminism's goals today.

assumptions in our premises, in our intellectual presuppositions, which need to be questioned in order to promote women's advance?"[64]

---

[64]   See chapter 1, note 6.

Joan Cocks, *The Oppositional Imagination: Feminism, Critique and Political Theory* (London: Routledge, 1989).

Cocks wants to preserve some opposites, reconcile some, and break some into fragments. Radical feminism is a 'counter-culture' that has risen up against the regime that rules over the sexed-body. 'Marginality' is a fashionable theme; we see power exposed in what it drives from the centers of life. The author wants to try to support 'the center'. Radical feminism, on the other hand, "stands as a great romantic refusal" (p. 10). She considers material feminism and psychoanalytic feminism. Radical feminism is "strangely enamored of the view that the genitalia are linked internally to thinking" (p. 18) and that "knowledge must come solely out of women's experience."

Feminists tend to be highly suspicious of theory, but Cocks thinks that theory is important (chap. 1), particularly since it has been oppressive, as any dominative power is (chap. 2). The writers she offers give an account of how they have cultivated a "pessimism of the intellect" (p. 63, chap. 3) The question is: Has human critical theory produced "the understanding of the world that is to make a difference?" (p. 94, chap. 5)

Masculine/feminine have been a cultural-political regime, and radical feminism is an antithesis to it (part II) Particularly, she questions the assumption that power is always a vice and powerlessness a virtue (chap. 7). She concludes: Power is always fractured; emancipation is provisional; and identity is forever on the edge of dissolution (p. 209).

Mary Daly, *Beyond God the Father* (Boston: Beacon Press, 1973).

Mary Daly argues that the women's revolution should be "an ontological spiritual revolution, pointing beyond the idolatries of sexist society and sparking creative action in and toward transcendence" (p. 6). Only the arch-reactionary could disagree with this and many have argued for it. However, as one reads her book nearly twenty years later, her rigid identification of all religious symbol systems as 'male creations' sounds outmoded, since gender roles have been, for both male and female, quite various in our history and seldom narrowly tied exclusively to sex. Woman's consciousness is emerging, and Daly sees it as the greatest single hope for survival of spiritual consciousness.

She argues that "if God is male, then the male is God" (p. 19). But the problem is that no known theologian has ever argued that God is male. Although both gender characteristics associated with male and female have been attributed to God, sex never has been. She sees the need for a "new language of transcendence" (which she will later go on to develop), but the issue is whether we are free to create languages at will. In this book Mary Daly sees the liberation of women leading to a new sense of ultimate transcendence, that is, God (p. 88), but years later she will move beyond God too. She argues that "no adequate models can be taken from the past" (p. 71), but just as in this book she sees the model of Jesus as a

We thank Greek philosophy for calling on us to question the foundations of thought, medieval philosophy for asking about the systematic function of 'God' in our theoretical constructions, modern philosophy for challenging us to follow what was then the method of science, Existentialism, Marxism, and Pragmatism for questioning Hegel's idealistic dialectic. Now we thank 'feminism' for asking us if any assumptions in our thought systems have in fact excluded women.

Of course, just as later Marxists discovered that all in the proletariat class do not think and act alike, in spite of the postulate of a universal material determinism, women are discovering that they occupy no single ideological position. Thus they have revived metaphysics. 'Positivists' once thought metaphysics was passé. Feminism asks us critically to evaluate our assumed philosophical basis. In so doing it re-establishes metaphysics, once again, as needed to escape the prison of unchallenged assumptions.

To do this, feminism need not be monolithic in theory, as some first assumed it must be in order to succeed. It need only challenge us fundamentally to ask us what philosophy is and does, that is, to question whether assumed theories contain biases or assumptions which need to be questioned and re-evaluated. To do this, all women need not unite to agree on one philosophical position or even

---

difficulty, so she will later be forced to see God as limiting the women's revolution too, and perhaps to a greater degree.

Andrea Dworkin, *Intercourse* (New York: The Free Press, 1987).

The 'murder' of women signifies the impossibility of physical love in a way that does not mean loss, sadistic celebration, the reader is told. There are those who are tormented by the depravity of the sex act. "Depravity, debauchery, dissoluteness, all connote this exploitation of women, who remain inferior because of it, for pleasure" (p. 10). After this 'repulsion' Dworkin goes on to consider the female condition involving power, status, and hate. It is, as one reviewer says, a 'shocking book'. The inferiority of women "creates a person broken and humiliated inside" (p. 169). Women are reviled as filthy, obscene, in religion, pornography, philosophy, and in most literature and art and psychology, the author claims.

approach philosophy in a single fashion. In fact, the opposite is true. It does not advance philosophy to challenge one dogmatism by assuming another. Furthermore, much practical advance may need no 'philosophy' at all, just consistent effort.

Metaphysics is reborn when monolithic assumptions are challenged and openness to new theory results. It is not necessary for all to have one theory in order to oppose a closed mind. It is enough to bring about a challenge to ways of thought which have been, for a time, taken for granted. In order to do this, we do not need to assume that in an earlier time all philosophers really agreed with any reigning orthodoxy, as for instance some feminists have sometimes assumed that all men have been Cartesian Rationalists. Dissent lies present beneath the surface of any uniformity of thought. A laudable revolution merely brings this fact to the surface, as Feminist philosophers have.

Reading through much contemporary feminist literature, and listening to the description of the repressed condition from which many feminist leaders demand liberation, for example a 'glass ceiling', one is strongly reminded of the Existentialist description of the human condition. True, existential writers such as Sartre and Camus thought they were describing the condition of every human creature, both male and female, whereas feminist 'protest' writers are sure that the most demeaning situations apply particularly to one sex. It certainly is true that women have suffered more from oppression than have males, at least from non-physical types of repression. Whatever redress and release women can obtain now is their due. Yet it is instructive to see how close the description of their oppression as a sex comes to the way Existentialists have described the general human condition.[65] Certainly, the forces that harm all human nature have often been used more against one sex than against the other, just

---

[65] See Simone de Beauvoir, *The Ethics of Ambiguity*, chapter I, note 4.

as they have been used against some groups more than others. However, when we think of 'women's liberation', it is instructive to see how factors that in fact apply universally have been turned more often against one sex.

If so, if the forms of oppression practiced against women are forces of oppression used against all, our path to human liberation is illuminated. We see that the forces of oppression are not themselves sex connected, even if they have been sex directed. First, consider physical sex itself. Many are guilty of using another person as a sex object for his or her own purposes (as Evita sings, we all use our lovers for our own advancement). That women have suffered with this more than men is probably true, since males have heretofore dominated politics and commerce. Perhaps the only way to prevent exploitation is to be sure women have sufficient political, legal, and financial power to resist becoming sex objects—unless they want to be. Using another male or female person as a sex object cannot be prevented as long as the sex urge remains primal, Darwin would remind us, but the unprotected should be given sufficient power to break out of any mold, if they want to.

Is our human situation just as it has sometimes been described? That is, are all human beings actually in the same existential condition? If so, women may have responded to this in different ways, and traditionally they have had fewer powers at their disposal to rebel, as Camus advised us all to do. That is, Camus wanted us to unite and to say 'no' to any degradation, in the name of our human integrity. In the Feminists movement, have we again discovered a universal insight from a particular condition? Using existential language to describe it, Simone de Beauvoir[66] observed that women offer a more graphic example of what can and does oppress all human beings. If so, we study women's condition and forms of oppression in order to

---

[66] See Simone de Beauvoir, *The Second Sex*, chapter I, note 4.

see more clearly what threatens us all. Certainly some unfortunate men have suffered suppression just as badly as any woman, and some women have been spared oppression when men have not been. Jails contain more civil and political male prisoners than women.

Some women have been powerful writers, artists, politicians. What then, we ask, enabled those women to escape oppression? From their example, can we see how all who suffer should respond? In reality, have more women than men suffered oppression? That depends on what forms of oppression we examine and how one evaluates the individual human condition. But even if women have recently been casting off the chains that hold their sex to an inferior status, observing this action should also reveal the forces that oppress any individual and how these might be countered. The condition may be particular and even presently sex connected, but the insight is universal, just as appreciating Shakespeare and the Old Testament has not been limited to Englishmen or Jews.

Is it ever possible to characterize 'all men' or 'all women' in a single statement, except trivially? Philosophers have always discussed the question of the universal vs. the particular. The Middle Ages was supposedly characterized by taking this as its crucial problem. The question arises again in the women's movement. Can we ever formulate a satisfactory and an agreed definition of 'women' that will cover all and do so universally? The answer depends partly on the distinction between sex and gender. If we are talking only of sex, a pretty good job can be done biologically to describe universal physical qualities. But gender roles vary radically and change over time, which makes us suspect there can be no universal description where gender is concerned—and this is precisely what many women have been arguing for.

Kierkegaard stressed the primacy of the individual over against Hegel's concentration on the universal. Feminism often seems to lean toward a Hegelian/Marxist love of universals. But should Kierkegaard be right, we may not be able to say anything of significance about real people on any basis other than the individual. If so, the individual does gain attention and importance, but universal movements become well nigh impossible. Women need not conform to universal norms. But if they stress individual decision, as Kierkegaard wanted, they give up any thought of a universal cohesive action based simply on sex.

It is possible that the philosophical theory we hold, or should hold, is dictated to us by our time and culture, or even by our sex. This proposition is in itself questionable and needs to be argued against the whole range of the history of philosophy and all of the options available to us on the present scene. Although surely not all, many Feminist writers often simply state a philosophical position, for example, 'skeptical', 'empirical', or 'deconstructionist'.[67] All such theories have vast histories behind them, and nothing automatically establishes one over another. That is a matter of philosophical discussion or dialogue. True, certain philosophical positions may seem appealing to certain groups on certain days, but philosophy, since Socrates, has resisted establishing any one theory over another simply by popular vote.

Furthermore, unless 'feminism' is merely a label for a group who share a certain ideology, it should be clear that not all women hold any philosophical premise by virtue of their sex. In the first place, as with men, many women are a-philosophical and could care less about such abstract, intellectual questions. Thus, we know that no 'Feminist position' based on any philosophical premise will hold universally for all women. Some will not understand it; many are absorbed in other matters. There is, of course, no reason that a 'Feminist' writer should not work on the basis of any philosophical view which she finds

---

[67]   See Sallie McFague, *Models of God*, chapter I, note 23.

congenial, much as Thomas Aquinas used Aristotle. But surely its truth should not be assumed as a confessional statement.

One way in which feminists have sought to ground their theories is to tie 'feminism' closely to what we might call 'body talk'.[68] Differences of sex are relatively easy to note. Thus, if what is distinctly 'feminine' could be tied to differences in the female body, it might be easier to get agreement on a single feminist perspective and also to promote it as something that men could never share completely. The cycle of a woman's body is distinctive and different from the male. There are rhythms and aspects which could easily affect the psychology, even the intellectual outlook, of women. But the issues are two: (1) Do all women respond to their bodily differences in the same way?; and more importantly, (2) Do women really wish to be limited in what they can say by 'body talk'?

This does pose a dilemma, since the major aim of the feminist movement is to release all women from rigid sexual stereotypes. Now, if the uniqueness of the feminine perspective is to be linked to physiological characteristics, will feminists not ironically end by limiting themselves far more than some males might? Our bodies may 'talk' to us and should be listened to, but to confine all that we

---

[68] Paula A. Cooey, et al., ed., *Embodied Love: Sexuality and Relationship as Feminist Values* (San Francisco: Harper and Row, 1987).

The editors claim that 'embodiment' and 'relationality' have been devalued in patriarchal strains of Western religion (p. 1). They state that women are more tied to their bodies than men, and they repeat the assertion that mind has been valued over body and the spiritual over the material. Women, they state, have been associated with the devalued realm and this added to their repression. Patriarchal societies value the public realm more than the private, they say. But gender constructions have the potential for change.

The emphasis is on touch and body language. And silence must be broken. Redemption must be perceived in social terms. There is a tendency to accept the assertion that there is no absolute truth, but the irony is, as the editors point out, that women authors suggest "that their visions are grounded in ontological reality" (p. 6). They opt for the spoken word as more embodied for communication. These are "feminine essentialists," and they confirm women's difference and root it in the body.

Pauli Haddon, *Body Metaphors* (New York: Crossroad, 1988).

can say to only what can be so based is, ironically, a very rigid stereotype.

Women, one would think, would not want to be limited by their bodies. Furthermore, we have Plato's question: Do we perceive some things through the senses (bodies) and others directly with the mind? If our world is not limited to the body, that would seem to offer us all, men and women, a great deal more creative and intellectual freedom. Of course, we have to learn how to become free of our physiological limitations; but that is the primary aim of all successful education.

Some feminist theorists argue that Modern Philosophy has unfairly excluded emotion as a source of insight,[69] and this undoubtedly is true for the Rationalist tradition beginning with Descartes. This may be true for some empiricists and positivists too, although David Hume give us a detailed account of the passions. In the light of the failure of Modern Thought to establish itself as outmoding all previous philosophies, early scientific thought, which might have wanted to exclude the role of emotion in understanding, has been replaced by new views about the role of theory which would seem to preclude any final scientific theory based on reason or sense experience alone. There undoubtedly is a need to re-examine the role of emotion in our lives and thought, and Feminist theory may be right to call this to our attention.

However, at least since the time of Plato, philosophers have also worried about the uncontrolled and the destructive qualities of emotion. Certainly our courts, jails and newspapers testify to the daily destruction unleashed by uncontrolled emotion. Questions about the limits of sanity need to be brought in too. Philosophy, as "the love of wisdom," has always sought a reasoned approach to issues, although it is wrong to say that this has meant banishing emotion to the realm

---

[69] See Elizabeth Dreyer, *Passionate Women: Two Medieval Mystics*, chapter 2, note 41.

of psychology. Plato's *Phaedrus* could serve as a model, although *The Republic* and other dialogues take up the issue too. Plato is aware of the destructive potential in emotion, yet he feels that it is necessary to use it in order to attain insight. Its power lifts us, or it can lift us, above the mundane. However, Plato's classic picture is one of reason controlling and moderating emotion's power.

To be committed to the life of reason is not necessarily to be attached to any one view, or to shun the influence, of emotion. Philosophers differ as philosophers on what 'reason' means and how it is to be interpreted. Thus, they are always obligated to give an account of their reasons for their position, in spite of the fact that their argument may not be universally compelling. But the role of emotion may divide us even more than reason, somewhat ironically. All attempts by Freud and Spinoza to reduce emotion to a form of reason, or to control it by rational understanding alone, have not gained wide acceptance.

Feminists, in their quest to restore emotion often seem to have overlooked Existentialism which has stressed passion and its primary role in all decision. In reaction to the Rationalists' exclusion of emotion as a producer of insight, perhaps feminists' philosophies have shied from Existentialism because of its radical individualism.[70] If emotion is central, but if it isolates us and renders universality and uniformity impossible, then it cannot form a basis upon which to unite all women behind any reform. In fact, emotion's individualistic tendencies are precisely why the Rationalists wanted to exclude emotion from philosophy, or at least to domesticate it.

Thus, a dilemma appears for Feminism as a movement. If the Modern hope to found understanding on a fully rational basis is opposed, if Feminists can claim that the prejudice against women is due to their supposed emotional basis for thought and action and that

---

[70] Simone de Beauvoir is, of course, a striking exception.

97

this is wrongly based and that emotion should rightfully be considered an avenue to insight, then all hope for universal agreement must be abandoned too. Reason is our best bet to find a basis for universality, as logic and mathematics attest. But women feel the totally rationalistic approach has been prejudicial to their interests and that it is also used as a basis for anti-feminine discrimination. As they argue for restoring emotion's place as a guide to thought, any goal of universality in feminist theory must be abandoned too.

One example: The Berkeley 'flower children' of the sixties and seventies drew contempt from orthodox Marxists who were bent on revolution in social structure too. They knew that uniformity and finality of theory alone gave them the solid base needed for an effective revolution. Emotion leads to individualism, and Existentialists have never been revolutionaries, except perhaps in Camus's Rebel and in Sartre's attempt to reconcile Existentialism with Marxism, both questionable moves.

If emotion may be appealed to as a basis for our insights and for the decisions we take, we have no basis to enforce uniformity of thought. Furthermore, women may press their option, but we have no evidence that emotion plays any lesser role for men, only that it may take different forms. Thus, the good and bad, the positive and the destructive role of emotion in all human beings must be opened to examination once again.

C. The Feminist Challenge to the Life of the Intellect

Can only one who has physically experienced something (e.g., childbirth) articulate that experience or claim to understand it? If so, the edifice of drama, the novel, and of literary authorship either comes tumbling down or must be drastically revised. For example, Shakespeare was neither a Danish prince nor a young Italian girl in love.

The life of the intellect is based entirely on the assumption that some sensitive ones, not all, can understand, and then can present to us experiences which are not their own, particularly when offered in a form which makes the experience 'come alive'. All sympathy in human beings is based on this possibility, so that those who cannot appropriate experiences in this way are the 'unsympathetic' ones, as we say. And we know this fault is not restricted entirely to one sex, although it could be that on some issues (e.g., childbirth) women might begin by being closer to it than men. But certainly it is false to say that all women view the experience of childbirth as 'enlightening'. It is of course true that no human experience is equally appreciated or enlightening to all in any group or class, particularly if that group has the scope of half the world's population.

Acting is another field we should look to in this regard. I know a famous actor who plays roles quite distant from his own life. When I asked about this, he said simply, "It's called playing a role!" The finest actors, both male and female, are capable of giving us insights into persons and events that even the people who experienced them probably could not articulate. And when it comes to male vs. female, "M. Butterfly" is enough to illustrate that the clever male can portray the feminine role with a grace and skill that many a female might lack. Furthermore, women have been authors, and usually their skill has not been restricted to describing or appealing to a single sex. Authors have been predominantly male, at least in the past, but surely no one who plays Lady Macbeth thinks Shakespeare did not have insight into that lady.

Few of us have ever treated each other as the cast of "Who's Afraid of Virginia Woolf?" does, and it is quite likely that Edward Albee does not live that way. Therein lies his dramatic skill. If all women actors refused to play roles not written by women authors, our theaters would be considerably more drab. I never heard Bette Davis say that she could not play a role because the script was written by a man. Likewise, when women authors portray men, or when men act roles written by women, the sex origin of authorship becomes insignificant. Are there certain insights which women offer about their lives and experiences that most men might be able to capture as well? Certainly; however, the insight does not come simply from the sex of the author but from her rare skill in making it available to others in print or in script or on canvas.

Will women now enter all creative fields in greater numbers? It would appear so, at least in advanced industrial societies. What will the result of the changed ratio of women to men be in creative, intellectual, artistic endeavors? It is doubtful that any product can be called good or insightful simply because its author is a woman, any more than men could complain that, if their work did not gain acceptance, it was because they were male. Men are just as capable of prejudice and shortsightedness in relation to other men as they are to women. True, like the color line, sex has often been used as a negative factor rather than simply as an 'objective' evaluation. Everyone must work to get a hearing, and only a few persevere long enough to succeed. If creative women have had artificial barriers placed against the judgment of their work, we should work to remove these just as we should remove any myopic vision that cannot recognize new talent. But the unimaginative one will always fight to preserve his or her privilege.

If the life of the intellect is now to be claimed as much by women as by men, although a few famous women have always had their share, we must do this by removing the judgment of their effort from any connection to sex. In the long run it will be self-defeating to claim quality or insight simply from the sex of the author, since we know that cannot possibly be true. Although a man, Spinoza is still insightful for both sexes: "All things excellent are as difficult as they are rare," he said. Any society, any culture, needs excellence and must seek to remove all artificial restraints from both human production and its evaluation. It is the life of the intellect that we seek to free, not to tie it to new restraints of sexual identification.

Feminist writers often come back to the theme of their objection to a mind-body dualism, which on the whole they consider detrimental to feminist causes.[71] However, it is not always clear why. Perhaps bodies seem closer to women's psyche than to men, due to childbirth, etcetera. In any case, Descartes becomes the whipping boy. Philosophers have often agreed that his form of rationalism leaves us with a division between mind and body which is unbridgeable. But Descartes is not the only philosopher in our history, and few who read him, much as they argue with him, believe him. His theories are challenging, but they have not been widely adopted as 'truth'.

Mind will never be identical with the human brain, and intelligence will never be identical with emotion. 'Behaviorism' as a solution to the mind-body distinction is probably less believed than is Descartes. Since our experience is full of dualisms, it helps little to reject 'all dualisms'. The issue is how to relate mind and body, emotion and intellect, so that they are not divisive. Plato offered a theory of the importance of the emotions, just as Spinoza did. True, the age of Rationalism and Empiricism often tried to eliminate emotion from philosophy; feminists are right about that. But the issue is whether to find a theory that integrates emotion, which Existentialism does, we need to attack false dichotomies as if every male were antithetical to the body and to emotion and that only women could see their body's value in our life.

Are there oversights in Western (or Eastern) intellectual/scientific history or creative effort which have slighted women's actual contributions? As is always the case with shifting perspectives in teaching and research, these slights should be compensated for. Each new generation attempts that. However, if women were in fact not in

---

[71]   See Pauli Haddon, *Body Metaphors*, note 67 above.

prominent intellectual/scientific and artistic roles but wish to be so today, there is no need to distort a modest past in order to open a wider future.

D. Practical vs. Theoretical Feminism

It has often been felt to be important, if not crucial, to achieve unity in theory in order to effect social change. Certainly Marxism-Leninism has thought so. The Cultural Revolution in China was an attempt to correct deviation from theory, and the official response to the recent student-led protest for increased democracy in China has been to reinforce a conformity to orthodox political thought. On the other hand, in the U.S.S.R. the granting of permission for dissent has led to challenges from every minority. This has been welcomed as an evidence of greater openness to new ideas, but it can cause such disruption that the unity of the country is threatened ("The Moscow Problem").

In ardent democratic circles, Plato is derided because his *Republic* advocates strict training for each individual and the establishment of distinct hierarchies as the means necessary for this. It is not clear that fundamental change can be implemented if there is disagreement over how to bring about the needed improvement. Intellectual debate, the clash of differing ideas, is at the heart of a liberal education, but it may paralyze the political process unless controlled.

Women as a group, due to their numbers, can hardly be classed as a minority. Yet the record of their status in most societies has been that of a group who must struggle for their rights. To gain the right to vote, to achieve economic and political parity, these demands cast them in the role of a minority. To study the history of the crusade for 'women's rights' is to realize how long and hard the road for them has been. Yet particularly in the light of recent advances in feminist goals, we have to ask: "Is uniformity of theory necessary if we are to achieve women's liberation?"

It is easy to catalogue the issues that face women: (1) Voting rights and economic rights, where these have not been achieved; (2) Political power commensurate with their numbers; (3) Equal opportunity for advance in professions and in all forms of employment; (4) Special consideration for the time and for the attention children require; (5) Equality before the law and, particularly, agreement on the issue of abortion. But in the area of ideology, should the attempt be to develop a 'feminist perspective' on all issues, a goal which has been talked about today in the stress on 'sisterhood'? Should ideology be added to the list as essential to achieve equality and a full voice for women?

At first sight it might seem so. 'Women's voice' has been missing in large part in our intellectual-cultural-political past, it is claimed. We must now come to understand the feminist point of view and give it due attention. In the area of intellectual-educational affairs, this argument is stimulating, and it offers the kind of challenge to reigning ideas which philosophers should welcome. How do we need to define what is uniquely "from woman"? And as we do, how does this change our perspective on a thousand other crucial social/political issues?

Like all groups pressing for their rights, for example ethnic minorities in countries where another race dominates, must all women unite under a common ideological banner in order to insure success? In spite of the power that lies in theory, we need to be clear as to whether the solution to the practical barriers blocking women depends upon their uniform agreement about some one theory. Must they, and we, come to understand what is uniquely and distinctly feminine before the needed power can be forged to break down the barriers that still limit women's freedom?

When it comes to biology, there are physiological problems in drawing lines between male and female in certain unclear cases. Beyond that, there is the problem of trying to outline psychologically and sociologically how men and women are found to differ in approach and in outlook in various societies.[72] But when we get beyond physiology, we know that we have left sex for gender issues and that gender is nowhere near as fixed as sexual identity. In fact, it is crucial to women's press for change and improved status that gender roles must not be limited or defined entirely by sex.

Although many in the past have argued that there are stereotypical roles for women based on sex, we know that the very success of the women's liberation movement depends on the flexibility of gender roles, the assumption that these are not entirely dictated by sex, however the two may be connected, such as in the case of nurturing children. We know that definitions of the 'eternally feminine' have been used as much to restrain and to suppress women as the supposed universal attributes of their sex have provided a base for their liberation.

We come, then, to consider the philosophical role of the 'universal'. Is the universal dominant over the particular so that the grasp of

---

[72]   R. Hare-Mustin and J. Mareck, ed., *Making A Difference: Psychology and the Construction of Gender* (New Haven, CT: Yale University Press, 1990).

This book concerns feminist theory and post-modern approaches to psychology. In that sense it is about psychology and philosophical theories. All social categories are constructed and so is gender, they assume. Cultural ideologies influence these constructions. The editors outline a considerable overlap in gender characteristics between men and women and believe these will increase. They challenge the idea of stable gender differences. Androgyny research has reached an impasse. The politics of gender has become the politics of difference.

"The overreaching question is the choice of question," one author reports, echoing Plato (p. 2). Gender is an invention of human societies. Emphasis on gender roles obscures the commonalities between men and women, she asserts (p. 17). "Male-female difference is a problematic and paradoxical way to construe gender difference," another set of authors conclude (p. 54). Humans have a capacity to learn virtually any response, and this throws into question labeling any behavior as 'masculine' or 'feminine' (p. 71). One author goes so far as to argue against the study of sex difference (p. 102). Sex accounts for little of the variability in human behavior, she concludes. We are asked to move "toward the unimagined, rather than to be bound by existing categories."

the universal is central to power and control? If so, women must work for ideological uniformity as the necessary power base to effect reform. However, if the individual is paramount, any attempt to achieve universal agreement may actually lead to the repression of dissent (even among women) and stifle intellectual debate in the name of a particular cause. 'Woman' may be a universal category, but gender and ideology tend toward the individual.

If so, what are the consequences of our press to achieve practical, actual improvement, to initiate a change in women's status? It may be necessary and strategically important to divorce the practical goals of feminism (political, economic rights, etc.) from the issue of theoretical agreement on what 'feminism' means. The quest for uniformity of theory may, ironically, hamper the achievement of practical goals by plunging women (and men) into an endless philosophical debate. What is 'feminism' is an issue that, if the universal is not dominant, may divide more than it will unite.

Perhaps, then, the practical way to success is to divorce theoretical feminism from women's rights. Perhaps American Pragmatism (or Continental Existentialism) is correct here: Do not demand uniformity of thought. Set your practical goals and outline the strategy necessary for their achievement. Regis Debray argued in the same way for a *Revolution in the Revolution* in Marxist thought.[73] He said that theory had to be adapted to local structures and so strategy could not be outlined in advance. Perhaps the women's movement is ready for its revolution in their revolution: Achieving practical goals must be cut loose from the attempt to get uniformity in theory, or even universal agreement in principle.

This cannot, however, be said without recognizing that theory has also been used to exclude women from equal participation. For this

---

[73] Regis Debray, *Revolution in the Revolution*, trans. B. Ortiz (New York: Grove Press, 1967).

THE DESCENT OF WOMEN

reason, Orthodox Jewish women must go back and critique the religious doctrine which has separated them from equal participation in religious ceremony, for instance. Close as this may seem to be to the area of theory, it is perhaps crucial to recognize that, to question theories that exclude or block women, to point out questionable assumptions involved in theories that lead to religious or racial segregation—this is quite different from requiring theoretical uniformity.

In fact, the best strategy against any rigid exclusionary policy is often to point out that its theoretical assumptions are not as necessary or as absolute as they are made out to be. Thus, a critique of any obstructive theory that is detrimental to women's rights or status depends on showing that no theory has exclusive truth without alternatives. To do this may shake prejudice loose, if its rigid foundations are called into question. To do so demands a cohesive effort on the part of women (or of any group), since prejudice does not yield easily. But does it demand theoretical uniformity?

E. Should We Stress "Women's Ways of Knowing?"[74]

Would such a stress paradoxically limit women to one way, to "women's way," when the whole aim is to break the limiting stereotypes that hamper women's movement into all fields? The box that women want to escape from is the one that would limit them to the dimensions of their bodies. If one cannot understand women's ways of knowing (or of dealing with conflict) unless one is feminine, can one expect to understand what males say? We would have to ask at the same time if there is anything special about males' ways of knowing and whether this is open to both sexes to understand. For instance, a Feminist critique of Patriarchy certainly seems to suppose that women can understand male orders. Why not vice versa?

---

[74]   See *Women's Ways of Knowing*, note 59 above.

It must work both ways. If women can see how men perceive the world, at least in order to critique its deficiencies, men should be able to understand women's ways of knowing and to ask if that too is subject to any limitations. More than this, we have to ask, "Do all women necessarily understand in that one manner, or might some understand from 'a male perspective'?" If so, all men might not see the world as it has been outlined for, say, patriarchy and actually be more sympathetic to "women's ways of knowing"? If there is no universalism which restricts all women to one way of knowing and all males to another, this is important to know.

This is partly because Feminists strive to be released from stereotypical roles that limit women. If so, they must be able to see the world as men have and not be limited to, say, "domestic perspectives." The dilemma is that feminists cannot urge a distinctive way of knowing for women without risking being limited to that. If they admit that women's ways of seeing the world are not fixed by biological sex but are flexible, we may be at best reporting tendencies: some men in some societies seem to have these perspectives, but these are gender roles, not strictly determined by sex, and men may adopt these (and probably have) on occasion.

Beyond this, we have to ask if the 'Feminist Revolution' succeeds and if women are now found in all walks of life, in all offices and professions, will this "special way of knowing" change as gender roles change? If so, any "women's way of knowing" speaks only for a limited time-bound, perhaps culturally determined, perspective. If so, we are talking about individual ways of knowing and not about some perspective of the world limited to one sex. We also know that nothing about being of one sex prevents you from understanding any perspective. That is a matter of universal sensitivity, not of biological sex.

Although women have always written about women and their condition, it is only in recent times that a self-conscious 'feminist theory' has emerged. This change is undoubtedly connected to the emergence of revolutionary theory.[75] The notion of 'revolution' is of relatively recent origin in the history of consciousness. Just as Greek and Medieval philosophers tended to take the world of nature for granted, the possibility of other worlds, and thus of other orders than our particular one, emerged only when natural science developed its vastly increased ability to control nature. The Enlightenment and emerging political democracies seemed to put more power for change in our hands than previously had been thought possible.

'Revolution' involves the idea that basic structures regulating human nature and our condition can be radically altered, in the same way that medicine began to control disease. Feminist theory acknowledges its debt to revolutionary theory and to more recent liberation philosophies and theologies. Thus, it is not too surprising that in earlier centuries women tended to accept their condition, since men did too. Only as new horizons opened for all did women glimpse their own possible release. Thus, although some men in some societies may have conspired to keep women from understanding the new possibilities that might radically alter their status, women could not have become aware of their possibilities to create new conditions until mankind in general was aware. Thus intellectually, men opened the door for women as new doors opened for us all.

However, women seldom thank their brothers for inaugurating the possibility for radical change in nature, which had for so long seemed fixed. As anyone does who realizes that release is now open to them, the first reaction of many feminist theorists is anger. It is as if men had purposefully held from them the secret of the possible release from nature's confines, whereas in fact men had not assumed this was possible for men much earlier either. When women examine history and point to all the negative descriptions of women's estate given by

---

[75]   See Charnie Guettel, *Marxism and Feminism*, note 59 above.

some (not all) men, they forget in the heady flush of intellectual release that many men were negative about the state of all humanity, their own as well. True, in accepting the chains that seemed to bind us all, many men (and we must remember most women too) thought women even more bound to their state than men, due primarily to women's physical condition and the considerable trials of uncontrolled childbearing. Now that we can finally lift some of these burdens, it is hard for us to realize how difficult it was for anyone to see that women's condition could be other than what it was. Some feminist theorists write as if men 'lied' to women, concealing the possibility of release. But like modern physics, the changes that have come about could hardly have been forecast. Certainly women did not see their future opening until recently.

In feminist theory, then, we must be careful of making present changes appear as if they could have been seen earlier but were withheld by some conspiracy. Surely men have been as startled as women by the explosion of revolutionary theories and the unexpected possibility for change in our common estate. If, insofar as public freedom goes, women suffered to a greater extent than men, now as they realize the possibility of change it is understandable that their anger might be more extreme. Looking for a reason for why their release might not have been made known earlier, men in general form a logical target for women's rage. This is true in spite of the fact that men did not, until more recently, foresee their own possibility to live in a less dangerous situation.

In the anger that explodes upon release, women forget that although men have not been burdened with childbearing and home care to the extent that women traditionally have, men have been slaughtered in wars and tortured more frequently than women. Thus, men have had their own battles to fight for to achieve liberation, which in the flush of women's anger often tends to be forgotten. If we consider the human race as a whole, it would be hard to say which sex has suffered more. A case could be made that men hold the edge on suffering, if taken together, which seems to have been overlooked in feminist rage. Perhaps we have all suffered in union, each in our own way. Nature has shown no discrimination according to sex in the reign of terror, much like the rain that falls on the just and the unjust alike.

In fact, a good case could be made that women have often occupied a protected, a privileged status, one which they will shed as they reject patronage from the opposite sex. Thus, as women assert their equality with men (which can be achieved now in many areas which before were closed), they should agree to accept their share of war and death and persecution and suffering. This comes with equality. To emerge from protection is to emerge into a dangerous position. Formerly women's danger had centered on pregnancy and restriction to the home. Now the danger grows as the areas of freedom enlarge. Women must serve on the front line in all areas, not just the privileged and protected ones. Men should yield a share of the first rank, now that childbearing need not be compulsory. But women must accept some front line dangers "in the trenches."

Feminist theory, then, has in its development shown that human nature is not fixed in its roles but can be self-determining, that is, assuming the right conditions.[76] Given past restrictions, this is a more

---

[76]   Naomi Black, *Social Feminism* (Ithaca, NY: Cornell University Press, 1989).

Professor Black studies 'feminism' as it is shown in feminist organizations. 'Feminism' she defines as a desire for increased autonomy for women. What are the values and experiences identified with women? 'Social Feminism' she takes to include equity feminism, maternal feminism and radical feminism. Women have always had universal involvement with domestic activities and a relative lack of public power and authority. She sees autonomy as the central impulse of feminism (p. 9). But feminism as a movement lacked an ideology, she feels. Yet as a movement, feminism emerged only within relatively modernized societies. And underlying all demands there is a shared impulse for women's self-determination (p. 23).

The crucial feminist press is for the abrogation of men's authority and control over women. Yet women's social activism has covered a wide range of political views, never one.

important discovery for women than for men. However, the issue remains as to whether women can gain as full a release as seems open to men, at least on occasion and for some. The question remains open as to whether women's physiology will allow all of them as great a freedom for self-determination as many men have discovered. Furthermore, since all men do not actively seek release, it is even less clear that all women seek all of the more vulnerable roles now open to them, granted that some will. For all that we have discovered in revolutionary possibilities for change, it is still not clear that women are as open to radical change as men.

Feminist theory has shown women, and all humanity, what is possible: We need not be bound by nature. But it has always been true that only the brave venture beyond established confines. The Nietzsches are few, and they tend to be rejected in their time. Conservatism, the Golden Mean, is the norm—unless vigorously challenged.

F. What Shall We Say About 'Feminist Philosophy'?

If 'Feminist Philosophy' is not a single thing, as this account will insist it cannot be, there is no single answer to this question. However, in the tradition of philosophy, we want to thank anyone who raises crucial questions for us in our time. As we will argue, where the issues of human nature are concerned, 'Feminism' has done this for us, if we will listen with perception, and if we will extend their concerns from 'women' outward toward all humanity. Women face

---

In history it is easy to see that women's groups have had many ideologies and aims, not one. The only thing specific about feminist theories is that they are about women and, increasingly, are formulated by women (p. 45). "Women can articulate women's standpoint in a number of ways" (p. 52). If equal rights conflict with the institution of the family, then feminism becomes a way to reform the family. The great benefit of Naomi Black's book is that it documents the wide variety of feminist movements in the past as well as in the present, and the multiplicity of theory. She sees no reason why advance today needs to depend on a monolythic feminism.

certain special problems connected to their sex and have faced centuries of repression. Still as their status improves, their demands become more like the quest of all human beings. They are real, irrespective of sex, although raised by the special concerns of one sex. And it is often true that from special circumstances a general concern arises and is made clear.

What then is the role of Feminist Philosophy? If it were unified, as Marx and Lenin assumed all revolutionary theory must be, it could unite all women in a common program. But if Feminist theories are diverse,[77] or if all women are not entranced with theory but many in fact remain disdainful of theorizing, there is little hope of unity being achieved by means of any theory. In spite of Marx and Hegel's hopes, theory in fact ultimately tends to divide more than to unite. Ancient philosophers took this as the function of philosophy, that is, to present diverse options. But revolutionary, even utopian, theory demands concerted, united effort to achieve radical change, as every dictator who wants to induce change knows and then moves to enforce a new status quo.

Thus, what we say about 'Feminist Philosophy' is that theory alone cannot achieve the unity necessary to usher in change. That is, it cannot, although one can achieve some consensus on practical issues and programs, for example, abortion, voting rights, access to professions, and so forth. However, this does not result in utopias or revolutions in existing structures, only in alterations and perhaps an improvement in the present order, always subject to reversion.

What options are open to feminists, if philosophical unity and revolutionary change in social structure are no longer as conceivable as they once were? We discover the human limitations within which we all exist, as well as the human possibilities, and also the struggle we each must maintain if we want to achieve self-realization. If evil

---

[77] See "50 Ways to be a Feminist," chapter I note 32.

is not totally in our control or subject to final removal, if corruption knows no limitation to one sex, if all males are not bad and all goodness does not reside in women, the final solution to all human dilemmas is not as easy as nineteenth-century revolutions, and eighteenth-century utopian projections, thought. Only a few human beings, male or female, have achieved their desired fulfillment, and often not in their public roles.

So what should we say about Feminist Philosophy? We should beware of any theory which seems to present the source of evil, of corruption and sin as too neatly divided along any universal, obvious, publicly observable line. And we also are suspicious of any theory which claims special privileges for itself based solely on the sex of its author. Have women no complaint connected to sexual discrimination? Certainly they have. But it is true that race, class, education, physical beauty or ugliness, many observable, identifiable qualities, have equally been fastened on as responsible for discrimination. Thus, if we want to argue against, and to eliminate, all overt qualities as a basis for discrimination, we are left only with the qualities of the human spirit, which unfortunately are often undetectable by our eyes, as the basis for discrimination.

Since we do and will find observable surface qualities used as a basis for prejudice, primarily due to our efforts to raise ourselves by putting others down, discrimination on the basis of sex remains an ever-present possibility in spite of our advances to remove sex-based prejudice. This leads us, of course, to our common human problem, to the dilemma of how to free each person to fulfillment in spite of the handicaps of outward circumstances. Race and sex are proven examples of the external and the obvious barriers we face, and they always threaten to return if we relax, just because they are so obvious. It is human to try to put down another person for our gain, unless we are spiritually sensitive and eternally vigilant.

Is all the Feminist Philosophy propounded, all the books written, of no avail? That pessimistic conclusion does not follow. Theory retains the same function it has always had: to enlighten the mind, to provide new approaches to constant problems. Theory is valuable and is to be prized, but it just may not radicalize social structure (or philosophy itself) beyond return, as women may once have hoped. It may locate evil in existing structure, but if it is too simplistic in its delineation of a single source (e.g., located in males), it actually creates an additional problem because of the false optimism it creates about a found solution. Theory is helpful if it is self-conscious of its limitation and its alternatives.

Theories in their challenges or assumed orthodox positions are necessary to provide insight into our human situation, if any improvement is hoped for. But the sources of evil of deteriorization and destruction are not easily contained, nor are the dogmas of reigning popular doctrines. In fact, it may not be possible to eliminate them. In every society, we always face fashions and customs assumed to be unchangeable. Feminist theorists, dissenting philosophies offering new outlooks and challenges to entrained ways of thinking, in our day these recall us to philosophy's critical task.

G. The Feminist Challenge to Philosophy

The question, "What is 'feminist' philosophy?" and what distinguishes it from any other mode of philosophy, is simply philosophy's ancient question of self-doubt about itself in a new guise. But does this make the classical function of philosophy, constantly to question its own discipline and its mission, any different for a philosopher who labels himself or herself as 'feminist'? Of course, all philosophers of significance have been different, else we would have one philosophy and no history of philosophy. The change is that, as in so many professional fields, women have in recent years entered philosophy in greater numbers. There have been women in philosophy's history, but are today's 'feminist philosophers' any different from males who enter the field?

In ethics and in politics it is fairly easy to answer "yes." Specific questions in ethics, such as birth control, abortion, domestic violence, equal pay and access to all political and economic levels—these issues have special concern for all who are female. And it is probable that philosophers in earlier times did not give them sufficient attention. Although like slavery and human rights, it is not the case that only women can claim discrimination or repression. Their concerns may, however, take on special 'sex linked' forms. Once the rights of every individual are established, women can explore their special concerns as 'feminists' in ethical or political theory.

However, once we recognize these philosophical questions as being specifically 'feminist', we must add that, as women approach or consider any traditional issues in philosophy's past, there is no necessary reason why their treatment or conclusion will or should be any different due to their sex any more than men either now or before need think alike due to their sex. Thus, we will omit the practical issues in feminist philosophy which stem from ethics, politics, economics, and legal issues. We ask the harder question of whether, in other traditional areas of philosophy, we can identify any questions or answers as specifically 'feminist'.

Of course, if we or others argue for any perspective or doctrine as uniquely 'feminist', we must recognize this as creating a potentially self-defeating dilemma. Why? Would all women regardless of background or individual interests be predestined to adopt that stance, and would it be restricted to 'women only'? If so in any restrictive way, it would work against the primary feminist aim to be released from any stereotype of women's role as being required of them or as necessarily imposing restrictions on their activity. Every person who enters the philosophical arena can, or perhaps even should, attempt to offer a new perspective or a fresh approach. Women philosophers may do so too. But if they are restricted to a specifically defined 'feminist' viewpoint, such a limitation is as equally stifling to freedom of thought as was their earlier categorical exclusion from the field of philosophy.

Simone de Beauvoir might offer a good test case. She was active as a philosopher before specifically 'feminist' perspectives were staked out. Yet she also wrote one of the early texts in feminist thought, *The Second Sex*. As events developed, she went on to support many women's issues in seeking equality and openness. But in *The Ethics of Ambiguity*,[78] which appeared in English as early as 1948, is there anything which marks her arguments offered there as specifically 'feminist' in distinction from her colleague in Existentialism, for example, J.P. Sartre? She speaks of the 'tragic ambiguity' of our human condition. "Let us assume our fundamental ambiguity," she recommends (p. 9), but she seems to take 'humanity' together, suggesting no difference between men and women.

"Individual freedoms" can forge laws valid for all, she claims (p. 39). Thus, she admits the possibility of a human universality which some feminists have rejected as potentially limiting. Freedom is the source from which all values spring, but this depends on having a valid philosophical structure. We feel anguish in the face of our human freedom, we are told (p. 34), but she never indicates this as different for women than for men. As a philosopher, then, de Beauvoir is simply that. Stressing individual freedom, she could not lock herself into any fixed perspective without contradicting the most cherished existential notion, the centrality of individual freedom and the dilemma of decision that it necessitates for each of us.

Obviously, Simone de Beauvoir is a woman, and almost equally obviously she offers ethical insights into the human ethical dilemma

---

[78] Simone d Beauvoir, *The Ethics of Ambiguity* (New Jersey: Secaucus, 1980). All page references are to this edition.

which she feels are applicable to all. Of course, later feminist philosophers could have discovered something more specifically feminine to offer us, perhaps derived from some special feminine insight, and they might offer this to all. de Beauvoir remarks: To will oneself free is also to will others free. Individual freedom is a central theme for Existentialism, but note that achieving it for oneself has a universal extension. If she is correct, any feminist proposal for women's liberation would be automatically applicable for all. And one supposes that for any male to seek individual freedom is also to see it extended to de Beauvoir's "second sex."

If "no man can save himself alone," as she claims (p. 62), it should follow that no woman can save herself alone. (Of course, by 'man' de Beauvoir actually means all humanity). All sexes, all human beings, all races and classes, must learn their existential identity of situation. Certainly, as de Beauvoir outlines her history of *The Second Sex*, women have their own account of the denial of freedom, but any protest should be in the name of all who are denied their freedom. To seek only the liberation of one's sex or culture is to set human beings against each other in competition and thus, ironically, to restrict one's own freedom in the process of restricting another's.

Is there, then, such a thing as 'feminist' philosophy? Yes, of course. In what sense? In the sense that 'philosophy', since its inception, has always had itself as its first question. Philosophy, it is said, is the only discipline which always starts by questioning itself, its mission, its aim. Thus, as Feminists do this they question what philosophy is, has been, and should be. In this case it now comes as women's turn to question a discipline which has heretofore been primarily practiced by males. Insofar as women who now enter the field in numbers question the mission and the enterprise of philosophy, they join all the innovators in philosophy, from Socrates to Hegel to Nietzsche, who have questioned whether philosophy is doing what it should do if it is fulfilling its mission.

Thus, feminists radicalize philosophy by once again questioning the tradition handed down to them. Such challenges are, or should be, always welcome, given philosophy's tradition of self-questioning. However, one complexity is that some, not all, feminist philosophers come to philosophy with a perhaps legitimate program of social, political and economic change. In doing so they raise Plato's old question in *The Republic* of the ideal of the philosopher-king. That is, can philosophical insight be combined in one person who also has the governing powers and political astuteness of the King? Today, we might call it: The search for the philosopher/queen. Our question: Can women in philosophy achieve significant social change?

Some, of course, would say that they do not seek to convert philosophy into an instrument of social revolution. But if not, then it does not seem to matter if the philosopher is male or female. It is simply the pursuit of another academic discipline. But next we are forced to ask: What power do words have, since all philosophy is written or spoken? Wittgenstein thought we could 'dissolve' philosophy's traditional problems, reduce their puzzling aspects by the use of a proper method. But most feminist philosophers want philosophy to become a more powerful tool for change than that. Then, can women now use philosophy as a social powerful force? But how powerful can written words be? "If words could kill...," but in actuality they are weaker instruments than that. So what then can 'feminists' in philosophy accomplish, other than carrying on its traditions, perhaps questioning and revitalizing them by their reconstruction?

We, they, must be aware of the danger of becoming "lost in the jungle of words." Their philosophy, all philosophy, tends to lose itself in esoteric concepts. There is nothing wrong with this. Neither Hegel nor St. Thomas has written best-selling works, yet they are influential. But only the very few who write philosophy have been, in the long run, paid much attention to, as is the case in most academic disciplines. Only a few read any philosopher's thoughts, whether male or female. A handful of devotees does not a social change make. To whom, then, do feminist philosophers wish to speak—other professional philosophers, whether male or female?

Feminists as they challenge philosophy's past, its procedures and its doctrines, raise for us once again the question of the mission of philosophy. Since Socrates' time, those who follow his lead feel that philosophy's self-questioning is both useful and necessary, else we proceed blindly without asking the fundamental questions. Thus, post-feminism philosophers cannot proceed without questioning the aim of the enterprise, once again, just as early feminist philosophers did. Yet as feminist theorists become involved in esoteric doctrines, for example, 'structuralism', whatever value such theories may have, the more technical, the more esoteric, the less likely are the philosopher's words, whether male or female, to reach into the wider political-social arena and be effective.

Can we, then, find in feminist philosophers one or more who can combine subtle thought with effective political-social change? If not, then certainly feminists may offer or espouse new or interesting doctrines, but they are merely at one with all previous philosophers, ones who have from time to time challenged reigning theories, for example, as Nietzsche did. With these questions in mind, let us review the work of a number of advocates of feminist thought and see if we can discover what is unique or original in their suggestions—or shall we simply take them as one more instance of philosophy's questioning of its purpose and the revising of the doctrines and the approaches which we have inherited?

Jean Grimshaw in *Feminist Philosophers*[79] says that "questions about women are central to philosophy" (p. viii), and that the

---

[79] Jean Grimshaw, *Feminist Philosophers* (London: Harvester Wheatsheaf, 1986). All page references are to this edition.

questions arise out of the tensions and contradictions in women's lives, just as Existentialists (and Hegelians/Marxists too) have said. Of course, in one sense our first question is in what sense all previous theories are 'male', except in the obvious sense that most philosophy in the past has been written by males (p. 3). It would be odd, really, to reduce the immense variety in philosophy's past to a single common denominator, given the great controversies in our intellectual history. Are there any concerns central to women's lives which are not the same for men? Of course, just as all men do not share the same concerns, Kant notwithstanding.

Grimshaw finds that women have been in philosophy since the eighteenth century, coordinate with the Enlightenment and the search for freedom and democracy, not simply since the recent Feminist movement (p. 7). Thus, one might link the rise of women in philosophy with the press to open all enterprises to the people at large, not merely the nobility or the privileged. We had to open the possibility of a different life for women, as we first did for the majority of men. The "growth of egalitarian political ideals" (p. 8), then, as much as anything opened the discipline to a wider group of men and then eventually to all women too. The 'rights of man' next had to be extended, by the same logic, to women.

However, if the rising number of women in philosophy challenge traditional or reigning views and simply replace these with some new dogma, there would be little advance. Yet as the feminist movement has grown, it has embraced diversity, so there can be no uniformity in feminist philosophy. Still, is philosophy 'gendered', Grimshaw asks (p. 36)? Women have been frequently 'devalued' she concludes, but that does not quite make all of philosophy 'male' in its theory, true as that might be, since many men once held theories which now are widely challenged, for example, on slavery. To stress 'women's experience' (p. 75), however, is another thing, since both Pragmatism and Existentialism claim that all philosophy is based on experience.

'Childbirth', obviously, is central for women in a way that it can never be for males.

If 'human nature' is not unalterable, as Grimshaw reports (p. 105), then new changes are always admissible. A consistent theme in feminism has been women's need for independence and autonomy, and this is easily shared with males (p. 140). But where ethical theory is concerned, is there any difference in the approach for women than for men (p. 188)? There easily could be so that ethics is altered by feminism's approach. But, she concludes, "There is no non-contested or unsolvable paradigm of female values or priorities which can be seen as a source of feminist philosophical thinking" (p. 259). Josephine Donovan writes a history of American feminism.[80] Women were often oppressed and excluded both politically and socially, so that 'feminism' as a search for status and rights is clearly definable.

The Enlightenment liberal feminists sought to change this, and as a group they shared certain basic tenants, including a faith in rationality and a belief in education for women (p. 8). However, Grimshaw in particular believed that "the intellect is not sexed" (p. 16). The Social Gospel and the Protestant Awakening supported the women's cause. Yet as women were 'romanticized', many men argued for the "feminization of culture" (p. 35). Thus, in no sense were women always denigrated. Of course, the necessity for 'consciousness raising' among women borrows from Marxism (p. 63). Freud has been taken as both a positive and negative influence (p. 91), and Existentialism has often been ignored, in spite of many notions perhaps useful for individual advance (p. 117). Of course, there are 'radical feminists' too, borrowing from the New Left (p. 141).

---

[80] See Josephine Donovan, *Feminist Theory: The Intellectual Traditions of American Feminism*, note 57 above.

Several volumes have tried to bring together a variety of perspectives, which shows the diversity of feminist thought:[81] Conservative, Liberal, Marxist feminism, etcetera. But this leads to the conclusion that, although the oppression of women may have been near universal, "feminist consciousness is not" (p. 23). "There does not seem to be any one quality which all images of the feminine must have; in this may be found that the feminine is not a Platonic universal" (p. 97). Should there be a distinctive feminist way of thinking? The authors conclude: "women should not erroneously think that in order to overcome their oppression they must learn another language" (p. 155).

In *Feminist Theory*[82] the editors of the essays claim that "feminist theory is fundamentally experienced" (p. vii) which in time would separate it from some philosophies but not from all, nor would this necessarily be unique to 'feminism'. In contradiction to what has just been stated, they feel that 'we feminists' must "devise our own language" (p. xiii), but at least we know that not all feminist philosophers accept this as a necessity. Yet they are sure that as a critique of ideology, it "must also criticize itself and counter the tendency to congeal into a new ideology" (p. ix). There is a danger of 'idealization' of the idea of a female point of view, Grimshaw argues in another work.[83] The danger is in offering a false universalism, and so "there are immense problems with the idea of a distinctively male or female point of view..." (p. 17).

Some women activists, of course, take their mission as exclusively practical and find that "feminism on the whole is still relatively

---

[81] Mary Vetterling-Braggin, ed., *Femininity, Masculinity, and Androgyny*, (Totowa, NJ: Rowman and Littlefield, 1977).

[82] Naunell O. Keohane, Michelle Z. Rosaldo, Barbara C. Gelpi, ed., *Feminist Theory* (Chicago: University of Chicago Press, 1981).

[83] Jean Grimshaw, *Philosophy and Feminist Thinking* (Minneapolis: University of Minnesota Press, 1986).

little concerned with philosophy" (quoting Janet Richards) (p. 28). So feminist philosophers—or any philosopher—should be wary of assuming a too great importance for philosophy in the feminist agenda, or in any social agenda, although Grimshaw herself feels that feminists cannot avoid philosophical questions (p. 34). But "there is no non-contested or unsolvable paradigm of female values or priorities which can be seen as a source for feminist philosophical thinking" (p. 259). Yet certainly that same fact would be true if we tried to establish a male point of view.

Moira Gatens argues[84] that not enough work has been done on the tensions *within* the methodologies of feminist theory itself" (p. 1), and that "there is not a feminist theory, but feminist *theories*" (ibid), various theories which feminism makes use of or 'borrows'. Yet rather than theorizing about women's experience, she sees their task as "a radical reconstruction of basic assumptions in philosophy" (p. 37), just as all radicals in philosophy have thought. "If there are no fixed natures then there is no 'eternal feminine' which dictates women's social role as wife/mother" (p. 48), as Existentialism argues and as de Beauvoir points out. "The project of philosophy is necessarily open-ended" (p. 89).

"Feminists, like philosophers, do not speak with a single voice" (p. 4).[85] "We do not think that any particular content in philosophy can be identified as female," the editors report (p. 6). "Femininity or masculinity are not fixed, nor are they independent of each other" (p. 7). "Women's views need to be considered and then synthesized with men's to find a human whole" (p. 20), Paula Buddington concludes. It is necessary, Lorraine Code states, "to break out of the stereotyped perceptions of women's nature" (p. 181). If so, then there is no given nature of women which can be appealed to as a distinctive source of

---

[84] Moira Gatens, *Feminism and Philosophy* (Cambridge: Polity, 1991).
[85] Morwenna Griffiths and Margaret Griffiths, *Feminist Perspectives in Philosophy* (London: Macmillan, 1988).

philosophy. "The notion of women's experience (in the singular) is an artificial construct" (p. 188). Lorraine Code concludes that feminist epistemology, then, should remain in dialogue with tradition.

A number of anthologies stress a wide variety of views within feminist philosophers. Mary Mahowald, for instance, incorporates a variety of classic and current concepts.[86] And Carol Gould concludes that women's liberation must not be considered alone but in terms of "the liberation of all human beings from varied forms of oppression" (p. 445). Germaine Greer, for instance, sought a transformation of sexual relations which would also liberate men" (p. 6).[87] One Irish feminist says: "I don't want to be called a feminist...I want liberation from all oppression" (p. 173). Cora Kaplan says of Feminist Literary Criticism, "The focus of feminist analysis ought to be on that heterogeneity within the literary..." (p. 347). Social division and ideologies "if they are understood they can be changed" (p. 360), she concludes.

Yet one of the most interesting—and different—phenomenon is the involvement of some feminists with Modern French Philosophy. [88] Why? First, because it is clear that this is in no way an original 'feminist' invention; the innovative thinkers were primarily male in the beginning, with the exception of Simone de Beauvoir, of course. Second, fascinating as it is and suggestive as it is for feminist philosophers, it is esoteric in its appeal and, for many, off the main stream of conventional philosophy. There is nothing 'wrong' about this, except for the fact that this is hard to see it becoming a broad basis for wide-spread feminist thought. The editors stress 'wonder' as the characteristic emerging from 'feminist' philosophers, but that is traditionally where philosophy was always been said to begin, in

---

[86] See Mary Briody Mahowald, *Philosophy of Woman*, note 59 above.
[87] See Sandra Harding, *The Science Question in Feminism*, note 58 above.
[88] Jennifer Allen and Iris M. Young, ed., *The Thinking Muse* (Bloomington, Indiana: Indiana University Press, 1989).

a sense of wonder (p. 1).

Existentialism and Post-Structuralism both have features which are attractive to some feminists as a base. In Existentialism, the stress on lived experience appeals to feminist themes, plus the stress on the individual and freedom. Emotion has a central role for Existentialism too, as does the notion of the alienation of the other. Post-structuralism advocates 'destabilizing' traditional thought, and this lack of fixity in philosophical norms is congenial to the newcomer. Women must put themselves into the text, and both philosophical movements stress the centrality of the individual to philosophical writing. However, in no way can that be claimed as a unique 'feminist' discovery. Rather, they are only human discoveries, slightly at odds with much of Modern Thought, and which at least some feminists find offers a congenial approach.

Thus, as the editors report, "what it means to be a feminist has become more problematic than it once seemed" (p. 12). However, the assumption of universal human experience 'devalues women', some still think (p. 16). 'Difference' is a primary metaphor for the female. Yet Donna Stanton cautions that attention to difference also has its dangers for feminists. "If we have female differences, we risk becoming entrapped in the patriarchal structures we are challenging," she reports (p. 17). In spite of every attempt, there seems to be "No Exit" for feminist philosophers form the context of historical philosophy with all of its variety. Teffner Allen suggests a paradigm of women's lives that emerges in the turning of women to one another (p. 78).

But how will the eventual necessity (at least if we want peace not war) of all human beings turning toward each other be accomplished, if women really form exclusive networks? For instance 'oppression' is said to be a fundamental fact of women's experience (Julia Murphy, p. 101). This involves 'devaluation', but how are oppression and devaluation to be dealt with whenever they appear, in whatever

THE DESCENT OF WOMEN

sex, since surely not all women universally in history have felt this, although many more have in recent times. Donna Stanton replies: "We would expect man to take and understand the difference woman is discovering" (p. 157). Yet Namascar Shaktini's suggestion that "Lesbian metaphor must overwrite phalogentric metaphor" (p. 192) would seem to turn us back to a 'difference' that would be difficult to extend.

Of course, one other block to extending women's experience is now widely recognized. As Linda Nicholson remarks: "From the late 1960s to the mid-1980s, feminist theory exhibited a recurrent pattern: Its analysis tended to reflect the viewpoint of white, middle-class women of North America and Western Europe" (p. 1). "To try to identify unitary themes in the experience or in the perspectives of women may require the suppression of voices different form our own" (p. 6). Appealing to Post-modernism, she believes that feminists must reject the universalism of Modern Thought, just as that movement has. Does, then, Post-modernism mean both relativism and the abandonment of theory (p. 9)? Ironically, 'gender' and the very categories we used to liberate, "may also have their controlling moments" (p. 16).

"For many feminist theorists there is by no means a consensus on such (apparently) elementary question as: What is gender" (p. 43)? We are back to Socrates, who finds in the Dialogues that our most important terms have multiple meanings. Feminists, then, would seem to be opposed to Wittgenstein's hope to find simplicity in philosophical language. The social/political conflict, so central to feminist concern, does not seem easily resolved. "Consensus has become an outmoded and suspect value," Seyla Benhabib claims (p. 108). "The bonds of womanhood are a feminist fantasy," Susan Bordo reports (p. 133). "For no theory...can place itself beyond danger" (p. 140). "Is it ever legitimate to say 'women' without qualification?" Nancy Hartsock asks (p. 159).

126

There are oppressive implications in the assumptions of the unity of women, Iris Young reports (p. 301). Thus, "reconstructing our 're-visioning' philosophy is a very large, open-ended project," the editors of a collection of essays in feminist epistemology conclude.[89] Marilyn Frye suggests a 'lesbian epistemology', and Alison Jagger suggests that emotion is indispensable for knowledge (p. 110), although Plato and others have suggested this as well. Sandra Harding sees "two conflicting feminist epistemologies" emerging (p. 189). "We need to think in ways that deliberately break the rules," Gail Stenstad suggests in agreeing with Nietzsche. "One of the most subversive things feminists can do is to think anarchically and then to speak and act from this thinking," she concludes (p. 332).

Lorraine Code asks: What can she know?[90] and offers one suggestion: "There are advantages to endorsing a measure of epistemological relativism that makes of it an enabling rather than a constraining position" (p. 3). Yet the sex of the knower is only one of a cluster of subjective factors (p. 4). In questioning whether there are in fact ways of knowing that are 'distinctively female', she quotes Ruth Bleier: That the variability within each sex is greater than the variability between them (p. 16). And so: "My principal conclusion is that questions of whether a feminist epistemology is possible or desirable must be left unanswered" (p. 314). Thus, feminists join the Socratic dialogue in that discovering the questions are more important than the finding of an answer.

And in discussing 'feminist philosophy' we must not forget that in social/political circles "Theory is a highly contested term within

---

[89]   Ann Garry and Marilyn Pearsall, ed , *Women, Knowledge, and Reality* (Boston: Unwin Hyman, 1989).
[90]   Lorraine Code, *What Can She Know?: Feminist Theory and the Construction of Knowledge* (Ithaca and London: Cornell University Press, 1991).

feminist discourse" (p. xiii).[91] The editors' conclusion: "We end up offering a set of essays that will not settle the question of 'theory', but that will instead appreciate the unsettling power—and politics—of theory" (p. xvii). Denise Riley remarks: "'Women' can also suffer from too much identification" (p. 122). And Jane Flax leaves us again with a question rather than an answer: "What are the relationships, actual and potential, between feminist theorizing and its practice of feminist politics?" (p. 446). "Rationality" is replaced by the more episodic and unpredictable connection of networks," Linda Singer concludes (p. 466).

In addition to its political connection, most feminist philosophers seem to agree that "the women's movement is deeply ethical in nature" (p. xi).[92] "Feminist ethics begins with female experience," the editors state (p. xiii), but they add: "There is no homogeneous women's experience. (p. xv). Since "sisterhood is complicated" (p. xix), the editors insist, "We must develop an analysis broad enough to account for the experience of *all* women, not merely a few" (p. xviii). "The diversity in women's experiences can lead to ideological splits within feminist ranks" (p. xxiv). And "the diversity among feminist perspectives is reflected in the diversity of feminist ethical theories" (p. 211). So that, in spite of the centrality of ethical concerns, we can expect to find no uniformity there. However, Carol Robb widens the perspective: "feminist ethicists are loyal to women in a way which is consistent to a loyalty to all of humanity" (p. 213).

The authors of *Women's Ways of Knowing*[93] state: "We searched for a single voice..." (Preface). But the differences they found in *Women's Ways of Knowing* "do not necessarily divide along gender

---

[91] Judith Butler and Joan W. Scott, ed., *Feminists Theorize the Political* (New York: Routledge, 1992).

[92] Barbara Hilkert Andolsen, Christine E. Gudorf, and Mary D Pellauer, ed., *Women's Consciousness, Women's Conscience* (San Francisco: Harper and Row, 1987).

[93] See *Women's Ways of Knowing*, note 59 above.

lines" (p. 8) in our self-definition. They found five major epistemological categories for women, but these overlapped male ways of
knowing to a large extent (p. 13). "Women become their own
authorities" (p. 54), they suggest, but surely all involved in a quest for
knowledge share that goal. "Truth lies hidden beneath the surface,"
they say (p. 94), as Plato also claimed. Nor is what the authors heard
an 'exclusively female voice' (p. 102). "The women we interviewed
were not limited to a single voice" (p. 103).

Chapter IV

Theories of Liberation and Revolution

A. The Feminist Dilemma, Our Dilemma

Hanna Arendt was right when she reported that 'revolution' is a new thing, a Modern concept, unknown in the Ancient or Medieval world.[94] It also seems to be primarily a Western product, since none of the traditions in the Eastern philosophies or religions offer to bring about the complete transformation of society, and thus of all persons within it, as an option, or an avenue of human release. Social reform, yes; revolution in structures, no. We recognize the association of revolution and liberation theories with the Enlightenment, with the development of democratic political processes. These concepts are also connected to the rise of the universal press for liberty, for the rights of the individual, for the overturn of barriers such as a caste system, slavery, or serfdom which restrict the rise of persons to their natural level of achievement.

Thus, as revolutionary theories fall under question, for example, the rejection of Marxist thought in the former U.S.S.R., terror and repression emerge again. Not only were they not eliminated, they had actually reached new levels of destruction. This helped to precipitate the downfall of the revolution intended for the good of those formerly suppressed or held in bondage. Revolution and liberation as a theme is linked to that which is perhaps best in Western civilization. This makes it hard critically to reappraise our enthusiasm for all proposed theories of human liberation. Instead of ushering in Utopias by eliminating all former sources of evil and destruction, these 'noble ambitions' often turned out to breed their own corruption. Thus,

---

[94] Hanna Arendt, *On Revolution* (New York: The Viking Press, 1965).

eventually they deteriorate rather than producing new liberties.

Into this scene of radical change and reassessment comes one recent version of the Women's Movement. Following feminist writers' recent exploration of women's history, we know that women's movements have appeared before in our past, and sometimes they achieved their goals, such as voting rights, legal and financial equality. But then, oddly, once successful they often become quiescent. Although not all women in the recent renewal of feminist demands were radical in their intent, a number made a conscious connection to Marxist proposals. This is partly because Communist theories seek to overturn some of the same social, political structures which women saw as oppressing them too. It seemed obvious and easy to borrow Marxist notions such as 'alienation', 'oppression', and 'class warfare' and to substitute 'Women' as a universal in place of the Proletariat.

But one issue which arose was whether 'women' could be treated as a class and whether that notion, rather than 'the workers', could be the chief power behind a social revolution. Materialist theories of social and political structures, not to mention thought and culture as determined by economics, by the ownership of the means of production, these are hard to reconcile with 'sex' as the primary social determinant and so make that the target for the removal of oppression. Still, even if all feminist theory did not parallel Marxist ideology, many did borrow from the history of revolutionary changes in social structure and in human relations. They pictured Utopias, idealized societies transformed by the revised relationship between the sexes which they demanded.

Studying the origins of women's press for their denied rights, we recognize the connection to 'equal rights' theories as these developed earlier and were fought for primarily by men. As medical advance, birth control and optional abortion liberated women from the tyranny of uncontrolled childbirth that was often life-threatening, this non-ideological, purely physical change began to release women to allow them to seek the rights they had encouraged men to argue and to fight for. Biology had almost been destiny, but technology and education, plus advances in medicine, released many women (not yet all by any means) from total bondage to their biological role. As this happened, instead of everything becoming easy, the same bondages which had inhibited men now became women's restriction too.

Of course, old prejudices, old patterns do not die easily; they do not even fade away gradually. In competition for scarce resources and for limited financial, political success, human beings have always seized on any powerful prejudice in order to strike against their opponents. As women become competitors for leadership in all fields, as had hardly been conceivable in the centuries before, instinct works to use any weapon available to undermine one's opponent. Women had known that "all was fair in love and war" and had, as a matter of fact, done rather well in the battle of love. To paraphrase Harry Truman's saying, they now found the heat in the public kitchen more intense than that in their homes, but many did not want to "get out."

Some feminist theorists have seen that women simply face all the 'put downs', all the failures to accept change, all the resentment against new competitors that reign in politics, in economics, as well as in religions. In response, they wanted to change the rules of the game. True, advocates of democracy had fought to remove artificial barriers to fulfilling human potential that were based on class or race. Thus, women could easily feel that all restrictions based on sex could go next. But examining how women had been exalted and protected, as well as how they had been abused and held down, the virtues we celebrated as women's, for example, love, caring, noncompetition, discussion vs. confrontation—it was argued that these admired qualities could be moved from the home, from child care into education, into professional fields, and even into revising social structures along improved lines.

A dilemma appears: If you argue for complete equality of opportunity, in church, state, commerce, and education, does the rejection of gender roles, now considered more restrictive than admirable, also do away with any claim to virtues specifically gender or sex linked? Of course, you can argue to take away any virtue once considered admirable and to build new social relations around that, as monks and nuns, Utopian theorists, and Marxists had done. But what odds for success can we give to such a proposal to transform present societies? Here feminists face the crux of their dilemma. This proposal for radical change in social roles and practices stands or falls depending upon our appraisal of theories of revolution and liberation: How far are people and societies open to radical alteration?

We know that it is possible to found small communities on radically Utopian schemes—the Shakers, the Quakers, new orders of monks and nuns, Zen monasteries, Buddhist temples and Hindu ashrams. However, the theories proposed in the Modern Era were not content with that. Some women have proposed new matriarchal, all-female groups and communities.[95] These may have the value of promoting solidarity for the participants, but they do little or nothing

---

[95] Mary Daly, *Beyond God the Father: Toward a Philosophy of Women's Liberation* (Boston: Beacon Press, 1973).

Reading Mary Daly is like reviewing the evolution of the women's movement in the late 20th Century, particularly in theology. She intended this book as a sequel to *The Church of the Second Sex*. The same anger and the same hope animated her. Women have a low caste, masked by sex role segregation. The task of the women's revolution is to spark creative action in and toward transcendence. The language of the sexist world must be castrated.

There is an emerging women's consciousness such as never before has taken place (p. 14). Women's consciousness is being wrenched free to find its own religious expression. God has been oppressive against women. There needs to be a new language of transcendence. Yet she agrees that women's liberation is "essentially linked to full human liberation" (p. 25). Self-transcendence must keep alive the question of ultimate transcendence, that is, of God. This is a bit ironic when she concludes that "women will be forced. . . to confront the most haunting of human questions, the questions of God" (p. 33), because her later books will reject Christianity when she has found it beyond the very reform she here proposes as women's task. She has said it depends on a leap in human evolution, but that leap took her beyond Christianity.

to change the patterns of the public world into which women have increasingly sought entry. Thus, women must either settle for consciousness raising and isolation in small groups capable of developing their own spirit free from the contamination of current civilization, the feminist version of Walden Pond and the Desert Fathers, or they can side with one of the revolutionary theories of the Modern Age and argue that it is possible to find universal solidarity by sex if not by class. But they must base their hope on our ability to reconstitute social structures.

Of course, accomplishing all this is also predicated on the Modern euphoria, that is, on the feeling that power not heretofore available has come into our hands. If this has not happened, it is foolish to argue that we can do what has not been possible in any previous age, that is, to rebuild human nature and control societies in order to prevent their decline into corruption. In the *Republic*, Plato argued for using his model as an ideal and for trying to reshape societies to it. Education was and is a key tool in any such program. But except for turning Plato into a Modern, we know that he depicted the countervailing forces as being balanced against the ideal, always threatening its decline.

The basic question, then, concerns our newly acquired ability to eliminate evil, to eradicate human sin, to control corruption, to train human beings away from old and destructive, even self-destructive, habits. The enthusiasm over our capacity to do this has much to do with the decline of religion, at least among the intelligentsia and the leaders of society. God is truly unnecessary, if we can really become our own superman or superwoman, break old human limitations and revalue old values. Nietzsche had proposed this and Hitler endorsed him publicly. All we need to change in Nietzsche's plan is to eliminate his negative, even vicious, comments about women, change his theory to allow the Superwoman to rise above old restrictions placed on her sex, and we have a basis for belief in an ability to recreate ourselves.

135

What is the problem with this proposal, since it has attracted many of "the best and the brightest" in recent centuries? It has even given old religious doctrines new life by advocating them as an avenue to social transformation, for example, Liberation Theology. The problem is that, as we look around us for the evidence of the success of these Utopian transformation theories, we find not only no unqualified success but actually many major catastrophes. How did Stalin go wrong using Lenin's theories? How did Mao's 'cultural revolution' destroy much of value in Chinese society rather than purifying it? When the Berlin wall came tumbling down, when the U.S.S.R.'s union fell into violent division, why did we seem to see so little of noble goals to admire in these situations and so much misery and descension?

In trying to assess the success-failure record of theories of liberation and revolution, in order to see how this might lead to feminism's major dilemma, we should pause and ask ourselves if the United States, or any other Western style democracy, is an exception to the recent Utopian failures. And if so, does this leave us with any 'way out' for feminist proposals or any new means to appraise their agenda? Again, Hanna Arendt gives us a lead clue: In contrast to the French revolution whose ideals still attract many (witness the international success of "Les Miserables") but which admittedly deteriorated into destructive terror (revolutions tend to eat their own children, it is said), the United States began with a constitution, a declaration, and soon a Bill of Rights. This prevented, or at least moderated, the tendency for the victors to destroy their supposed enemies in that massive paranoia which we so often witness.

An ideal society cannot be built on hatred for another group, it is also said. Does this mean that all revolutionary groups must become practical, if not theoretical 'Christians' in order to succeed? Mao, Lenin, Stalin, Che Guevera, Castro have certainly not said or acted so. Some theologians have connected Christian promises with the need to implement social change, and it is true that Christianity has, in its most attractive forms, offered 'new life'. But until more recently this has not been applied to societies or to institutions, not even to churches, but rather to individuals. To see Christianity otherwise means to move it from its founders' role and to reinterpret it in revolution/liberation terms, since Jesus did not transform his society or release his people. He was crucified.[96]

The assumption must be that we possess various powers of radical reformation that were not available to Jesus, Buddha, or Confucius. If so, it is certainly more attractive to offer transformation for massive

---

[96] Denise L. Carmody, *Seizing the Apple: A Feminist Spirituality of Personal Growth* (New York: Crossroad, 1984).

In spite of the widespread attack upon Christianity's attitude toward women, the author still believes that Christianity is a treasure house of spiritual resources. She joins Christian faith to women's liberation. In their history, all religions have not promoted women's status. Women have amassed a store of spiritual resources whose time to shine may well have come, she states.

Joan Chittister, O.S.B., *Women, Ministry and the Church* (New York: Paulist Press, 1983).

There is no Christian justification for the oppression of women; this is the author's beginning premise. She sets out an agenda of nine points for change in church practice, including the elimination of sexist language and the ordination of female priests. There is a new need for leadership in religious life, she claims. Sisters, she concludes, "Let us celebrate together the resurrection of the Lord, and our own" (p. 130).

Regina Coll, C.S.J., ed., *Women and Religion* (New York: Paulist Press, 1982).

The author realizes that women face greater problems in a patriarchical church, such as hers, and her aim is to speed 'socialization' in change. She is aware that gender roles can be modified, and family life too, and she wants to find a way to accommodate the church to this. Since culture plays such a large role in our behavior, we can consider changes in what we call 'appropriate' and 'inappropriate'. The authors who are included approach the task from a wide variety of background and perspectives.

Mary Collins, *Women at Prayer* (New York: Paulist Press, 1987).

In an era when the popular image has shifted to women in action, in politics, etc., it is a nice contrast to any extreme to read an account of women at prayer, since the spiritual literature of women is long. Traditional spiritualness comes to us through women at prayer, she reports. But she knows that the church was often been hostile to their wish to communicate this. Collins has chosen Annie Dilard, the writer, the poet Anne Sexton, and the painter Meinrad Craighead as examples. Women have gone to "the edge of the rim" in their quest for God; this is her theme.

social groups than to individuals who still live within a corrupt society or church. The goal of our liberation from racial discrimination lies in the same situation. Where violence was concerned, Martin Luther King preached classical Christian pacifism. But the Black Power movement replaced him, and we have ironically seen mass violence in the racial scene in the U.S. as much as we have seen mass improvement. Christianity must have something useful to say, even to the non-believer who shares its desire for release but who does not act on faith. The Women's Movement is in the same situation. Insofar as it has retained any base in a hatred of men as a class, vs. the bourgeois for the Marxist, such hatred undermines its goals.[97]

Jesus advocated love, not only for friends but primarily directed toward our enemies. The practicality of this difficult doctrine, both to accept and to act upon, seems borne out by the self-destructive tendencies built into any revolution that draws its strength from the ancient passion of hate. Love promotes compassion, but it cannot fuel massive revolutions. And it is (or it should be) suspicious of trying to achieve the power necessary to seize control of the channels of social and economic reform. Thus, revolutions are caught in the same dilemma which some recent radical Feminist demands face: to draw power from the tested avenue of painting vicious pictures of universal villains (e.g. 'patriarchy', or in some cases proscribed 'hetero-

---

[97] Mary Condren, *The Serpent and the Goddess Women, Religion and Power in Celtic Ireland* (New York: Harper and Row, 1989).

Church and state in Ireland, the author states, depend for their life blood on the subjugation of women. Condren wants to trace out how this came to be in pre-Christian, early Christian and then in contemporary culture. Sexual politics dictated the exclusion of women from religious officiations. Women could only sacrifice themselves, and plunge so themselves into powerlessness and particularity. But today there is a voice of women calling for renewed religious consciousness. Women represent the world of nature, men the world of history or culture, that other battle ground in Ireland. But the myth of "objectivity" has served to conceal a hidden agenda of those in power. Sex and spirituality have too long been polar opposites in Christian teaching, she believes.

sexuality'), or to accept a less divisive love for all human beings but one which often lacks political force, sweet as it sounds.

Reinhold Niebuhr talked of 'the children of light' and 'the children of darkness', and he knew full well that 'dark forces' have an advantage in seeking power. He wanted 'social Christians' to retain their purity of light but to assume the cunning of 'the dark ones' in their ability to gain and to control power. He did realize that power tends to corrupt, but he was a child of his optimistic times, convinced about our ability to build at least semi-utopian social structures, and he thought this new light could be kept from becoming dark.

Yet the record of those who gain power is not an optimistic one. Few women like to use recent women political figures as models, Margaret Thatcher, Indira Gandhi, Golda Meir. Antonia Fraser depicts her *Warrior Queens*[98] as full of terror and fury. Kali is a fear-inspiring Hindu goddess. Pele spews out molten lava from volcanoes in Hawaii and elsewhere. As women gain power, they do not seem to remain exempt from power corruption.

Following the use of 'class' by Marx as the chief category for social economic analysis, we have to ask if raising 'sex' to the chief interpretive category is subject to any of the same weaknesses. That is, we see that by focusing on 'class' we often created an increase in class warfare, perhaps even hatred, and that Marxism has never managed to establish its goals of the 'classless society', its version of the kingdom of heaven on earth. The repression of one's ideological enemies, even their destruction, has never proved able to move beyond itself; it could never lead to the ideal society free from strife. Is sex or gender, as a new category for all analysis, any more likely to lead beyond "the war between the sexes," beyond antagonism against all who do not share one version of the relation among the

---

[98]   See Antonia Fraser, *The Warrior Queens*, chapter I, note 30.

139

sexes?

If prayer books are revised specifically for gay and lesbian emphasis, if biblical documents and religious songs and services are rewritten so that one is, ironically, necessarily more aware of sexual division than before, can the emphasis on sex ever lead beyond itself rather than simply to heightening divisions? In an ideal agenda, yes. The rights of minorities will not only be protected but in fact idealized; all American Indians portrayed as wise, sensitive nature lovers; all explorers or cowboys as ruthless destroyers. The point: The attack on any group as such, or even a public stress on any group, actually increases our sense of division and does not lessen it. Jesus said: "Come unto me all ... " He did not specify a favored group or castigate all of another, not even the Roman officials who tried to control him. The movements that followed him have on occasion developed vast power by focusing on hatred, heretics, infidels, and so forth. But it is a travesty to do so in the name of one who renounced hatred and destruction.[99]

---

[99] Joann W. Conn, *Women's Spirituality: Resources for Christian Development* (New York: Paulist Press, 1986).

The editor states that "the feminine" is a society constructed attitude and rejects a set of unchanging abstract qualities. Not feminine nature but "women's cultural evaluation of standards for maturity" is the norm (p. 1). Yet the mind reflected in the book is predominantly white, middle class, Western Women.

Women's spirituality is perplexing and difficult for three reasons: (1) their possibilities for mature spirituality are restricted, and (2) Christian teaching has contributed to this. Women are suspicious of self-surrender and seek autonomy, and (3) some women think the Christian spiritual tradition is so sexist that it is no longer useable for mature women. Can, then, women's spirituality only be accomplished by rejecting biblical tradition?

Doris Donnelly, ed., *Mary, Woman of Nazareth* (Paulist Press, New York, 1983).

Interest in Mary, long traditional in the Roman church, has reemerged, largely due to the rise of feminist theology. For many, Mary became an unhappy symbol of the subservient, silent, obedient woman. But it is also true that Mary was a symbol of wisdom and embodied the feminine dimension of God. These essays, offering a variety of approaches, seek to affirm that "Mary can indeed serve as a model of faith for all Christians" if properly reinterpreted. This, of course, involves layers of interpretation that are not simply present in the text.

The Women's Movement, then, insofar as it is a radical revolutionary proposals, faces its dilemmas that stem from the hubris of the Modern World: To seek the power that revolutionary social change requires but to resist focusing hatred on any group for fear of introducing the inner decay that hatred subjects us to. And more importantly: To highlight the role of sex so that its prejudicial uses can be opposed but still not frame our entire intellectual agenda on an analysis of sexual opposition for fear that this will in turn cause an even greater sense of division vs. a unity of all humanity in our common condition. The slogan: "Everything is gendered" is not only not true in any uniform sense; it may actually work to heighten tensions and opposition.

But to say to women that the Modern revolutionary theories have not fully succeeded and were questionable in their assumptions might seem to be arguing that we have not advanced and are in our ancient human condition, which certainly has been the source of innumerable dilemmas heretofore. But that is not really true, as well as not being what feminists want to hear, since it appears as an excuse to hold women in their ancient, often repressive, condition. To deal with this we have to consider another Modern icon—Progress. Just as we are partly chastened by the failure, or at least the terror, of radical revolutions, so our optimism over 'progress' has been dampened. Science was our model here. Women have been released from ancient bondage by modern medicine. Technology has given them equal powers, often equalizing strength differentials.

However, we know 'technology' not to be an all-good word. Industrialization has transformed societies and, with science based technologies, revolutionized the conditions for life but not always for the better. In addition to 'revolution', human 'liberation' and 'progress', the Modern Age based itself on 'universalism' too. If classes, types, kinds, races, sexes, religions could all be categorized and described, evaluated or dealt with on the basis of universal concepts, if all of one race or sex or religion or class really were alike, then we would possess powerful tools to divide the world according to sweeping categories, Jew vs. Aryan, Black vs. White, Bourgeois vs. Proletariat, Christian vs. Muslim. But these massive categories for change are at the same time massive categories to promote hatred.

The failure, or at least the less than fully promised success, of the Modern Utopian agendas calls into question the potential destructiveness of wielding these massive universal concepts, all women, all science, all anything. If we are forced back to individual assessment for all truthful judgments, if not all men are oppressors and not all women are virtuous, if not all of any category share either common values or common ideologies, then 'revisionists' (that hated Marxist concept) are the order of the day, not an exception that can be wiped out. Values do not fall in universal categories for our convenience. Good and evil are falsely attributed in blanket fashion to any human group no matter how constituted. If so, ease of appraisal, simplicity in our understanding of the world, all go out the window. We may change and we may work for change, but not very realistically if based on universal classifications.

The adolescent luxury of having a fixed target for hatred disappears. 'Post-modernism' is not quite a good name for this approach, since that has become connected with some rather esoteric theories,[100] while what is here proposed is not that abstruse. It is just painful in its refusal of simplified answers. Our conclusion is not particularly 'religious' either. Yet on the other hand it does not of necessity deny God in the name of human progress as Nietzsche, Freud, and Marx felt they must. However, it cannot be the God of Rationalism that returns, since this is not the neatness and resolution of old dilemmas which the Rationalists or the Empiricists hoped to offer. It is certainly not anti-scientific, although it finds all good, all necessary progress, in no one location.

---

[100] See Shulamith Firestone, *The Dialectic of Sex*, chapter I, note 15.

But if recent well-advertised feminist demands have led us to this situation of dilemma and to our need to reappraise all theories offering liberation and revolution on a mass scale, what then is the 'future of feminism'? If in fact it has raised to new prominence every traditional problem, God and religion for the feminist theologians,[101] social change as an agenda for all societies, and quotas of fairness in our political system—then projecting both feminists' achievements and the impossibility of final solutions could provide the key, the illustrative example, of our future in a world post-Progress. Since progress is not an automatic feature of our era, if in fact deterioration seems as prevalent as advance, how are the changes women propose likely to come out, especially since they turn out to be similar to the list of long-celebrated 'liberal' values which are at the heart of the success of some democracies?

The dilemma which the feminist agenda has encountered contains much that is instructive for us. The outline of the obstacles, the repressions, which women face in their search for new opportunities highlights for us the same barriers which all human beings face in their quest for fulfillment. Similarly, the impasse the Women's Movement has reached tells us about the barriers we all encounter. First, we know that no universal concept binds all women together, except a vague physiological identity. So all human beings should avoid thinking that race, religion, or nationality of itself creates uniformity—other than an artificial one. Furthermore, when we discover that universal transformation is not available, ideological repressions are often born in reaction. In response to frustrated

---

[101] Dorothy Sayers, *The Mind of the Maker* (New York: Harper and Row, 1979).

When it is argued that women writers have been overlooked, Dorothy Sayers offers a good counter example. Her mystery novels had wide circulation. Yet although she wrote a number of theological books, they are less referred to. True, she is by all odds a 'conservative' in theology, and thus offers a stark contrast to more radical theologians today. Yet she is an expressive and a powerful writer, one who makes theological issues come alive. She challenges her reader with questions.

revolutionary goals, "politically correct thinking" has recently attempted to restrict all who do not agree and who, by their descension, expose our inherent diversity.[102]

The attempt to impose universal beliefs inevitably leads to intolerance, inquisitions, new heresy trials. Hatreds are bred as we try to fix the source of the problems of any group on one source, say Blacks on Whites, women on 'patriarchy'. We now know that such focused hatreds do not provide the base for an improved society but instead often breed holocausts and an artificially induced mounting hysteria. Oddly, the extremes of any radical proposal, whether politically left or right, tend to increase animosity, not reduce it. Sadly, 'compromise' becomes a term of abuse, a sign of failure, and millions are sacrificed on that altar. When any oppressed group, whether of race or sex or class, vocalizes the source of its repression, that voice must be converted to speak for all who suffer in any condition. Negro spirituals form one of the great traditions in religious music, and they have been universally appropriated. Witness

---

[102] Nancy F. Cott, ed., *Root of Bitterness: Documents of the social history of American women* (Boston: Northeastern University Press, 1986).

The editor quotes Sarah Grimke: The root of bitterness is the mistaken notion of the inequality of the sexes. However, the editor thinks the essays presented "all bear the earmarks of the intellectual tide of 1970 and 1971. They are still too wedded to an outlook in which the male is the norm, she feels on later reflection. One theme absent is the conflict among women themselves.

The essays deal with the consciousness and self-consciousness of American Women (primarily white and middle class). They begin with the primacy that seventeenth-century colonists gave to religious awareness. Then preindustrial society altered work roles for women. In the eighteenth century the subject of women's proper roles was of great interest. The nineteenth century saw the cult of domesticity. The antislavery crusade brought up the issue of women's rights. "There is no slave, after all, like a wife."

However, biology was destiny to a much greater extent in the past century. Against the background of today's feminist theorists, these essays give a very clear picture of the shifting and vari d roles women have had in American history. The availability of higher education brought a great change.

144

the civil rights movement's use of "We shall overcome" as its theme song.

In contrast, any Black self-concentration which voices hatred seems neither to improve its lot, except for popular music groups or for movies that exploit it, and not to lead to much improvement for the impoverished. Some women have succeeded spectacularly, but not all women universally. If hatred is focused on any group, advance is not likely to be sustained, since we know we cannot get all women to support any universal indictment. Some women love men and feel protected by them, while some women can become more vicious than many mild men. The conclusion: Any suffering group must offer its agenda for release to all human beings universally, without restriction, and refrain from blowing up any image of a single villain or source of evil, for fear of being undercut by an unacceptable generalization.

This partially leaves open the notion that, practically speaking, it is advisable to love even one's enemies (and these are not all of any universal group) in order to avoid the self-deteriorating tendency which induces hatred. Yet as Kierkegaard remarked, love cannot be commanded. It must be voluntary, and it always works individually, never covering any group indiscriminately. All who have tried to force themselves to love, whether under the inspiration of Jesus or by following their sex drive, know that to be a futile enterprise. If, then, we cannot command love, and if hatred as a focus draws out amazing energies but proves uncontrollable and even destructive, can we offer no universal judgment, urge no uniform routes to liberation for whole groups? We are, it seems, in the weakened position of operating individually.

What if neither feminists nor radical revolutionaries nor 'social gospel' Christians want to accept this, since it sounds too much like giving up an admirable and attractive goal? Why would anyone, except perhaps the drug lords and rulers of the underworld, object if we brought the Kingdom of Heaven into being on Earth? No one; but the record of revolutionary theory, which was new with the Modern World as well as notions of Progress and our power to transform our natures, has lead to so much more destruction than advance that we need to check our basic premises carefully. The time has come, as Aristotle would say, for the metaphysical evaluation of our hidden assumptions and to ask ourselves critically: If destruction and terror has so often appeared instead of benefit, on what basis can we safely band together to seek human liberation, but not as based on any universal class whether for or against it?

To do this involves stressing the thesis that "women are not alone," that no single enemy can be universally defined, that only as Blacks, Jews, Muslims, Irish, Women—any group—put their liberation into the context of all human beings, only then can we avoid stirring up sub-surface hatred and frustration, fixing these on some image of sex, class, religion, or race, and so planting the seeds for terror tactics to emerge, as we see in countless instances around the globe. To seek the advantage, the autonomy, of any single group requires that it be at the expense of some other group; and thus ancient warfares are rekindled. 'Ethnic cleansing' breeds a new holocaust. We can point at what our group needs, what restricts us, what needs to be done, but we must then transfer that agenda away from sectarianism to the universal human agenda.

We can see this in the rise of the Women's Movement, since we recognize its early emergence from the pioneering men who struggled against their political and cultural tyrants, arguing "give me liberty or give me death." But the Statue of Liberty in New York harbor is famous and was a gift to America, not because it lighted a path for only women or only the proletariat, but because it was (and hopefully is) a beacon to all seeking freedom and a new life without oppression. We know only too well that this did not translate out immediately for Jews who arrived under its shadow. But at least the Bill of Rights was never rewritten so as to apply only to one class or sex or race or creed. If this universalism can be kept open and the general human condition can become our context, there is some hope that we will not let hatred trap our visionary ideals into ever new repressions.

B. Plato, Feminism and Sophistry
1. The Feminist as Sophist

Given the long-traditional account of the Sophists in ancient Greece, it is fascinating to consider that they might offer a sympathetic context for feminist concerns. Of course, the Sophists have been thought of popularly via the way Plato describes and opposes them. Since we know that Plato, as a creative artist, seldom gives a straight factual account but instead uses actual persons as symbols for points he wishes to make, his account should be viewed as historical fiction. Yet two issues are in question: (1) How can the art of Sophistry aid feminist programs; and (2) Did Plato revise his early view of the Sophists in a way that is more enlightening than his early attacks?

Susan C. Jarratt suggests that, because the Sophists were considered as 'the other', they share that situation with women.[103] However, one problem is that although this came to be true, the Sophists in their time were both quite popular and accepted, whereas it was Socrates who was excluded and put to death due to his 'otherness' from the reigning norms. Philosophy has tended to exclude rhetoric as an art, it is true, and in that sense women might share this exclusion. This fact is linked by Jarratt with the 'marginalization' which hierarchical systems cause, so we know one issue is the question of our norms in philosophy. Again, it was Socrates who was 'marginalized' by his society, not the Sophists. In our day this might include any man or woman who does not agree

---

[103] Susan C. Jarratt, "The First Sophists and Feminism: Discourses of the 'Other'" *Hypatio vol.5, no.1* (Spring 1990), pp. 27-41. All page references are to this article in this section.

with reigning orthodoxy in any dominant view, 'feminist' or otherwise.

Jarratt suggests that Sophistic rhetoric offers "a flexible alternative to philosophy for mediating theoretical oppositions among contemporary feminism" (p. 27). Philosophy of course never claimed to be the only avenue, at least in its Platonic/Aristotelian embodiment, so that rhetoric, or the art of persuasion, has never been excluded but only contrasted to the method of philosophy. Aristotle is known to have said that one must pick a method appropriate to the subject matter, so it is conceivable that rhetoric is appropriate for many situations. Plato only wanted to cast philosophy in a different role from Sophistry, but that depends on how broadly or narrowly we define 'philosophy', which is always an open question.

It is hard to say that Plato wanted to make rhetoric 'subordinate' to philosophy: certainly he wanted to contrast the two approaches. The Sophists did teach effective public speech, and in this regard they might be compared to teachers of homiletics in seminaries, who teach the important skill of effective sermonizing. On the other hand, theologians specialize in the analysis of theological questions. Perhaps more important: "For the Sophists, human perception and discourse were the only measure of truth, all of which are contingent" (p. 28). So, the real issue is the existence of Plato's Forms and whether in knowledge we seek fixity.

Jarratt correctly points out that the basic question is whether there will be any rank ordering of knowledge. And lest we think that either Plato or Aristotle dominated all of philosophy, we need to remember the Skeptics, who denied all possibility of finality. Also, both the Stoics and Epicureans took philosophy as simply an instrument to make possible the achievement of their ethical goals. It was not an inquiry justified for its own sake but for its practical effectiveness. There always have been alternatives in philosophy, even though Plato may have gained a wider significance later on. Still, philosophy in Plato's time was not monolithic, which is exactly why he argued against the Sophists. The underlying assumption, sometimes detected in feminist theory, that all of philosophy has been of one kind, is hard to reconcile with the vast variety in its history.

Most important, Jarratt points out parallels between Plato's rejection of the Sophists and the cultural stereotype of the feminism. Irrationality, subjectivity and emotional sensitivity are 'devalued' in favor of rationality and objectivity. But as we will argue, one must look carefully at Plato's later and serious treatment of the Sophists. We must consider not only the *Republic* but the *Symposium* and *Phaedrus*, which stress the insightful qualities of love and divine madness. Jarratt points to a parallel oppression of women "within the same system" of Western thought (p. 30). But if philosophy is "the love of wisdom," it is hard to see how women are automatically shut out. For Plato, love is crucial to achieving insight.

In response, Jarratt suggests that the Sophists difference from philosophy "could simply be named 'feminism' and valued as such" (p. 32). An emphasis on practice, on historical contingency "characterize the rhetoric of the Sophists" (p. 33). Thus, if women wish to rewrite their history, the Sophists' non-fixity is helpful. And if story-telling is to become an effective method, both Sophists and feminists stress sensual pleasure in the sound of words and poetic effects. As a literary interpretive device, this importance is clear. Women need to "break with explanations, interpretations and all the authorities" (p. 34, quoting Cixous). Style cannot be separated from substance. A new history must be invented. There is a drift toward narrative. Feminists can take a revision of logic through narrative as their central strategy. There is a political significance to narrative.

Jarratt's concluding theme: Current feminists are becoming Sophists . . . by describing rhetorical solutions to crucial problems of defining a theory with the most power for changing women's lives. Sophistic rhetoric enables a "feminist reading/writing practice of breaking into the received histories of the discourse of man" (p. 39). It provides a way to recover a range of marginalized voices in the history of rhetoric. It may offer increased leverage for dislodging the patriarchal institutions whose foundations were laid during the Sophists' time, she contends. Yet, in his later writings, how did Plato come to view and even value the Sophists?

We know that in the early and middle dialogues Plato took up questions which he treated casually. In the later dialogues he refined and formed these into serious theories. Susan Jarratt has argued persuasively for how a re-evaluation of the Sophists can help feminist causes. But it is also true that Plato himself revised his early antagonistic opinion and learned a great deal from the Sophists. His detailed discussion, of course, lies in the dialogue, the *Sophist*, which supersedes his earlier more polemical treatment. Let us see how Plato revised his opinion, claimed to have learned profoundly from the Sophists, and how, if this is the case, it might shed light on feminist projects.

We need to remember, too, that the Sophists were 'hired teachers' who taught for money, so that Plato/Socrates felt they might compromise truth (as he saw it) for popularity and for pay. Philosophy always has to consider its task in comparison to popular doctrines of the time. In this sense, philosophy today might contrast itself to "politically correct thinking," feminist or otherwise. More important yet, if Plato/Socrates did not claim to possess truth but only to love its pursuit, no fixity of doctrine is possible, and he thought that the Sophists' claim to possess knowledge which they could teach to others constituted such fixity. Plato, you recall, thought he could only ask students questions and that each student could only teach himself/herself. Thus, the inconclusive nature of the dialogue method.

We need to be clear about why Plato objected to the popularizing of the Sophists and then contrast this with what in the later dialogues he reported to have learned from them. Oddly enough, *the Sophist* contains Plato's most detailed statement of the philosopher's art. Realizing that Plato and Socrates were in fact 'the other' in their society, we can see Plato's objection to conceiving of philosophy as popularity. What is 'marginalized' in one day may become orthodoxy in another and vice versa. So that rather than teaching truth for pay, Socrates wants philosophy to be only the love and never-ending pursuit of wisdom. However, if feminists want a lack of fixity in doctrine, Plato's inconclusive dialogues offer a model. Still, Plato learned from studying the Sophist's art, just as we may learn by evaluating feminist demands.

The similarities in the discourse of post-modernist feminists and the Sophists is a case in point. We see this when Jarratt says that "sophistic rhetoric offers a flexible alternative to philosophy as an intellectual framework" (p. 27). She seems to assume that 'philosophy' is some one, fixed doctrine. It cannot be so for Plato, and its myriad variations in history (although some philosophers are certainly 'rationalists') tell us that philosophy's meaning never comes to us fixed but must be worked out by each individual. Plato did that for himself, but there is no evidence that he considered his conclusions fixed for others. And there is much evidence that he thought each person must work this out for himself/herself. If Protagoras, the Sophist, was exiled, so was Socrates. Thus, both stood outside 'the system'.

2. The Sophists Teach Plato About Philosophy

A feminist theorist learns from studying Sophistry. Plato also learned from them. What was it that he claimed to see, and how might it illuminate the feminist use of Sophistry? In his later dialogue on *The Sophist*, Plato does not have Socrates as the main speaker but "a stranger from Ellea"[104] (p. 265, 216A). Such men appear in all sorts of shapes, sometimes as Sophists, he suggests. Plato begins to admit that understanding the philosopher involves understanding the

---

[104] Plato, *The Sophist*, trans. H.N. Fowler, Loeb Library. (New York: Putnam's Sons, MCMXXI).

Sophist's art; the two are linked (p. 271, 218B). The Sophist 'hunts' new and promising youths, teaches primarily for pay, and claims to give an education (p. 289, 223B). He is argumentative, controversial and pugnacious (as is Socrates himself) (p. 299, 226A).

The art of discrimination is what one wants to teach, Socrates suggests (p. 301, 226C). This requires first a 'purging', "to make him think that he knows only what he knows, and no more" (p. 313,230D). But what is the magical power of the sophisticate art? "It is a sort of knowledge based upon mere opinion" (p. 325, 233C). The issue of 'Socratic ignorance' comes in at this point, for Socrates does not claim wisdom but only to know that he does not know. "And when a man says that he knows all things, and can teach them to another for a small price in a little time, must we not consider that a joke?" (p. 327-9, 234A).

The Sophist's claim to possess knowledge and to be able to teach it—it is this to which Plato objects. The philosopher does not make such knowledge claims; and Jarratt wants that too. Plato suggests however, that the Sophists are 'entertainers', and that comes closer to Jarratt's interest (p. 331, 235A). It is an art which produces 'appearances'. And this leads Plato to ask how falsehood can be believed, since it is clear that many are impressed and/or misled. Thus Sophistry must have power, which leads Plato to "the bold assumption that non-being exists, for otherwise falsehood could not come into existence" (p. 337, 237A). Sophistry has led him to the metaphysics of 'being' and 'non-being'.

How can this be? How can what started as a diatribe against the popular Sophists lead Plato to such a difficult issue? Because, I suggest, if he wants to oppose philosophy's method of an inquiry, which clarifies by means of questions, to the Sophist's claim to teach knowledge, Plato comes up against a difficulty: How can they be so widely acclaimed? Anyone who opposes a popular, long-held belief must confront that question. It does not make sense to dismiss a belief that is widely held without accounting for its power. So Plato is forced to decide that his world of Forms, which represent the objects of knowledge, do not exist in pristine purity. Rather, they involve non-being in their very being.

If this is true, things are not quite so easy or so obvious as he supposed early on. And if not, this allows not-fully-accurate beliefs to be attractive, but it also makes the philosopher's task of searching for the truth far from easy or obvious. Without going into detail on Plato's analysis of 'non-being' and how it is linked with 'being', the Sophist 'hides' in these difficult questions, for example, makes things appear easier to understand than they are, whereas the philosopher accepts the limitations on finality and thus the difficulty in all teaching. Oddly, this puts a feminist such as Jarratt closer to Plato's 'philosopher' than to the 'Sophist' at least on this issue, since fixity of knowledge is what she hopes to prove impossible.

Sophistry has forced Plato to say that 'not-being exists' (p. 351, 240C) which makes the doctrine of the pure knowability of the Forms anything but simple. False opinion, which Plato opposes, thinks that things which are not "in some way are" (p. 351, 240E). Plato has been forced into a difficult metaphysical position, one which frustrates the simplicity and clarity of knowledge. But he could not avoid it. He must explain the Sophists' attraction and power, even if he does not accept their knowledge claims. If not-being is, then "on the other hand in a sense being is not" (p. 355, 241D). Nothing could be more compromising for a rigid believer in the immutability of the Platonic Forms to admit.

The Sophists have forced Plato to revise substantially his basic theory of knowledge in order to account for the effectiveness of Sophistical teaching. It had a power which must be accounted for. Plato changes his definition of 'being', which is a rather fundamental compromise. He now defines being as "nothing else but power" (p. 379, 247E). If so, the Sophists have power, and so the objects of their knowledge, their teaching, must exist. Like feminist theorists, Plato gives up all claim to exclusivity and finality in knowledge. Our objects of knowledge must be more complicated than he had thought, if the power of perceiving 'being' lies in no single formula.

The philosopher still has his task, for Plato, but it cannot be a claim to possess all knowledge. 'Motion' comes into play in knowledge, whereas before Plato had at first wanted only what was motionless as objects of knowledge (p. 387, 249D). And if motion is admitted as characterizing being, knowledge cannot have a 'Platonic' fixity. Learning from the Sophist's art has indeed forced Plato into a non-exclusive philosophical position. Rather than the fixity of the Forms, Plato now says that "all the classes or genera also commingle with one another, or do not commingle" (p. 401,253C). 'Dialectic' is born: the task of tracing motion and the manner in which objects blend or do not blend with one another. In other words, the Forms no longer live in splendid isolation but can move and change in their relation to us.

Philosophy asks the question: How can individual things be associated with one another? The answer is not simple and cannot be fixed. The Sophist, Plato feels, "runs away" from these complex and confusing matters and offers a simplicity which cannot be accurate. However, 'Sophistry' would not be possible, nor could it be believed, if the objects of knowledge were as simple and fixed as the Platonic Forms had been thought to be. 'Otherness' comes to pervade all things, Plato is forced to believe. Each thing is not "just what it is and not another thing" but in fact includes relationships of infinite complexity. The 'otherness' involved in all being, and the complexity which results, is precisely the 'non-being' "which we were looking for because of the Sophist" (p. 421, 258B).

The Sophists have clearly upset the 'neatness' of Plato's theory of knowledge, which is a goal some feminist theorists also seek. But oddly, this is more true of Plato than it is of the 'simplicity' in Sophistical thinking. Rhetoric is not the issue. The art of persuasion is actually much advocated by Plato, and philosophers must learn this in order to be effective in the market place. The philosopher must blend the king with the politician. Mixture is both important and difficult. "The attempt to separate everything from everything else... shows that a man is utterly uncultivated and unphilosophical" (p. 425, 259E). Given this definition of 'philosophy', the Sophist teaching is faulted as too easy.

"Our power of discourse is derived from the interweaving of the classes or ideas with one another" (p. 427, 259E). The idea that the Forms 'interweave' was repugnant to the early Plato, as was Sophistry. Now he has learned from the Sophists how difficult it is to speak the truth and that to fix knowledge in speech is impossible. 'False discourse', then, can come into being because final clarity is an impossible ideal. Plato will still accuse the Sophists of 'false discourse', that is, of taking the easy way out, of simplifying excessively what in reality is both difficult to state and complex to grasp. 'Falsity' is to "speak of things that are not as if they were" (p. 439, 263B). But because of the otherness in all things, that is, the involvement of not-being in all being, this is easy to say and difficult to make out.

It is instructive that the dialogue, *The Sophist*, tends toward triviality at the end, as if Plato were telling us again that finality in human knowledge is impossible, so complex is our task, so involved in multiple relations are the objects of our knowledge. Plato does not have Hegel's version of 'dialectic' to comprehend all the myriad complexities within one system. So that in fact most feminists have more in common with Existentialism and Socratic Ignorance than with the surface simplicity of the Sophists, even if it is backed with rhetorical skills. Perhaps this is the real lesson Feminist philosophers can derive from the Sophists, just as it was for Plato.

3. The Sophistical Function of Philosophical Theory

Having understood Jarratt's interest in the Sophists due to their relevance for feminist concerns, and having examined how the 'late Plato' changed his appraisal in order to learn from the Sophists a crucial insight into philosophy from—let us review Jarratt's major points. Then, comparing these to Plato's lessons, can this shed any additional insights into Sophistry and feminist prospects? The 'other' is the key term. So that if we ask who was the 'other' in Plato's time, it turns out that Socrates most certainly was. Thus, any novel doctrine will in its day mark its author, male or female, as the 'other'. What, then, can reverse this to give the new, the odd view acceptance, we ask?

Were the Sophists relegated to the margins of the serious public work of knowledge, as Jarratt suggests? Are not all creative people at the margins of their time, philosophers in the lead? Were males in public roles dominant? Undoubtedly, but philosophers are not kings, much as Plato advocated this union, so that philosophers are always at the margins of serious public work. 'Women' and 'philosophers' who are both serious and novel, seem linked in this regard. And if the Sophists taught citizens to participate in democracy, this certainly was Plato's goal too, although he held different views about how the knowledge necessary for this should be acquired. For him it involved a more arduous path than it did for the Sophists.

More important: Did the Sophists "challenge the elitism of philosophers and their suppression of difference?" Remember that the Sophists were paid teachers of wealthy families, whereas Socrates spoke to anyone in the marketplace. Nor is there much indication that the Sophists taught anyone but young men, so their clientele was both restricted and elite. Still, did they share with feminists an interest in the historical situation and the use of rhetorical solutions for theory building? Aristotle and Plato were certainly interested in their historical situation, and Plato nearly came to grief trying to get the rulers of his day to educate their young to philosophy. Socrates was put to death for his challenge to the existing beliefs.

However, the question of the use of 'rhetorical solutions' to theory building is more complex and difficult to deal with. Rhetoric was not so much 'excluded' from philosophy as was the art of persuasion contrasted with the philosopher's more arduous and technical inquiry. For both Plato and Aristotle, the two were linked. That is, they felt that the more rigorous investigations of philosophy were necessary for insight, but both of them wanted philosophy eventually to be effective in public discourse. Feminists, of course, may have other goals than pursuing 'philosophy'. But in philosophy, what is the role of rhetoric?

In dealing with this question, we come up against the perplexing link some feminist make between theorists and 'deconstruction'. Post-modernism and deconstruction are highly esoteric and 'radical' proposals for a change in our way of reading/interpreting texts. There is nothing 'wrong' with this. It is just that to tie feminist concerns to any theory, which (like most radical proposals) is unlikely to have wide acceptance, is to jeopardize the cause by its link to a theory probably acceptable and understandable by only a few intellectuals. This can be done, of course, but the problems involved need to be recognized. Women wish no longer to be 'marginalized' but to be at the center of philosophy (and the world). Will this goal be hampered if deconstruction proves not to have a wide or a long-lasting appeal? This is an important question.

True, Jarratt lists rhetoric as a 'flexible alternative' to philosophy. Philosophy has many alternatives in its mode of approach, and no one would disagree that we find few 'philosophers' in public life, in spite of the fact that bits may creep into public utterance. Then, do feminists wish to reject philosophy as a medium, or do they seek to revise it after a newer (really older) model? The revision of philosophy has been proposed and tried many times. Some proposals get themselves ingrained in the classical canon, for example, Hegel and Wittgenstein. But none captures the whole field and sustains itself unchallenged. 'Public discourse' need not depend on deconstruction for philosophical reconstruction.

Promoting "unusual rhythms and poetic effects" (p. 28) is, as others have suggested, to tie philosophy to poetry. And if the issues of truth were 'contingent' for the Sophists, it is interesting to see how Plato changed his own view about 'finality' through studying the source of the Sophists' power more carefully (see Sec. 2). Of course, a rank ordering of knowledge does carry gender implications, but I can see no argument put forth that tells us why "all conceptual organization" (*ibid.*) is therefore subject to men. Women may argue for anarchy, but they may also argue for any rank ordering which they suggest. And if the character projected onto the feminine is unsatisfactory, it seems clear that that is now also under serious revision. Philosophy has had many definitions. It can be modified again. It modifies itself continually. It can (should) do no other.

Emotional sensitivity is not 'devalued' by Plato, if we read the prominent place given to 'love' and 'passion', even in his very definition of philosophy. Rationality, objectivity, detachment—these have been opposed by men as well, for example, Kierkegaard and Nietzsche. So it seems impossible to link these traits as being exclusively 'male'. If some 'trivialize' women by identification with "sensuality, costume and color" (p. 29), this does not include Plato. But perhaps the most serious issue is to understand how feminists turning to rhetorical possibilities leads to "understanding different directions for feminism" (*ibid.*). "A discourse of equality" and "a discourse of difference" (*ibid.*), these all seem possible without rhetoric.

Jarratt does see the problem involved in the post-structuralist theory. If it leads to 'undecidability' or the loss of 'essential sexual difference', then it too is unsupportive as a base (p. 31). "The identity of a woman is the product of her own interpretation and reconstruction of her history" (p. 33, quoting Alcoff), but Camus, Sartre or Kierkegaard could say the same. This alone does not justify a turn to rhetoric—although all did use literary styles. If you want to celebrate sensual pleasure in the sound of words, turn to philosophy as story-telling (e.g., Elie Wiesel). If that is 'rhetoric' as opposed to 'philosophy', possibly we have begun with too narrow a definition of philosophy. If women are to break "with explanations, interpretations and all authorities" (p. 31, quoting Cixous), that goes far beyond the Sophists, whose success depended on their popularity.

Did philosophers want to separate 'style' from 'substance' and the Sophists not? Sartre and Camus wrote plays and novels and Plato's dialogues are essentially literary pieces. So some philosophers shun style as a mode of communication; others celebrate it. Can philosophical discourse not be "isolated from the operation of social customs and political power?" (p. 36). Hegel and Marx are much stronger advocates of this impossibility than the Sophists. If Cixous thinks it is time to change, "to invent the other history" (p. 37), Nietzsche's diatribe against the heavy hand of history is perhaps a better ally than Sophistry.

If the aim is "a revision of logic through narrative" (p. 38), this can only mean 'logic' in a very broad sense, since symbolic/mathematical logic is incompatible with narrative. Yet if feminists are "describing rhetorical solutions to the crucial problems of defining a theory with the most power for changing women's lives" (p. 39), the connection is really more between 'feminism' and 'religion', since that is the aim of the evangelist. Will this 'dislodge' "the patriarchal institutions"? (*ibid.*) That depends entirely on how much acceptance one gets for these methods. And the irony is that many, both male and female, may not be able to understand what the issue is. Both the theory and the project are essentially 'esoteric'.

Can Plato's later insights into the significance of Sophistry help us in this project? Plato came to accept a complexity to all theory, and he thought the Sophists tended to settle for not-accurate clarity in order to court popularity. But if Sophistical 'education' was based on an unreal perception of the real intricacies of the world before us, both human and natural, their clear, easy-to-learn proposals might be attractive but ultimately ineffective in achieving change, just because they remained superficial. If Plato is right in this, all of us philosophers—Sophists, feminists—face extraordinary complexities which cannot be captured easily in words.

4. Rewriting History, Revolutionizing Epistemology

In the re-evaluation of 'Sophistry' and the attempt to reverse its usual negative picture, are feminine theorists suggesting that, in order to achieve their goal, they must 're-write history'? In traditional accounts, the Sophists have had a negative image. Philosophers are 'the good guys', seeking truth and virtue, while the Sophists sell their wares and promise easy solutions where none may be possible. That picture could be left alone and feminist theorists could still go on to strike a novel position for themselves in present discussion. Yet it often seems that, in order to have a better future, feminists must first rewrite the past.

Of course, it is clear that women have not often been publicly prominent, philosophically or politically, in the past. If they want to reverse that in the future and either share or dominate the limelight, must they begin by rewriting history to prove that the standard interpretations have been questionably based? It would seem so, but why? We know why women have emerged in the present as a force to be reckoned with. We know why in the past they have not been publicly prominent (e.g. childbirth, prejudice). Why not simply try to correct this and let the past stand as previously recorded? It seems necessary for feminists to prove that they have not, in fact, had the status which, in fact, they seem to have had, or at least that any designation was 'wrong'.

Thus, if Sophistry once despised is now restored as valuable, is women's role in the present somehow rendered significant? How can that be? If the association of women and Sophistry can be made, if Sophistry somehow becomes intellectually respectable, can women as a consequence have a more important role? But why cannot the present role of women be improved without rewriting history? That which may have been undervalued, it seems, must prove this exclusion 'wrong' in order to justify itself in the present. The past must be reversed. If our view of history remained 'traditional', could women still have a better future?

If past evaluations need not be proven to be in error in order to give women the confidence they need to conquer the future, negative evaluations need not be totally revised. Self-confidence seems to be the issue. If women have not been emperors, explorers, political leaders, why not? If it is due to prejudice and false appraisal, we can reverse that and prove the past exclusions to be in error, thus allowing women the future which the past denied them. If the history of philosophy is left intact as traditional but never uniform, would it somehow make women's roles today seem aberrant, not normal?

The same is true of epistemology. Our ways of knowing, our standards for truth, it is thought, have excluded women.[105] Therefore, somehow traditional notions of 'truth' must be proven to have been in error. 'Truth' must be "opened up." The Sophists were accused of distorting or of ignoring 'truth'. Thus, could Sophistry be made 'legitimate', somehow all that has been denied could now be accepted. Of course, much of this rests on the notion that all previous epistemologies have been 'phallic', male centered, as if all the diverse and heterogeneous theories of knowledge become one by some mysterious connection to the penis.

Thus, we must ask if all epistemologies to date have been such as to exclude women automatically, in which case a revolution is needed. Are theories of knowledge 'sex connected', so that women must develop their own or else never find acceptance? If Plato once opposed Sophistry, must women prove Sophistry legitimate in order for their philosophies to be legitimate now? But is there a universal 'feminist epistemology', such that it unites women to oppose whatever men have constructed in the past? If so, feminists must

---

[105] See *Women's Ways of Knowing*, chapter III, note 51.

identify with all who have been excluded ('marginalized') and reverse that status in order to assure their own future.

However, what if our past proves not to have been monolithic, and what if all women today are not united behind a single epistemology? One might then choose one's epistemology without respect to its origin. If one does not treat history a la Hegel as monolithic in its dynamics, there is no need to rewrite it, since its judgments are as various as one might wish. If the past is not uniform, it can offer a variety of bases for any current enterprise.

Still, does 'feminism' require an epistemology different from any before it in order to establish "women's point of view"? It does if there is any such uniform thing. But if women have or will vary as much as men in outlook, there need be no 'new epistemology', because anything anyone wishes to say has either been said before or can be extended from some past phrase. Take for example our suggested re-interpretation of 'Sophistry'. If in fact it is not that novel and does not depart that far from known theories, can one let history stand? Epistemologies need not be radicalized, and all that women wish now to say can still be said and heard. Philosophers can still oppose an over-simplified popularity and any claim to finality in theory. They may not become popular in doing so, as Socrates was not, but theirs is still the critical function.

5. Exaggeration and Simplification vs. The Search to State the Truth

In seeing certain aspects of 'Sophistry' which may be congenial to feminist goals, it is important to consider Plato's central objection to the Sophists. The question he raised centers around how difficult it is to discern and then to state 'truth', or indeed whether it is even possible to do so with any finality or certainty. 'Sophistry', as Plato presents it, offered to teach the young for pay, whereas we know from Plato's comments on teaching that he felt no one can literally teach another. Each must teach himself/herself, although the teacher can serve as a spur, a 'midwife'. But more important, because Plato first

162

saw 'the truth' as embodied in the Forms, it is impossible ever to formulate what is grasped in final statement. Words cannot do that; truth remains always beyond the possibility of final conceptualization. But the Sophists made truth easy, or so it is as Plato presents—and opposes—them.

We know from the *Parmenides* and the *Sophist* that Plato felt truth involved the use of a subtle dialectic needed to achieve balance, a rare accomplishment which could too easily be oversimplified. If the search for truth is difficult and esoteric, that is, not open to all but only to the committed few, Sophistry must be opposed, because it presents what is immensely difficult as essentially easy and apprehensible by all. So before we can really appraise the feminist argument in favor of restoring Sophistry to respectability, we must ask what 'truth' is and how difficult it is to convey or to state. If it lies beyond our final grasp, then as philosophers we must oppose anyone who would present it as simple and stateable by all.

Of course, Nietzsche and Kierkegaard and others have argued for the use of 'exaggeration' as a needed instrument in our search for truth. How can that be, if Plato is correct about both the difficulty of accuracy and the impossibility of stating truth finally? Because, I suggest, what is exaggerated cannot be literally true. Thus, the impossibility of taking what is said literally makes it clear (to the one who understands this) that truth's grasp must lie somewhere else than within the literal statement. Our questions concern the Sophists' (and the Feminists') proposal that truth can be quite literally and directly stated. If so, this must be opposed in the name of increased sophistication.

What we need to ask of Sophistry and of Feminism is whether political/social influence is its aim. If so, then either exaggeration or literalness may be more effective, as a reading of the morning newspaper tells us. There is no question but that feminism aims at political influence. Does this mean that it will resort to statements not literally true but which may be politically effective? Feminism as a movement, then, must decide between its announced aim to wield political and social influence and its willingness to recognize the difficulty, if not the impossibility, of stating truth clearly and finally. Of course, were it possible to do this, the goals of feminism would be easier to achieve. No questions would remain, only the implementation of reforms. Unfortunately, if feminism must face the non-completion of its truth statements, it must turn equal attention toward the subtleties of stating truth vs. aiming for practical accomplishment.

To "tell it like it is" may not be politically effective. If so, the 'philosopher' must always choose between pursuing political influence and seeking to state truth as best it can, or cannot, be said. We know that good trial lawyers 'exaggerate' in their statements to juries. In that art lies the path to success. But as philosophers, our primary aim is (or should be) the path to truth. Politicians employ media people to embellish the truth for election purposes. Along that path lies winning elections. But the issue is: Does philosophy have a different mission in life? If so, we need to separate the feminist's political agenda from its philosophical goals. We ask: (1) How can an issue be made effective in the public arena vs. (2) How can we express truth most accurately?

Can we hold the line against politicization and preserve philosophy in an uncommitted role? Even so, as we try to do this we must admit that much of the Sophist's (Feminist's) enterprise is both effective and even necessary. If everyone held out for complicated, inconclusive statements, the world's business would not get done. How can we recognize the necessity of making practical evaluations and yet admit that truth may not have been fully stated?

Can we hold the line against the politicization of all philosophy and keep its critical independent role, all the while admitting that other enterprises are both necessary and perhaps also more effective? In asking this question we come to perhaps the most crucial epistemological issue in feminist theory: Is every enterprise, including philosophy, unavoidably 'political'; or can there be any such thing as a dispassionate search for truth? Let us begin by admitting that many causes require political action or else they fail. 'Feminism', in its attempt to liberate women from suppression and to release them to the full expression of their talents, needs political action or it will not achieve its goals.

No society needs philosophers in abundance. "Engineers make the world go round." But all political assumptions, including 'feminism', need constant critical evaluation—unless we assume that some one theory is truth itself. Given the fact that feminist theories are multiple and not all consistent, we must move 'backward' to critique as well as going 'forward' to action. For many this evaluative job, this 'metaphysical' appraisal of the first principles we assume, has been taken to be the philosopher's primary and special task. Any given philosopher may be politically active, but he or she needs a reflective, critical mode too. 'Sophistry' may hold certain lessons for feminists about effective action, but this need not exclude philosophy's traditional task of a neverending quest, a love and a search for 'wisdom' vs. the claim to possess 'knowledge' in any self-contained form.

C. Our Human Work Is Never Done: Or, It Should Not Be?

Polly Toynbee's article (*Times Saturday Review*, London, Sept. 14, 1991) at its time came as a breath of fresh air, full of common sense. It is not that this is totally lacking elsewhere, but some feminist voices are more strident, more militant, full of radical proposals to revolutionize societies and all human relationships. "The facts of life," which Toynbee wants us to face up to are that we know human nature to be flexible but not infinitely so. Feminists have made clear the need for many males to change. But Toynbee addresses both sexes together, a coordination that is all too often missing in some feminist 'attacks'.

Germaine Greer is fun to read. She can change her mind dramatically. Toynbee cites herself as one who found Greer's *The Female Eunuch*[106] revolutionizing for women's outlook, which is the kind of change all education seeks to accomplish. But as with every drastic proposal, Greer's flaws appear, for example, a Marxist, Leninist bias, magnificent in its conception and liberating for any restricted mind. Still, all depends on the theory's enactment, as we have recently learned again. Greer's book "held a mirror up to women," which is what every educational-religious conversion process aims for. But if as individual women and men we come to see our situation differently—which most certainly now do—how far can change in the relations between the sexes be instituted practically?

One ironic consequence of the feminist attack is that today, probably more than ever before, men and women are conscious of their opposition, of the great divide between them. "The war between the sexes" has taken on heightened proportions. Of course, just as the Marxist must seek to raise the consciousness of the proletariat in order to create a sociopolitical revolution, women as never before must become conscious of themselves and of their condition, both individually and collectively. True. But unless we still believe Leninist revolutionary doctrine about the total elimination of all class distinctions once the new consciousness is here, must we not work together to achieve change?

If the answer is yes, this will involve compromise. But 'compromise' is a four letter word in some feminist circles, since it does involve the fact that neither side will gain its full agenda. In the United States our founding fathers had to compromise on slavery in order to establish the union. So all compromise is not moral and does not lead to eternal harmony. But if we will accept none, the outcome is a constant warfare of every individual group's interest against

---

[106] See Charnie Guettel, *Marxism and Feminism*, chapter III, note 62.

every other. Is that not what we see today dragging half the world into destructive conflict, the refusal to compromise? Toynbee rightly sees that practicalities suggest that both sexes should settle for less than any radical agenda promises.

And if the sexes cannot make peace, can we expect races, small ethnic groups, social classes, political parties, unions, any special interest group, to do other than fight until, like Sampson, we bring the temple down upon our own heads? To say this is not to join the political-social extreme right. In every area you can name, women have legitimate, legal, moral, economic causes to press. Advances toward equity have been made. Practical issues are an open agenda, but the question is: Would we deal with inequities more effectively if we softened the male-female opposition and tempered the hostility?

Greer's enduring value, Toynbee recognizes, is to stop blaming men entirely (at least some men have been loving and liberating in their relationship to women, haven't they?) and to see how much women must first change their self image if they want to experience new life (something monasteries-convents said earlier while proposing different goals for the person). Toynbee does note that "husband and wife drag each other down." The fault for failure to achieve fulfillment is often mutual. Few can do it alone, neither male nor female, although males have had better odds most of the time. Greer ripped veil after veil from women's identity, but the question is "what next?" Mass lesbianism was one alternative. But Greer is not anti-male. Yet she did think men were human beings whereas 'woman' had been an 'artifact'. Existentialism (e.g., Sartre, de Beauvoir) long ago called for all human beings to define themselves. But perhaps women have not heard that call to 'authenticity' so loudly until recently.

Toynbee then turns to our present reality, and she finds the results not so glamorous. The statistics for women's financial-political 'success' are still not in their favor. Her complaint: Too many women "still expect marriage to deliver." The call of marriage and motherhood, to which many respond, she finds to be an "insidious fungus in the brain." But is this something peculiar to the female of the species? What are the statistics of fulfillment for both sexes, given what they expect from career-family, against how it turns out? Is the failure to embody our ideals any greater for women than for men?

Should we suspect that only the few succeed in romantic fulfillment—although we can hope for an increase and urge all to make the attempt? Given the feminist call for self determination, we have to ask: Is there a built-in assumption that we can achieve total fulfillment for all? If so, disappointment is built into the project for the majority of women, as it is for most men. Toynbee also blames women for their continued absorption in 'maternal mothering'. Childcare is a necessity, but women must first be "relieved of the burden of guilt," she argues. Yet Camus believes we all feel guilty by virtue of the human situation of mutual responsibility (read *The Fall*).

Toynbee offers a dismal picture of the negative rewards of motherhood. Granted that it was never all bliss, is it necessarily as unrewarding as she made it out to be? All children do not end hating-neglecting all parents; that is another false dichotomy. She is right: Children are no guarantee of "protection against loneliness." But we reply: What is? The 'true price of femininity', Toynbee claims, is "a life of poverty, despair and misery" for most. 'Marriage' may need to be reconceived, as it has been from time to time, but there is also the possibility that marriage needs to be restored more than abandoned. Is 'love' really universally "sold as a meal ticket"?

Women are as addicted to romance as ever, Toynbee claims. Are they alone in this? I find romance all over today's social scene, women-women, men-men, although a majority still opt for heterosexual bliss. Despite 'sexual liberation', students are just as nervous about sex and romance as ever, in spite of 'the cool approach'. As many men are interested in romance as women, although they perhaps express it differently. And I can't see that 'romance' will ever lose its attraction, although it may change its focus. Men may not "sit and pine beside the telephone," but anxious men express the same apprehension differently. Remember that today no woman is bound to a man for life, any more than a man is to a woman.

Greer does cling to "a bit of romantic stuff," which should make us ask how much of feminist theory has a 'romantic' base, which always sets one up for realistic disappointment, if we believe our dream to be reality. Toynbee's response is that human beings do not have a 'nature'. And she follows the Enlightenment theorists (all males) in seeing 'knowledge' as the key to release. But Toynbee thinks education will free us from determinism, which is an equally 'romantic' notion. Just consider the forces we face that threaten to enslave us all over again, for example, sex, egoism and fame. Do we really "have the knowledge to make of ourselves what we will"? That's shocking in its over-simplicity and unreality. Who will do this, all of us or only the valiant few of both sexes? "All things excellent are as difficult as they are rare," Spinoza ended his *Ethics* by reporting. Has that really changed, granted that some conditions have and can change and that artificial barriers can be brought down. Has radical feminism simply borrowed a Marxist form of Utopia and projected the total liberation of women as a class?—a brave proposal now discredited.

'Reactionaries' always claim that 'nature' is on their side; Toynbee is right about that. But isn't there a more sensible response. We should question any fixed definition of 'nature' but then move on to ask: what can be changed and what cannot be changed? What can we accomplish if humans really care enough to put forward the energy, not for total revolution but for reformation? After being Utopian, Toynbee moves on to a very down-to-earth note: "women are scarcely different from men." If so, we are tied together in our search for fulfillment and in the relationships we are bound to, for example, male-female, society-race. In these we find the outlines of our 'nature' within which we define ourselves.

We must thank the Women's Movement, the feminists and the post-feminists, for raising again the agonizing question of human fulfillment and of doing so in new ways that highlight the issues. Old problems, even if they have been dealt with in classic forms, need a fresh perspective if there is to be advance and not a quiet slide backwards. Women have highlighted dark areas which were known but not focused on intensively before. More than that, medicine, birth control, abortion and education now offer women a control heretofore largely unavailable. There are reasons why feminist demands were not voiced as strongly in ages where biology did more to fix destiny. Today, more doors are opened.

We need to thank the Greers and the Toynbees for admitting to a change in their agenda, for not becoming dogmatists of a new creed but remaining open to 'revision'. That hated term contributed to Communism's downfall and to its bad name, in spite of Marxist-voiced ideals. Most visions which may be beautiful in theory are betrayed in practice, violated in action. The feminist self-critique of their early hopes helps to forestall rigidifying another orthodoxy, which leads to failure when it occurs. We must become more cautious about the siren call of Utopias and become immunized against its disappointments in practice. Traditional 'American optimism' still infects U.S. feminism, especially when it is revolutionary and not individualistic in intent.

Differences will remain, Toynbee concludes. In spite of the radical feminist almost violent protest against stereotyping, Toynbee sees that they have stereotyped women (as "gentler, nicer, less competition") in their search for a distinctiveness in their gender, in order to push for altered stereotypes and at the same time offer female attributes as somehow fixed qualities. "Her life must be her own destiny," Toynbee asserts. Certainly, but Existentialism has held that to be true for all human beings.

In order to avoid further eventual disappointment, we need to point out again how rare this achievement truly is for either sex, how hard it is and how many will always opt for an easier road, or as least one that seems so in a limited perspective. And Toynbee may have an Achilles heel in her proposals. She wants not to moralize about "the passing of family values" and warns us that the clock cannot be turned back—a truism. But 'change' does not necessitate an irrevocable change, even if Hegel and Marx thought so. Given today's 'open society', open in different ways than Carl Popper once argued for, the context of the family must be different. And perhaps this is, in many ways, for the better.

Yet let us not think that earlier times had all options open to their view and then blocked some out in spite. Study the history of childbirth, the long agony of getting children through to adulthood, the medical dangers for women, death lurking for both mother and child. Abstinence was almost the only guarantee of stalling an endless cycle of debilitating pregnancy. Wars fought in armor and on horseback, the constant need for men to arm and train to fight, this went on almost without exception. No wonder monks and nuns sought refuge from a society which could promise them little peace.

But as control over the female body—that feminist slogan—becomes possible, does that really dictate the end to "marriage and the family" or just the need to rethink the basis for human relationships? To promote the family (ironically, still the basis for many feminist claims to possess a special gender-linked virtue) need not mean to demand it in a previous form. The benefit of recent research into women's history is that we know that both 'family' and 'women' have had a wide variety of forms and meanings. We need not deride 'Victorianism' and fail to see its good qualities, nor reject all family ties in order to try to forge new ones in a changed time.

As they were being driven from the Garden of Eden by an avenging angel holding a fiery sword, Adam is reported to have said to his partner in sin: "Eve, we are living in an age of transition." Since that time, societies have managed to hold fixed in their form for varying periods of time, but none has survived unchallenged, unchanged, in spite of the current romantic veneration of the 'noble savage' (e.g., "Dances With Wolves"). So Adam and Eve must both use the knowledge which Eve urged them to appropriate and play Prometheus today by stealing fire from our former gods (our cultural masters).

However, any pressure for change in our relationships[107] which argues that "all things will be made new" should realize that they have appropriated the Book of Revelation with its divine power and forgotten that such a drastic revision comes only "at the end of time." Existing still in time, what real options are open to the sexes that, realistically, seem likely to be appropriated by any majority? Minorities, now based on sexual preference, if you will, can retreat like monks into differently governed lifestyles. But there seems little evidence that love between the two sexes will vanish, or that the miracle of one's child being born will be abandoned—even though

---

[107]   Pamela Dickey Young, *Feminist Theology/Christian Theology: In Search of Method* (Minneapolis: Fortress Press, 1990).

In her attempt to reconcile Feminist Theology with Christianity, Professor Young gives a straight forward account, which she admits some have not been able to do. The virtue of her attempt is the clear exposition she gives of three authors, Rosemary Ruether, Elizabeth Schussler Fiorenza, and Betty Russell, two Roman Catholics and one Protestant. The deficit is that, like all methodological accounts, one needs more substance of the theology in order to judge the method. However, she indicates that as Roman Catholics, Ruether and Schussler Fiorenza have a more difficult time, since they face a hierarchical church almost totally male dominated. Russell has an easier task, since Protestantism has tended more to individual interpretation and democratic organization.

Women's experience as the source and norm (see chapter III) has the problem of defining what this is, as Young admits. "Our experience of ourselves and others as oppressed" is said to be the starting point (p. 68), but when theological issues are to be decided that hardly gives us a clue. She says the doctrine of God is no longer a doctrine of the all-male God (p. 14), but she agrees that no one has ever really said that God is male by sex. Our author wants to blend or balance both Feminism as a norm *and* Christian tradition. Young joins others in appealing to "women's body experience," but it is hard to see why men do not experience their bodies too, although admittedly in a slightly different manner. Where Jesus is concerned, she agrees that he does not reveal God as male but as love.

realistically we are aware of the potential heartbreak children can bring and the special restrictions childbirth involves for the mother.

Artificial walls can come tumbling down, if not by the sound of trumpets then by skilled political work in the heat of the kitchen, as President Harry Truman warned us. But advances have a habit of being quickly eroded. "Eternal vigilance is [still] the price of [women's] freedom." But we must remember that for centuries women were not biologically free to work equally with men, although that is now a possibility for many. Some women, who have not heard that their gender-virtue is a 'non-competitiveness', will still opt out of competition, leaving men in the majority even if no longer in a monopoly position.

Feminine beauty may be a 'myth'[108] for some, but we still seem to have within us an instinctive warm response to the appearance of physical beauty, whether in males, in females, or in the animal world. We always need to be told, and to relearn, that beauty comes in many forms, some physical, some spiritual, some artistic, some intellectual, some in practical skills. We do not all agree or appreciate exactly the same 'beauties', but our overall agreement is considerable, else models and athletes would not be universally so admired. Salome still seduces us with her dance; Cleopatra still uses her wiles to effect. Elizabeth Taylor still draws a crowd of photographers.

Let us try to make the best of our natures not the worst, and change our forms of expression as seems to suit our times. Let intellect and its alluring vision not blind us to the way the larger world lives outside our minds and our words. Let us also watch the way individuals, of whatever adopted gender role, treat those around them. If virtues are 'relative', they have to be relative to something. Decency, consideration, compassion, forgiveness vs. hate, deceit and the destruction of all who are in our way—these actions still contrast

---

[108] See Naomi Wolf, *The Beauty Myth*, chapter I, note 14.

and can be exhibited by both sexes.

Power corrupts. If women have been celebrated for their spiritual virtues in the past, as those pedestals are vacated, what is the evidence that power in the hands of women is any less subject to corruption? Note that feminists are not fond of the major female politician of recent days, Golda Meir, Indira Gandhi, Margaret Thatcher. Lady Macbeth plays a role not entirely lost in history. But if we are to adjust to changed sex and gender roles and make the best and not the worst of our new opportunities, we'll need to mute the hostility of female against male, check into the possibility of forgiveness and compromise as an accepted practice, and see what of beauty can now be rebuilt on the unstable soil of our often depleted souls.

Chapter V

Reading History Backwards

A. The Modern Notion of Freedom

Many today seem to want to read history as if our predecessors did see—or should have seen—things as we do today. Columbus is reinvented as an ecological tyrant, when his age could not possibly have thought in such terms. Feminists often act as if every woman before them wanted to occupy every public office, whereas most accepted the opportunities open to them in the society in which they lived. Of course, every age has its visionaries, its rebels; thank goodness. But they were 'revolutionaries' precisely because the majority of women then could not have imagined what is open to women today–and some might have rejected it if they had.[109] To reread history as if everyone should have had our values and goals makes hash of the intricacies of culture and the complexities of human life. It is also an ultimate form of cultural arrogance, far worse than the 'cultural imperialism' of which America is often accused.

Kierkegaard has a good saying for us: Never act as if what you think now was in fact how you thought in an earlier time. Once upon a time: slavery was accepted; colonialism was a high calling; empire builders were cultural heroes; and explorers were brave men. That is not how many see it today, given our new set of global conditions. Fine. But there is no need to try to read history backwards and pretend that Cleopatra or Columbus could possibly have conceived of radical feminism or ecological concerns or a romanticizing of native life. "Dancing with Wolves" could only be written today, not at the time of the Westward movement. We need to try to understand history on its own terms, try to think ourselves back into their vision,

---

[109] Barbara J. MacHaffie, *Her Story* (Philadelphia: Fortress Press, 1986).

not ours. If we do, it will actually be easier to move forward without first having to rewrite history.[110]

---

[110] Nancy F. Cott, ed. *Root of Bitterness: Documents of the Social History of American Women* (Boston: Northeastern University Press, 1986).

The editor quotes Sarah Grimke: The root of bitterness is the mistaken notion of the inequality of the sexes. However, the editor thinks the essays presented "all bear the earmarks of the intellectual tide of 1970 and 1971. They are still too wedded to an outlook in which the male is the norm, she feels on later reflection. One absent theme is the conflict among women themselves.

The essays deal with the consciousness and self-consciousness of American Women (primarily white and middle class). They begin with seventeenth-century colonists primacy to religious awareness. Then preindustrial society altered work roles for women. Next in the eighteenth century the subject of women's proper roles was of great interest. The nineteenth century saw the cult of domesticity. The antislavery crusade brought up the issue of women's rights. "There is no slave, after all, like a wife."

However, biology was destiny to a much greater extent in the past century. Against the background of today's feminist theorists, these essays give a very clear picture of the shifting and varied roles women have had in American history. The availability of higher education brought a great change.

Sara M. Evans, *Born for Liberty* (New York: The Free Press, 1989).

Sara Evans' large volume has received praise as an "outstanding book," and so it is. In an era of strident attack, she chronicles the experience of women in America. Her theme comes out of the "sentiments of American women," Philadelphia, 1780. And so women in the United States have carried the torch for liberty, as does the lady who welcomes newcomers to New York harbor. Women love the public good as much as men, even if they do not march to glory by the same path. However, what is most impressive, and most important, is to see the variety of roles women have actually had in American history, whereas much contemporary voice seems to say women have only recently come from a repressive situation.

If history is a narrative of public action, it is an arena where women have been little in dominance. Yet professor Evans catalogues a vast variety of intense activities by women. They did not have the freedom to engage in politics as men did, but women responded by creating new public spaces for their activities. They developed social control over public action by their effort. They "used voluntary associations to express their interest and to organize for public activity" – a significant fact about American women we now tend to forget. They took roles that originated in domesticity and created professions, teaching, nursing, and social work in particular. Even feminists historians have actually overlooked the unique aspects of our public life and our actions of citizenship, she reports.

"In real communities women could and did exercise considerable social power through informal channels" (p. 23). There developed in the nineteenth century a growing separation of men's and women's lives which had not characterized the early and revolutionary eras

We often seem to forget what the 'Enlightenment' meant. It was a discovery much celebrated later—not so much at its inception—because men found out that they could assert their rights and try to control their own destiny. Of course, 'men' had to discover this first, even though the notion of 'all human beings' was implicit. After that women or races or classes could discover that they too could seek to appropriate universal rights and individual liberty. Throughout the major extent of human history the world's frame seemed fixed to those who were born into it. The stronger dominated; women were destined to a seemingly unending cycle of childbirth; hierarchies were fixed; the powerful, whether tyrannical or occasionally compassionate, would rule; multitudes were destined to serve.

---

in our history. Men were thrown into competitiveness and idealized the role of women as outside that, as it had not been earlier.

As powerful bonds developed among women, their spheres separated from men's – a fact one often forgets. Christian benevolence became their sphere, versus abstract rights and justice. Contemporary investigations support this, but we have lost track of how this developed as men's roles changed and separated their role from women. Today, women talk of non-hierarchical societies, but such an idea began as early as 1848 among the Friends or Quakers.

The power of women, which developed in the nineteenth century, reached its apex late in that era in the push for political reform. The middle-class woman came into conflict with the developing "working girl." A new drive toward autonomy, p easure and consumption were at odds with earlier Victorian notions that had actually united women. The rise of women's colleges developed women with new ideas and split an earlier solidarity of women. "Nearly half of all college-educated women in the late nineteenth century never married" (p. 147).

"Young, hedonistic, sexual, the flapper soon became a symbol of the age..." (p. 175). But in the 1930s the depression brought women back into partnership with men in the struggle of survival. Women participated actively, powerfully, in labor and social movements. Yet the earlier widespread women's movement was now gone. We often are unaware of the vast changes which have shaped women's roles before today.

After the war, ideology defined women in terms of wife and mother, true. But this was not so in many earlier periods in our life, a fact we tend to forget in reaction to the era just past. The renewed public life for middle-class women in the 1960s was a far cry from the earlier era of domesticity, but it was not at all different from earlier roles for women. The feminist movement, "arose in a time of dramatic change and deep social conflict."

Why, then, do we now act shocked to look back and see how few thought that anything was to be done except to serve, while hoping not to be cursed in the process. Of course, you could seek dominance if you were born to power or could acquire it. Today the same philosophy prevails, but it has to struggle against the modern idea of democracy and human rights and the claim that each individual can or should achieve human fulfillment. This is a noble goal, one which took centuries of striving to produce and which only a few could envision. Many still cannot see the possibility of human dignity for all, or else they accept it verbally but proceed as if the world were still a jungle where only the powerful can claim rights. But the genius of reading history is to read ourselves back into a time when revolutions and utopias could not even have been conceived. These concepts are modern, recent, not ancient. Our ancestors should not be expected to have seen what we have finally come to.

Of course, for centuries the world's various religions served as our outlet for human aspiration.[111] Some allowed individuals to

---

[111] Juha O'Faolain, and Lauro Martines, eds., *Not In God's Image* (New York: Harper TorchBooks, 1973).

This is a source book, as the author's say, of women in history from the Greeks to the Victorians. They have drawn together writings that define the status of women in each age. The authors claim that the aim of the book is not polemical, and yet it offers a compendium of what can be called derogatory statements about women. They stop at the middle of the 19th century, since women then begin to assume control along with men on increasingly equal terms.

They omit the "unrepresentative women," female regents, queens and courtesans, yet these are a part of history. Women did not think of their interests as distinct from their male protectors until the 16th century, when complaints begin to emerge. The 17th and 18th centuries questioned; the 19th century began to demand parity; the 20th century began to grapple with the condition of women.

There were exceptions at the top and bottom of the social hierarchy. Women in courts had privileges, and women in peasant surroundings were of known importance. Men, the authors point out, were crucial to the battle women waged for emancipation in the 19th century. But there is no absolute uniformity. As they point out, "the female preference for the dependent life and its rewards is still with us" (p. xx). The authors, then, have collected representative writings from Greece until the era of revolution in the 1850s.

achieve release through ritual practice, but most depended on the power of a deity to achieve fulfillment, now or in the future. The notion of self-created human utopias took long to develop as a conceivable alternative, and as we know it was the rise of modern science that did much to spur our self-confidence, as well as our egos. The rise of the possibility of self-determination precipitated the decline of religious power, which of course had not always been used to promote human welfare. The new utopias predicted religion's total demise, for example, Freud and Marx. We do not build as many churches or shrines today as we once did. Yet our disillusionment over man-made utopias and self-created new societies, and the terror and destruction often produced by their rise, has made religious alternatives not seem so obsolete as we once thought.

Who could have thought as "Columbus sailed the ocean blue" that the world's resources were anything but unlimited for our use. Certainly most thought they were until very recently. The forging of an empire was a 'magnificent obsession'. The great empire builders of the world, whether political, financial or industrial, deserve our careful study and sometimes even admiration. Their dream of empire in their time was just as astounding as our dream of allowing every man and women to be free and equal. Those titans of the past probably wouldn't understand our values or visions even if we could explain these to them. Why whip them verbally for not seeing the world the way we do? And no political philosophy in the world's history seems to have been flawless in its execution. We should leave history as a magnificent and tragic drama and instead worry about the miscarriages of many of our 'more enlightened' plans.

Peace, race relations, and the women's movement offer us good case studies. Today some have claimed that peace, possibly even on a universal scale, is attainable if only we try. The sentiments behind both the League of Nations and the United Nations were admirable advances in human history, even if faulty in design or in execution. Until more recently, why would any general, emperor, or king have thought of anything other than war as a means to establish control and stability? And many wars did unite fragmented lands that today are disuniting once again. That vision of peace and unity proves fragile today, because the same spirit still lurks in the human breast that "might makes right." It is hard for us to see that all do not seek peace in their hearts, if warfare offers a better opportunity. Our cup overflows with violence in a time we thought peace might reign supreme. Why? Because not everyone can sit in the seat of power, neither in a family, in a company, nor in a country.[112] And many do so fearfully, constantly alert to put down any suspected challenge.

So in spite of the modern noble ideal of a new order of democracy, which has achieved some measure of success, our price for liberty is still eternal vigilance—perhaps coupled with an arsenal of atomic bombs or large quantities of money. So peace and democracy are possibilities which opened to us only relatively recently in our human history. The constant clash of armies and incessant death today is said not to be so inevitable as once was thought. Yet if we look around us, we seem only to see conflict breaking out in new ways on new fronts. The would-be Hitlers are still numerous, the threat of murderous Stalins far from permanently removed. The utopian total transformation of society and human nature no longer seems possible. We pursue utopian notions of democracy and individual liberty still, but we do so within the ancient context of empire and conquest, in modern dress but no less powerful and destructive.

---

[112] Toni Carabillo, and Judith Nevli, *The Feminization of Power* (Los Angeles: The Fund for the Feminist Majority, 1988).

Women need political role models, but Golda Meir, Indira Ghandi, and Margaret Thatcher had no compelling concern for the status of other women. The needs of ordinary people are unrepresented. We must take power directly, the authors state. A majority of voters are women, yet political decision making does not adequately represent women or their viewpoints. The authors offer a series of portraits of women in politics who might serve as role models in this political quest.

We must admit that the cries for self-determination of racial, ethnic, and other groups, for example, women, however genuine in their origin in the sentiments of their peoples, are still too often used as masks for those seeking power and control. The leader of the revolution will sacrifice lives for the goal of independence but then turn and crush those who oppose his or her newly installed authority. "All things excellent are as difficult as they are rare," said Spinoza, and that certainly seems true of our ideals of democracy and popular self-determination. The struggle of races for release from suppression and exploitation are subject to the same pitfalls. Once races simply fought to see who would dominate. The Hebrew scriptures have that story on every page. The notion of the inferiority-superiority of races simply reflected who rose to dominance at the time. In terms of science and education and general enlightenment, some were behind, others ahead. Should we not think of this as our permanent condition but work to do what we can for as many as we can?

The demand for the freedom of all peoples is a modern notion too. It echoed in the founding of the United States and in the French Revolution. Yet the French did not see the cry for liberty as applying to all peoples of the Earth. How could they have conceived of such a notion? To many in the American North as well as in the South, slavery was accepted as fact, all the while self-determination was fiercely fought for on other fronts. The ideal that every race and person is equal is a hard notion to accept; it is even 'odd', given the inequalities dominant in so much of the world. It is as much violated in fact as it is accepted as high principle. All are not born equal—except in theory—and not everyone of every racial group sets his or her race's advance above private gain or even accepts the limits of the law. We should pursue our notion of racial and sexual equality, but we should neither rewrite history nor be blind to a thousand internal inconsistencies in its enactment.

Our new perception about the status of 'women' may illustrate our dilemma in the modern world most clearly of all. We tend to forget that medicine only recently offered women release from an endless cycle of childbirth. How could anyone in earlier centuries—or women in a rural Indian village now—see much else for the majority of women but children and the home? This does not mean, as is sometimes said, that women's place was not honored or important, although of course this has varied in time and place. It was simply inconceivable that any but a brilliant, exceptional few could aspire to anything else but what they were born to. And we should not forget that women could not demand their release until men sought theirs and claimed it as possible for all to seek and to achieve. In previous societies most men probably had less possibility for self-determination than most women do today. Wars and fighting killed them, and their masters used their labor often ruthlessly. It is largely men who conceived of and fought for a new sense of liberty, self-determination, and individual worth. It was a magnificent conception and recent to the political scene. Neither Jesus nor Buddha told their disciples to rise against their political masters and demand democratic self-determination. But the concept is embedded in our psyche. Once it had appeared, women gradually appropriated it for themselves, with only a little less violent resistance than men had encountered. We are now interested in the history of the women's movement, which we had no reason to see as anything separate from our common human history before recent events. The problem is: Why did women not rise before, and also why were their early leaders essentially conservative in seeing woman's central role as still rearing children in the home?[113]

---

[113] Andrea Nye, *Words of Power: A Feminist Reading of the History of Logic* (New York: Routledge, 1990).

Professor Nye concedes that she is not a logician, and she documents her struggles to deal with logic. She starts by questioning the common premise that logic "is not a feminine subject" (p. 2). However, what Nye does from thereon is to outline the underlying assumptions in the history of logic, its 'metaphysics', which ends she believes with Frege's total emptying of content and formalizing logic by making it equatable to mathematics. Logicians have continually denied the connection of logic to the lives and culture of its

The answer is, in simple terms, twofold: (1) Pioneered by the Enlightenment and by emerging new political theories of democracy, the notion of a radical shift in cultural patterns concerning the individual roles of men and women did not and could not occur at first. Revolutionizing human nature and the family structure could only come as the thought of human freedom and self-determination gained ground. We must not forget how novel the idea of liberty was, nor how much we owe to those who proposed it and fought for it. But more important where women are concerned: (2) "biology was destiny" for all but the amazing few, and it could not be conceived to be otherwise until the yolk of childbirth and the tyranny of death among infant children and mothers came under control. Biology had to be altered before women could be released.[114]

Now the liberated woman often wants to rewrite history either to deny that a painful, burdensome past was in fact accepted by most, or to say women were denied what only became possible later and claim their history to be more glorious than the record indicates. Today that can be true if we work for it; but before recent times, hardly. Men have suppressed women, it is true, just as stronger men have suppressed weaker men. The strong, whether male or female by sex,

---

developers. Thus, the formalization of logic completes the divorce of logic from its content and it originators' lives.

Nye stops short of 'feminizing' logic, but she wants to set it in a cultural context and 'humanize' it. Logic began with Parmenides, she reports, as akin to poetry. However, Nye charts the continuous movement away from this connection toward lack of all connection to the vagueness of life. But she states: "There can be no feminist logic that exposes masculine logic as sexist or authoritarian" (p. 175). Nevertheless, women must plunge into the arena of discussion and demand the right to speak (p. 178). There is an escape from the 'logical dilemma' which she recommends: attending, listening, understanding" (p. 183), recognizing our common humanity (p. 184). All that seems odd in this account is Nye's failure to refer to Hegel's cultural, dialectical logic, and also Existentialism and Pragmatism, which argued for the human context of all thought over a century ago.

[114] Letty M. Russell, *Human Liberation in a Feminist Perspective - A Theology* (Philadelphia: The Westminster Press, 1974).

will automatically suppress the weaker, male or female, unless taught not to or put under restraint. Granted, women had fewer opportunities in the past, or at least they had to use means other than physical, financial power, but what they did and could do is well documented in history and in drama. The struggle for any author, novelist, or scientist to gain, first attention and next fame, has always been difficult, hardly less so for the aspiring male than for the female.

Women of course faced barriers that men did not.[115] There is no need to deny that. But there is also no need to rewrite history to say that women actually did make political, cultural history when in fact they were ever present, always quietly important, but seldom the dominant leaders. Biology until recently did not allow that. There are always neglected, forgotten artists, writers, teachers. Museums and libraries cannot preserve everything, let alone display it. 'Marginalized' is not a four-letter word. Most of us must always live at the margins of society. All cannot occupy center stage at one time, and we know that the lead actors in the drama do change. The only issue is whether what we choose to place at the margins of our vision deserves to be there and whether the spotlight shines on those whose talent and achievements have earned it for them by right.

Peace, race, and women, these three, are recent issues in ways they could not have been conceived to be before. Each age must choose its crucial issues, and I can see none more important today than these three—except perhaps ecology so that we have an environment in which to live in peace. But we should be excited, and proud, that these are our issues, that we now can see possibilities which others could not see. We should give thanks to those before us who opened up these visions, not abandon the traditions which have made us what we are, but rather mold them as befits our revised goals. We do not really need to rewrite history, to read it as if our

---

[115] Evelyn Reed, *Woman's Evolution* (New York: Pathfinder Press, 1975).

ancestors saw things they could not have seen and then neglected them, berating our predecessors because they did not value things as we do. After all, exciting as our opportunities may be, we are just as subject to tragedy and villainy as they were, whether at the hands of men or of women; and we will quite likely mishandle our opportunities if we think otherwise.

B. Universals: Useful in Science, Distorting in Human Nature
1. Plato, Darwin and Hegel

Everyone thinks of Plato as the philosopher who was in love with 'universals'. His 'Forms', for example, women, beauty, good, were timeless and eternal. Each and everything in the world 'participated' in them and drew its essential qualities from this relationship, not from its particular qualities in time. But in point of fact, the Modern Era is the true advocate of the power of the universal, building as it did on the successful rise of science. The natural world was not only being powerfully understood, it was yielding to some human control, as well as to exploration. The universality of science, symbolized in its growing dependence on an expanding mathematics, led many philosophers to assume that now, at last, the vagaries of all past philosophies could be outmoded once and for all.

The social sciences were born. Human nature, which once had been the center of philosophy, now was available to scientific universalization. Freud represents perhaps the most extravagant of these confidences, since for him even the unconscious could be rendered knowable and tamed. Spinoza saw philosophy as parallel in structure to mathematics, embracing even God in its super-rationalism. By contrast and in retrospect, Plato appears as part mystic, part skeptic, since he did not think 'truth' capable of fixed statement or even of final comprehension. The 'Good', at the apex of the world of the Forms, transcended Being. His navigator on the captainless ship, as he depicts that scene in the *Republic*, was capable of using the stars unfailingly to guide the ship safely. Yet the unruly crew would not accept his leadership, even at their own peril. Human nature thus thwarts the use of our knowledge to solve even those problems that it might, Plato reports.

Many overlook the increasing complexity which develops in Plato's late dialogues, that is, the way in which networks of relationships come to dominate his view of understanding. Even though he sees the One and the Many as generating an unstable drift toward infinity, Nature as it unfolds before him is fixed in its plan. The frame of the world, both that of plant and animal and human form, we may take as given, even as we seek to understand it, for example, 'explaining' it by constructing myths. Darwin's account of origins would be foreign to Plato, which is why 'evolution' caused such a disruption of existing frames of reference. The notion it requires of our thought, if we are truly to comprehend our origins, and comprehend how we came to be, frustrated the often assumed notion that 'knowledge' meant fixity not change. Actually, Plato could accommodate non-fixity easier than Aristotle, who stressed the aim of reason as rest. Yet both accepted Nature's givenness.

Evolutionary theories had been proposed from the earliest times as one explanation of our origins. But they did not become dominant theories, and none approached the complexity that Darwin sketched. Similarly, Plato understood the role of 'dialectic' in dialogue and in our progressive understanding, but he could not have envisaged the centrality of motion and time and change as Hegel's new account of 'dialectic' did. Fortunately for the aims of the Modern World, Hegel gave us a theory suitable for advancing science, telling us how knowledge is formed cumulatively and progressively. This seemed to fit modern science's understanding of its own progress and growing power. And if this final comprehension governed human life too, then a complex but still universal understanding of ourselves, of our developing nature, could parallel science.

2. The Exemption of Humanity From Science

What we must now decide is why this attractive assumption might not be true, why Modern science stops at the gates of the very ones who develop, control, and exploit it, refusing universalization to their self-understanding. In the first place, that which had been projected to come under our control, to enable the institution of Utopias and the eradication of suffering, refused to obey. Such understanding as the Social Sciences offered seemed neither universal nor capable of instituting radical improvements in human behavior. Democratic societies developed and human rights were proclaimed against tyrannies. But as the Modern drama unfolded, it disclosed little change in the drives which had so often destroyed both men and women and their societies. New societies were proposed; education was extended more democratically than before; technologies brought people closer; and communication was vastly speeded.

Still, the record in the daily newspapers, at least those in which fact appears uncensored, seems oddly similar to what was reported before the Advent of Enlightenment and Science. Somehow the universalization of our knowledge of Nature had failed to capture the psyches of men and women so as to yield control. True, greater forms of power wcrc developed thanks to science-spawned technology. But as this higher power was employed, it seemed to create just as much destruction as before—perhaps even more—and not to distinguish between 'good' and 'bad' in its employment. Increased power spawned increased subjugation seemingly with little twinge of conscience—at least at the time. If a moral law was universal within us, power once placed in human hands seemed oblivious to its control. Good and evil, destruction and creativity, seemed equally balanced, if not opposed, in our actions.

One can say, of course, that the issue is not so much the non-universality of human behavior, of our motives and of our character, as the corruption of power, a fact so often noted. The problem is that the good, courageous, admirable Utopias we offered were undermined in spite of the fact that we came to possess the promised power to recreate ourselves and our societies. 'Better worlds' were within our grasp, but we too often let them slip out of control. Our problem lies in further improving our techniques, some argued. But this line of happy thought leaves unanswered the question of why the knowledge and the ideals we possess seem no more powerful today against the forces that threaten human happiness than before. In the war to free the human spirit, we have not outmoded or outdistanced religions, as it once seemed that we would.

For all that the Modern World has made possible, which is far beyond the conception of the Ancients, it is hard to argue that we possess more power over ourselves for good than for ill. Of course, where the body is concerned, that is not the case. Medicine has not yet found the limits on its power to aid human life. 'Behaviorism', the reduction of the mind to the physiology of the body, is now little accepted. Psychiatry, based on Freud's scientific optimism, has solved certain complex cases, but it is not possible to say that it has relieved general human misery to any extent, except through the development of drugs, and that involves mostly our physiological aspects. The human spirit has refused our attempts to control it, except by violent repression, which always leads toward eventual destruction.

3. The Non-dualism Within Nature

Spinoza postulated that all the attributes of Substance or Nature parallel each other in their structure. It is hard now to see why he might have thought that it be so, except for his Rationalism and his scientific/mathematical optimism. His thesis: once one aspect of Nature was understood, the same form of understanding would apply to all aspects, a convenient thesis for one seeking simplicity. More than the fact that mathematics has not developed to be so neat or so complete as Spinoza thought, the whole status of 'theory' has turned out differently. That is, we have witnessed the development of new theories which are not entirely inconsistent with, but still replace, former ones.

Few now suggest the 'completion' of all theory. Its constant expansion, its revolutions rather than gradual evolutions, do not allow us to postulate a time for the finalization of all theory. This is true for physical nature as we have come to bring it within our grasp. If universals do seem applicable, although perhaps not a single consistent set (Plato's world of Forms has turned out to be more complex in its structure than he could have imagined), then as we move to reform human nature the failure of any universal theory to offer us a greater degree of control or guaranteed improvement seems to render the human future not subject to the degree of control which universal theories offered us over Nature's powers.

Our nature does not seem to parallel the structure of physical nature in any helpful way. And if our mind operates on forms of understanding more individual than universal, we can look for little prospect to simplify human understanding and human nature by the use of universal concepts. In fact, we should suspect that where men and women are concerned, universals are more distorting than useful, that no universal dialectic governs the development of human intelligence and action. Various philosophers throughout history have argued for the necessity of individual assessment, more recently Kierkegaard, Nietzsche, and American Pragmatism. But they were quickly discounted by many who rightly saw universals as the only way to develop knowledge powerful enough to induce mass change. The Chinese 'cultural revolution' specifically opposed tolerating individualism. The irony in this is that the attempts to reshape whole societies by the adherence to a universal theory have resulted in some of the worst destruction of human beings in our history.

Attempts have been made—'last ditch' efforts in the face of massive shifts in our outlook on the world, we might say—to hold 'knowledge' to mean only immediate empirically confirmable statements. This would require the exclusion of introspective psychology and all that is either unseen or might be said to transcend structures of the natural order. There is, of course, no way to enforce adherence to these restrictions, offered in the hope of 'saving' the universality of our understanding. Of course: (i) the depth of the human spirit which lies beyond sight and control constantly erupts destructively; and (ii) the only way to be certain that nothing 'transcends' nature would be to transcend it and to be able to report that nothing was 'out there' beyond our common reach. But transcendence keeps being suggested by our situation, its lack of completion, its constant disruption.

Mathematics, of course, presents us with a problem. For if it is powerful and capable of providing a tool to comprehend the structures of Nature, both those immediately visible and those only indirectly knowable, then all that is abstract and non-empirical cannot be unimportant to know. To try to render all mathematics as a construct of the human mind is to leave entirely unexplained why it has any coordination with Nature's structures at all. Kantian 'forms of the understanding' are universal. Time and space do seem to characterize most of our experiences. However, when it comes to the higher reaches of mathematics, we again approach esoteric knowledge, open to the few, which cannot be explained as a universal form of all human understanding, since it is not.

Universals, of course, have even lost some of their standing in the physical science, in the sense that no one theoretical structure seems about to capture an absolute hold on all physicists, for instance. Even in biology, powerful as Darwin's suggestions have been, few claim that we have, or can expect to, establish a single theory of evolution guaranteed beyond all future replacement. In fact, the challenge of new theoretical suggestions, ones not previously formulated or accepted, seems to be science's more fruitful form of advance, not the final adoption and expansion of a single theoretical framework held by all. Rigidity in theory appears as a block to scientific advance. This is not quite the individuality of approach that human nature seems to require, but it does argue for a non-finality, a non-fixity in our use of theory—that no one theory can yield us 'truth' itself.

4. The Absence of Necessity and Certainty

Theologians have long argued for 'necessity' and 'certainty' as qualities of God's nature which are required to support the divine understanding. This secured God's power and control, but it did so at the price ultimately of denying human freedom and fixing the outcome of the future. Thus, when the Modern Era of science arrived, the new Promethians were simply proposing, as Nietzsche suggested, that enlightened human beings now seize these expanded forms of understanding and thus control much (not all) that the tradition had reserved for God. Spinoza suggested that we improve our understanding until we come to see things as God does, under the aspect of eternity. Even Kant's skepticism about our inability to know God or the world directly did not seem to alter his conviction that science could achieve finality.

We can see "the camel's nose under the tent" in the form of developing democratic theory, in the assertion first of the rights of man, and next those of women, of claims that we are all created equal and endowed with inalienable rights. For if human beings increasingly assert their freedom and right of self-determination, as they are doing, it is hard to see this as the product of necessity. Instead, it appears as based on a growing sense of individualism and of self-determination. If so, this is hard to reconcile with the Early Modern notions of an absolute fixity of nature. Even dialectical systems, whether it is the idealism of Hegel or the materialism of Marx, are not able to account for the way history and peoples have developed outside a single plan. And certainly no monolithic proposal in recent decades has worked out as predicated or with any apparent necessity in its outcome. Freedom and the intrusion of chaos destroy every certainty.

Confusion arises partly because human thought can let itself be governed by a necessary dialectic. We can design patterns, speeches, logics, theories which operate according to this account. Moreover, this sometimes seems to render human activity, particularly in masses of people, understandable, even enlightening. We can arrange all the known philosophies of the world into a scheme of dialectic development; we can see human behavior as governed by economics or by class, or more recently by sex. The problem is that, while these theories tend to be intellectually compelling, in actual fact we have to urge groups, individuals, masses into accepting such patterns, often by violence. The volatile qualities of human nature do not stay within any controllable theoretical boundaries except by force. The power needed to gain predictability comes only from an applied external coercion and by the exclusion of any dissonance. Oddly, necessity seems to be imposed by thought rather than discovered by it. This distinction is easily overlooked, since no one maintains that the regularity of the physical universe is sustained by our thought. The interposing of human individuals into the physical pattern of predictability is what invalidates the desired parallel. Evidently, we are not easily governed by universal regularities. Although societies and groups do fall into using customs which maintain themselves, we know that these are still subject to change and also that certain individuals can always "opt out." 'Revolution' is a modern notion, but it rests on the assumption that human beings can modify both their conduct and the structures created to control and to regularize it.

'Anarchy' as a political theory has fascinating implications for our attempt to control/understand human nature and human actions by the application of universals beyond physiological description. As a political notion, it rejects all social structure as inhibiting to human freedom and self-determination. And so it is. Most accept the need for social/political regularities, even after we have discovered that nothing we name in our presently governing social patterns needs to be as it is. Possible worlds are paralleled by possible modes of human behavior. The important difference is that the observable universe cannot elect to change itself into another optional form. But human nature, we have discovered, sometimes can.

The entry of theories of self-determination, of the divine ability of individual choice and thus for the individual appraisal of all cases which simply do not conform to expectations current at the time – these novelties in human thought and creative effort give us everything distinctive about human life and open its possibilities, when striven for, to all that enhances life. However, all forms of social control, while necessary to keep human life from chaos, cannot be seen as universally governed by any pattern external to human decisions, whether corporate or individual. At any given time most human beings, fortunately, live regular, even partially predictable, lives. But the independence, the creativity, the volatile potentials in our natures...this keeps open the possibility of change. It also makes universal understanding impossible. But it is the source of both the best and the most destructive activity in the human, as opposed to the physical, realm.

5. Description is Universal, Understanding Individual

The power of language lies in its ability to universalize; appraising the individual depends on grasping what is individual. This opposition is the source of much confusion. The irony is that we must tend to universalize in order to express ourselves at the same time that we must separate out the individual if we do not wish to distort. Art, drama, music come closer in their ability to capture individuality. Direct experience does too, but it defies expression, except for the gifted poet/writer. The poet is the one who can make words bear the burden of individuality while still conveying a sense of a universal application. Philosophers have the greatest trouble. They have witnessed the beauty of abstract universalizing. They are entranced by what the power of mathematics can do for them, could they understand all in the world by its use. Yet they recognize the enigma of the individual.

The philosopher, everytime he or she speaks or takes up a pen, tends to distort the individual perception. Yet at the same time he or she is entranced by the powers of universal description, which work better with flowers and stars than with men and women. The Empiricists knew this and tried to direct us back to immediate perception. Aristotle had told us that the individual is grasped, if at all, by immediate intuition. But the problem with this is that they, the Empiricists, can never agree on the exact description of any individual perception, just because it is linked to the individual, to words, and to the universal. Furthermore, sensory impression, unless extended, confines us to the exterior and so to the superficial qualities of the human being. We miss what is most important, that is, what we need to define by its individuality in order to understand.

Yet sometimes, although we can never grasp all, we must select out and focus on the memorable and general aspect of a group, if we are to be able to express and convey it. Every description is a stereotype, a partial distortion at best, inaccurate for the whole, overlooking non-conforming individuals, and yet often powerful in its expression just because of the focus which the exclusion of conflicting detail allows. The powerful writer and the graphic artist embody the paradox, defy the contradiction. Through the insight which makes genius, some detail is singled out which is capable of giving universal expression to what otherwise would seem lost in particulars. The individual, and its perhaps unique quality or characteristic, becomes a medium to depict a universal in non-abstract terms. The philosopher, not being a poet or novelist, finds this harder to express and so tends either towards individual concreteness as inexpressible or to unanchored abstraction.

The inescapable problem which keeps us from the final understanding, which we keep being convinced we really could record once and for all, is that anyone coming after the author or the artist can take that combination of words or sounds or artistic expression and grasp it in its individual meaning—or in its universalization—and show that it is not entirely an adequate expression, or even claim it as a distortion by treating it literally and not symbolically. All blacks are not...; all farmers are not...; all students are not...; nothing is all anything that is important in our lives. But we are forced into using the loose combination of particularity with a universal quality in order to achieve graphic expression. It is just that this can breed misunderstanding almost as easily as understanding, and thus it is inherently unstable. Philosophy, if not accepted as a symbolic expression, is either misleading or tends to triviality, even more so than sacred scriptures, since we know they must be symbolic. The 'fundamentalist', of course, can distort both scripture and philosophy in his or her hope to reach an unobtainable personal certainty.

C. Prejudice, Discrimination and Hierarchy

Anarchy is the ultimate revolutionary theory, the logical outcome of democratic struggle extended to its limit. It rightly recognizes that all political/social structures can be, and often are, used to repress opposition and to protect privilege. Like Utopian theories, unfortunately, Anarchy also fails to recognize the existence of destructive evil. It is this negative thrust which requires hierarchies in order to control violence and to recognize the brute fact that we were not all created equal, although we may strive to be. Societies, all enterprises, thrive if talent is located and allowed full expression, a fact which implies that all were not equally born to begin with. Beauty and talent exist and must be recognized: They are not uniform but multiple in their manifestations. Once recognized, they tend to entrench themselves—if they can—against all competitors, just because they are always under challenge.

Our problems begin with two: (1) There is no single, rigid absolute value structure; but instead there are multiple values, many—not none at all. Driven by human effort, these can be differently recognized by different peoples at different times. Anthropology in its cultural studies illustrates this. Yet it is radically opposed to say that we rank values differently than it is to say that none are given in nature, although all values need human recognition to become established; and (ii) values, talents, beauties, virtues, all are rightly granted higher rank in our recognition as we establish hierarchies.[116] But immediately they tend to become reactionary and to react against any challenge to their position. Yet all the while, ironically, health and vitality in a society, in a civilization or in any enterprise, rest on allowing new talent constantly to challenge for position. Also, sadly, any privilege not based on strength and talent but on weakness and on an insidious cleverness will move to ingrain itself against challenge, just because it fears it cannot sustain itself in open comparison.

In recent years, women have made us most aware of the vast and limiting aspects of prejudice and discrimination which operate as natural forces to establish hierarchies. The profound question which haunts all societies, all peoples, is how to allow for hierarchies based

---

[116]   Carol P. Christ, and Judith Plaskow, eds. *Womanspirit Rising* (San Francisco: Harper and Row, 1979).

The editors offer a diverse collection of essays which argue for reconstructing religion to speak to the experience of women. But for some, society has outgrown its need for religion . An enormous sense of injustice follows the discovery that religions are sexist. Sharing experiences, women began to realize how fully the world had been defined by men. But women will call themselves and the world into new being. Some will reform the past; the revolutionaries are beginning to create a new religious future. Some advocate equality, others female ascendency.

If women are to overcome their oppression, they must reject the male God and also all hierarchies and dualism (p. 24). The women's revolution can and should "change our whole vision of reality," Mary Daly argues (p. 54). "The ancient mother goddesses are being resurrected. Yet much of women's 'herstory' in early Christianity is lost" (p.92), Professor Fiorenza reports. But she also says that "the Goddess of radical feminism spiritually is not very different from the God which Jesus preached" (p. 138). Goddess symbolism undergirds and legitimates the concerns of the women's movement, Carol Christ concludes (p. 276). A woman's will is not subordinate to the Lord God as king and ruler.

on genuine qualities and talents to become established and at the same time to prevent these from immediately closing themselves off. They either reject all challenge from new talent or become so fearful of failure and of holding onto power, so afraid of not being able to meet any challenge to their privilege, that one who is established becomes blind to a virtue different from one's own. The openness which allows talent to rise and to be recognized turns rapidly into the repression of new candidates and closes in against all challenge (IBM, General Motors, Sears take note).

Of course, it is difficult to recognize a talent or a beauty that lies outside our current standards of reference. Just as we were not created democratic by birth but must fight to establish and sustain that spirit, so only a few are able to recognize true talent, virtue, and beauty when these appear. Popularity, whether promoted by drum beats on T.V. or by local 'talent shows', tends to fix the public standard or standards. How, then, can the prized few be allowed influence against a vulgar democratic popularity in order to keep open our ability to recognize and to accept new talents without appointing cultural tyrants?

The irony and the difficulty in all this is that the surface qualities which are used to assert prejudice—are just that, surface features and not the underlying factors. Thus, we can make progress in anti-discrimination laws, in abolishing slavery, in opening societies to wider options. But then prejudice simply moves to take more insidious forms. "Politically correct thinking," so much recently a focus in the U.S., has always been with us, because in any field the ultimate challenge to insecure leaders has always been felt to come from those who differ ideologically. This is particularly true after a reform or a revolutionary movement fails to achieve its goals, or falls into repressive terror. Oddly, when physical, racial characteristics no longer discriminate, ideological purity is often the court of retreat.

So we must discriminate, seek to form hierarchies according to genuine values and accomplishments, but we should know that the last defense of insecurity is to reject all who do not adhere to a similar ideology. The very factors needed to build a creative, memorable society, one that allows the production of works of enduring merit, these same factors cause its decline. This begins when those who recognize what has been achieved of real merit turn and force a conformity to what itself was once novel and difficult to establish in its originating time. The transvaluation of values, which Nietzsche recommended, works against the grain of all who enjoy privilege based on once achieved merit, hard won though it probably was.

We must accept the fact that all societies, all races, all religions, all political structures, all individuals, are not equally creative and exemplary, and so are not all deserving of outstanding merit or of being used as models. We must establish rank between cultures and individuals, and this requires discriminatory judgment. But we know in advance that this will not, cannot be, agreed upon by all. Much must remain to private not public recognition. Yet such modest recognition can be equally satisfying to one who seeks significance in life, a quality not necessarily reflected on a public, economic scale. All these evaluations, which we must make for the health and vitality of a culture, can seldom be seen as clearly justified at the time. What endures is often unsuspected in the age.

We need to recapture 'discrimination' from its recently negative status in our public vocabulary and distinguish it clearly from 'prejudice'. Hierarchies should be built on sensitive discrimination, on a judgment that is capable of accepting a wide range of values and is able to discern these in as yet undiscovered individuals. Prejudice is quite another matter and involves constructing negative appraisals based purely on one's internal regard. In any field, those who offer public appraisals often indulge in displays of their personal valuation, not in order to open new forms of appreciation but simply to gain recognition and status for themselves. We can never, in the nature of the plurality of all values, get agreed universal standards. But we can seek to establish these which allow for the new at the same time that old values are not abandoned totally.

Once again, the Women's Movement offers us insight into these matters and at the same time exposes their difficulty.[117] Women always had high value as the producers and protectors of the future of the race and of society's ethics. But they were held to this narrow virtue long after it became evident that they could be released from the all-absorbing burden of motherhood and exhibit new, more diverse, talents. Negroes freed at last from slavery could offer talents other than religious fervor or physical labor. Yet old evaluations, perhaps factual at one time, were used to confine these challengers to non-change. As one barrier falls, we do not always find the result to be total openness. Other grounds for rejection immediately arise. Black athletes, musicians, singers are beyond denial in their unusual creative talents, but all barriers against individuals do not fall when this is publicly recognized. Society cannot afford a 'fast fluidity', it seems.

To gain acceptance for the principle of evaluation based on individual talent alone, whether latent or publicly evident, is still the greatest barrier in the way of our human fulfillment, male and female. Of course, the ultimate irony is that our problem is not so simple as that each individual knows his or her talents and has only the problem of gaining recognition from others. For many individuals their major talents lay unrecognized, unexplored even by them. It is not only the existing society which judges individuals by established standards without regard for innovation. We each begin appraising ourselves by the known standards around us, not by what we might achieve if only we looked further.

---

[117] Eva Feder Kittay, and Diana T. Meyers, ed., *Women and Moral Theory* (Totowa, NJ: Rowman and Littlefield, 1987).

If race, sex, and religion have been the most blatant and pervasive objects of prejudice, as the rise of the Women's Movement (or the Civil Rights movement) makes plain, when obvious discriminatory grounds are removed and legal rights established and anti-discrimination laws adopted and enforced, all prejudice does not disappear. It simply moves to less obvious grounds—'glass ceilings,' as we label this. Modern Feminism is right: Hierarchies still move to defend their privilege, even if this cannot be done on legal or obvious grounds. Every person, male or female, of any race who is denied a recognition or a privilege they feel they have earned, can claim this is due to some hidden bias. Yet millions who comply to the obvious standards of the day for inclusion are also denied.

Virginia Woolf thought she and other women needed *A Room of One's Own*[118] in order to develop as writers. Yet millions of every race and sex have no such privileged situation available. Life is too dreary, too all-consuming of their labor, to allow this except for a small number. No society can set up ideal conditions for everyone, except perhaps in small, highly controlled groups. Thus, conditions much more serious than sex or race hold every group back. It is a rare leader, male or female, who having attained prominence will look backward and aid those who are behind him or her in their climb. In this age we are intently aware of the limitations on the earth's resources. We often neglect to see that talent outside the established routes for its expression is much more limited in supply than are our natural physical resources.

And so Radical Feminism has argued against all hierarchy, against all restraint. Yet no society, large or small, religious or lay, can survive and serve its people unless it accepts rules of restraint and order and fixes some means to establish authority in hierarchy. We

---

[118] Virginia Woolf, *A Room of One's Own: Three Guineas* (Oxford: Oxford University Press, 1992).

need "courts of higher appeal," since local bodies notoriously reflect local mores. But to set up such a higher court of appeal beyond provincialism requires a carefully ordered hierarchy, which is at once just as open to being used for the repression as for the liberation of a rising human spirit. The answer to this fundamental dilemma may be the concept of the "perpetual revolution." We seek to overturn hierarchies which impose intolerable restrictions, ones which not only cut off individual opportunity but work to suppress all non-conforming alternatives. "No taxation without representation," we cry as we continue to dump the tea into the harbor.

Revolutions can, of course, turn into terror and wreak destruction, and this they do perhaps more frequently than they initiate a vital society capable of expanding individual opportunity. Revolutions seldom build their new power into a hierarchical structure (of whatever form) allowing avenues for constant challenge to the potential abuse of power which any hierarchy possesses. But it is dangerous to romanticize revolutions, since they so easily run amok and simply replace old tyrants with new. Still, any hierarchy which does not find a way to accept constant challenge, to revalidate its right to hold decision making power, simply sets itself up for failure or for eventual despotic control. We need to question every exiting hierarchy, but not the idea of our basic need to establish one that is responsive to new needs, to undeveloped talent.

'Democracy', we argued at the outset, may offer the best societal means to ensure constant self-criticism for an evolving hierarchy. But there is no single agreed form which political, social democracy must take. Any artery for reform, once unlocked, has an immediate tendency to 'silt up' again, after the enthusiasm of the initial liberation passes. No political, social, or cultural democracy can keep itself open for constant total reappraisal. That is exhausting and can paralyze all action. But democracy, where it is practiced in a form not merely to conceal power but to encourage popular critique, may be the best alternative to keep prejudice from reigning simply under a "thousand points of envy." 'Discrimination' has to be practiced and cultivated, else new talent cannot possibly gain recognition. There is, there can be, no perfect system.

Public utterances are no easy indicator of the author/speaker's mind. How can one "read between the lines" and discover where prejudice really operates as it assumes new forms which are expedient in that hour. As has been recommended, we need to watch action carefully and always see it in contrast to the written/spoken word. This can be done neither on a mass scale nor in a hurry. Those who are insecure and so avoid open challenge must be skillful in keeping a separation between act and word, using a verbal cover-up. 'Truth' is not easy to find but hard, in physics or in human psychology. Prejudice conceals itself behind acceptable current 'truths'. Can value discriminations, while they build up needed hierarchies, be kept from closing off challenge and so remain open to constant reappraisal?

D. The Ash Heap of History is not Gendered

About an equal number of men and women are consigned to one ash heap or another every day. On the other hand, the "slaughter bench" of history is sex biased. Vastly more men than women have been and are brutally exterminated every hour. What we are talking about is the few, the very few, who are salvaged from destruction and immortalized in the written records or in the artistic representations of fame. If women were not brutally killed in wars and skirmishes to the same extent as men, the same forces that protected them, for example, motherhood, also made it impossible for more than a handful to get free of that burden to compete with men by exercising talents other than the womb.

When we say that women's history has been 'silenced', we do not mean that every living male was unaware that he had a mother. Everyone knows women were part of the human family and many celebrated that. We also forget that, if today many women can get free to compete for top spots and take a shot at immortality, until recently those who could or did compete for public spots were disproportionately few. If we want to say that sex bias prevented their entry into the competition, that probably was largely true. But to argue that somehow women were more prominent than the record indicates is to ignore the burden which confined most women. If women are on the verge of escaping today, let us celebrate the success of that long struggle. But there is no use forgetting that, until recently, biology was almost their destiny.

If modern medicine and social customs have only advanced or changed recently in order to free women from their biological destiny, the same primitive conditions of medicine consigned men who were injured in war or in dangerous work to pain and death in greater proportion than women. The traditional cry "women and children first" indicates that in many instances women were protected by men. It is not the case that all men always brutalized all women, even if far too many did. What women who protest their recorded history mean is that the 'glory spots' were awarded to few women. But we must remember: the evaluation, the competition for that 'paper immortality', is just as fierce for men. And they have been rejected for 'valorization' in even greater numbers than women.

If you reply that men have been the judges and the evaluators, it is also true that all the positions of "assigned relative merit" in the record, in the teaching of our cultural-scientific history, change from day to day. Men also fight over who from the past deserves our attention, and new candidates emerge in every era. That is what we mean by "the new generation takes over" in any field you can name: industry, education, art. Look in the libraries, in the churchyards, at the public monuments; more men are there who once were thought more important or famous than women. There are more buried there than any of us could have thought of or have time to consider. Our selection process is fallible and constantly shifting, but it is necessary in order to prevent 'intellectual overload'. We can preserve only a few.

If in reviewing the historical record, those women now freed from biological destiny want to make us aware of how unstable our selection process for glory is, if they want in greater numbers to run fast when the starting gun is fired in the competition for entry into the winner's circle, that is fine. Men have been facing brutal, prejudiced evaluators for centuries—and still do. Have male editors always accepted male writers for publication on the basis of their sex? When any man has tried to write, dream, speak, act, create, think along new lines, has he always been welcomed if he is male? Rejection letters shower down on those equipped with a penis too. Everything may be 'gendered', but in many cases that is a trivial factor. I never saw a novel idea ignored that made mention of sex in its rejection. But I have faced plenty who are blind to all novelty and who are rigidly glued to nothing but existing convention. Both sexes are equally subject to blind bias.

As women enter onto "the glory trail" in greater numbers, any illusion that cultural immortality is gained by intense effort is a grand illusion. Repressive forces have an advantage over innovation, always. Too many want public rewards. Only a few who control public access are ever determined that new ideas, practices, techniques, discoveries must be given a hearing. But before screaming 'gender bias' too loudly or too automatically, all who compete in this often crooked race (a universal Siena Palio) should check out how male innovators have fared in their bid for recognition. In almost every case, history reveals that they were overlooked to begin with. Every man who has gone to a male professor or boss with a new proposal has not been told that he is a budding genius and that the "man in charge of admission to prominence" will abdicate in his favor. On the contrary, most men are ignored and put down if possible.

In the very top echelons of any profession, we usually are not too uncertain about relative rank. Yet we do not remember all presidents, generals, scientists, artists, equally well. Remembered fame rises and falls, fades and reappears. Academic reputations are made by arguing for recognizing someone heretofore under-appreciated or overlooked. The work of an artist or a writer of a past generation receives new attention only to find that that book is bypassed on library shelves next year. The top spots are fluid but not entirely disputed. There is deservedly a "Court of the Immortals" at Forest Lawn Cemetery in Southern California, even if we might dispute the 'immortality' of its occupants. What most women who argue for a rewriting of the historical record mean is that, in the second and third rank (not such a bad position, actually, in view of how many millions die out of sight) there are women there who might be given more recognition than they have had in the past.

This is true, but it is also true for the males who crowded the middle rungs on the ladder. So we thank the Women's Movement for making it clear that our criteria for the evaluation of prominence are slightly unstable, subject to change, that the codifiers of the canon are not infallible, and that fashions change rather quickly. Fame is fleeting, except for the very few. Most of us will be forgotten, women too, except that no man ever forgot that he had a mother. Were women 'unrecognized' in the past? That is simply false. They did not have too many shots at running the world's affairs, that is true; that can change. But the number of men shut out of memorial glory, who still reside in some 'obscurely remembered' file, exceeds the number of women arguing for recognition.

Most men I know who occupy top positions, who control the gates of access, move either subtly or viciously to keep down any who challenge their position or judgment. Males have been, and still are, in numbers much more subject to such 'discrimination' than women. What the women's protest has, thankfully, highlighted is that all kinds of blocks exist to any who would advance, the easiest excuse used to shut someone out being that of race, religion, and sex. The real reasons for rejection are often concealed beneath that gloss, are often more subtle; sex is surface, an excuse. The gates of recognition are narrow, and steep is the way thereunto. As evidence of this, is it any clearer that women who achieve power or authority are any more open to accept a challenge to their position, or a reevaluation of their standards, than men, or any less ready to use every device to fend off the challenger? "Ask Imelda." Some men, some women, are open, compassionate, visionary. The harvest is plentiful; such workers are few—of either sex.

The Hitlers and Stalins have slaughtered more men than women, although the Nazi holocaust of the Jews seemed to have been indiscriminate as regards men, women, and children. Women's pressure for recognition, once they are released from their sexual destiny, makes it painfully clear to us how difficult it is to have a new idea recognized, how closed the avenues of reward are to so many, how even the insignificant will use any means to guard what privilege they have. We need constantly to try to open the doors for every new talent to audition for history.

Many men have in fact loved their mothers and credited them for much of their success. But it is not clear that family ties carry over when mothers leave their spinning wheels for the halls of fame. Their tenderness, like the noted Godfather's family sentimentality, may not extend beyond home and hearth. Some women see this and argue to change the rules of the power game. We wish them "Good luck; Godspeed." But we ask them to study the results of earlier attempts at radical social engineering. Human nature may be "socially constructed," but that in no way means that we can redraw 'nature' according to our dreams. The continuity of history does not argue for that; neither does the admirable qualities of some small utopian communities.

Chapter VI

Tomorrow's Women

A. Sweet, Soft and Weak?

"A sweet soft nature that comforts him by its contrast to his own"
—said by Anton Trendellsohn, (p.192).

"Yes; she was a weak woman—very weak; but she had that one strength which is sufficient to atone for all feminine weakness— she could really love,"
—said of Nina Balatka, (p.189).

There is much in Trollope's portrayal of male and female nature in *Nina Balatka*[119] to stir anger in the modern feminist. Of course, this is a male author writing on women's nature, and so we cannot expect him to understand the opposite sex, you say. Trollope paints his male hero as wanting women to have a "sweet soft nature" in contrast to his own. And he paints his female heroine as gifted with the single passion for love. "Gender roles indoctrinated by society," of course, we say. But in the rush to open and to accept new gender roles for women, is there any reason to look backward in nostalgia, or is there only a need to have done with the limits of the past? How will tomorrow's women look at today as past?

In the rush to escape confines and open new frontiers for feminine exploration, there is a tendency to paint all the past, and much of the present, as if it were 'all bad', women always subordinated, men always dominant. Traditional romance, the classic love story, is reinterpreted as a relationship of dominance. A strange connection is often made between the penis and the brain which seems to require

---

[119] See Anthony Trollope, *Nina Balatka*, chapter II, note 56.

all men to think alike, to taint everything they think or write or create with a 'male gender bias'. It reduces all of history and our intellectual/artistic life to a sexual uniformity. In an instant, this makes all that we have struggled to comprehend, the amazing diversity of life, suddenly homogenous.

Of course, women have been mistreated, just as men have, although women perhaps more systematically according to sex. Today new careers and possibilities can be opened to women. And for those who pursue them, this involves a 'revolution' in women's roles.[120] Legal, economic restrictions on women can be lifted. This opens new lifestyles for them and new positions of public prominence vs. the private prominence a majority have always occupied. "Good riddance," many say. "No retreat, no reversal of fortune, no reactionary pressures permitted. What has been gained must not be lost." We paraphrase the World War I song for women: "How ya gonna keep 'em down in the nursery now that they've seen the seats of power?" If consciousness-raising can achieve its goal, will all women seek to be released from their position and never look back?

The tendency of recent feminism has been to look forward, quite rightly, toward the goals they seek, abortion rights, equal pay, etcetera. Actually, there is a great deal of looking back, but it is mostly to rewrite history to expose women's hidden roles or to document in horror the negative ways in which women have sometimes been portrayed or treated in the past. If the picture presented is positive, it is to reveal a lost matriarchal role in religion, or to recount a prominence that has been overlooked in a forgotten

---

[120] Nancy M. Henley, *Body Politics* (New York: Simon and Schuster, 1977).
The author wants to see a radical restructuring of our social organization. Some have privileges others do not have, and this is evidenced in non-verbal behavior. Humiliation is experienced when one is ignored or interrupted. It is quite possible that women experience male dominance in this way, but surely the general situation is one that all who are in a subordinate position experience do so for a variety of reasons, sex being only one.

ancient past. This, then, spurs the campaign today, because we realize that there were times when women were more prominent. But casting forward, in the future when feminism's agenda nears fulfillment, can we envision the way tomorrow's women might look back on today's women's view of her past and her future?

In the rejection of any present confinement to past roles, feminists tend to reject the entire past for the sake of women's present concerns. True; yet given the burden of childbirth, there is no way history can be rewritten to make women equally powerful on the public scene in past societies, with some exclusions for matriarchies, of course. Thus, if the press is for public office and an equality in the governance of societies and institutions, for example, the church, then no past role is a candidate for nostalgic remembrance by the women who struggle to be free from it. But what I suggest is that 'tomorrow's women' may, in their turn, look back and see this sad history in yet again a different light. How could that be, if their hard won liberation is not abandoned? How, once the new opportunities are open, could any think of going 'backward', rather than 'forward'?

The possible answer lies in role reversal, in seeing the 'protected' status of women differently, in a possible recovery of the romantic novel. How could that happen? How could a woman be so mad as to long for what the generation before her fought to escape? Because, in the harsh world of constant power struggles, whether academic, political or financial, the 'soft' nature that was appealing and gave one a quiet, a less public role, might again appeal. In fact, it probably never did stop appealing to many who shunned the limelight, or as the New Testament says, did not seek the chief seats in the synagogue. 'Weakness' is what recent women have sought to throw off as a gender image.[121] Still, the weak are candidates for protection

---

[121] Stanler Phelps, and Nancy Austin, *The Assertive Woman* (San Luis Obispo, CA: Impact Publishers, 1987).
This popular book was printed in 1975 and updated in 1987. It is a "how to" book for

by males (or abuse, true). Strong, powerful women are not candidates to be sheltered.

Can there be, is there any possibility for, a return so that 'tomorrow's women' would find that the romance of love (even if not heterosexual) leads that person to want to be cared for, to appreciate tenderness and protection? It simply is not the case that all men act destructively and use force to subdue or to abuse all women. Most women, I would guess, have benefited from male protection as 'very weak' women, as Trollope phrases it. A love relationship is certainly seldom built on two powerful competing egos. This is not to say that the woman who is a leader in public office cannot "turn a different face" to her home, to her personal life. We need not make all females, or all males, of one uniform type. Love breeds on contradictions. But will some still want to hear "women and children first" when the ship is sinking?

Will tomorrow's women, any number of them, read of the Victorian Age with fascination and then daydream of a return to elaborate dress and decorative manners to live the life of *Orlando*?[122] Will any number of tomorrow's women read of courtly love and fantasize again of knights riding to their defense? Or will every woman want to fight in the front trenches for herself? If "the grass is always greener on the other side of the street," after the street has been crossed into the area of 'women's utopia', can the grass on the side of the street from which they have just come begin to look greener than when they left? It has happened before; it can happen

---

women who want to develop "personal freedom and strength." It goes along with the insistence of many women that they must become more assertive in their move toward a greater share of power. One needs to demonstrate that you are "as good as everyone else." It is, thus, a confidence building manual for the woman who needs to develop self-reliance. It has only a support role to play in the development of the feminist movement. It does not offer a major contribution to theory, but its "pop" psychology/sociology adds life to our understanding of feminist theory.

[122] See Virginia Woolf, *Orlando*, chapter I, note 9.

again, unless one still believes in an irreversible theory of Progress. Will women look back and again find an attractiveness in the romance of hearth and home and seek a softness in their nature as a virtue?—that which attracted Anthony Trendellsohn.

This question is tied up with the notion of 'Progress'. For a century or two, we believed that we had risen above our collective past, or at least that we could do so by spreading education and the Enlightenment. But for many reasons, chiefly the attempted extermination of the Jews by the most 'enlightened' nation on Earth, plus atrocities associated with Marxist and some other revolutionary ventures, we have lost our belief in non-reversible progress and have come to agree with Existentialism that, as far as the human condition is concerned, we have been and are in the same situation as all before us and all who will come after us. This does not mean that improvements in our situation cannot be made or wrongs rectified. Quite the opposite. It means that all that enhances the human condition, whether for male or for female, is very fragile and is in need of constant care, lest human corruptibility send us backward again.

On the positive side, this constant threat of being sent back to conditions which are "nasty, brutish and short" also means that all good in previous societies and customs need not be rejected in the name of Progress, that all improvement need not come by a blanket rejection of our past. Selectively, we can eliminate faults, injustices. But since all change is neither automatically for the better nor permanent, Tomorrow's Women need not always "look back in anger." They may find something appealing in a lost past, one which still stands open to them just because all 'progress' is not necessarily Utopia Unlimited. Thus, as inevitable faults appear—along with improvements—in any advance, one looks back to qualities which a hasty rejection and a blanket optimism about change may have caused us to miss. Tomorrow's Women may look back selectively, appreciatively.

211

B. Thirteen Difficult Pregnancies

In *A Room of One's Own*,[123] Virginia Woolf argues that a woman must have money and a room of her own if she is to write fiction (p.8). 'Women' and 'fiction' are unsolved problems, she tells us, although it never occurs to her to extend her analysis to the economically non-well-to-do. She talks about the daughters of 'educated men', that is, to extend to women the privileges which sons of well-to-do men already have, principally education and leisure. However, in contrast to militant feminists today, she feels that "one cannot hope to tell the truth" (p.5) where any question of sex is the subject. Since it is controversial, one can only show how one came to hold that opinion, she reports. 'Rightness' is not an issue. Yet there is a need to come to some conclusion on the subject. Thus, coupled with the essential uncertainty, the irony is that, whenever 'sex' is the topic, all lurking prejudices and passions are aroused.

No women could, she asserts, bear thirteen children and make a fortune at the same time (p.28). No one woman could stand that. Now the fact that this dichotomy need no longer exist shows us how radically the situation of women has changed. There is no need to endure "thirteen difficult pregnancies," as she puts it. Woolf adds the interesting observation that "women do not write books about men" (p.35), but again we see that this has changed radically, given all the accounts we have now of 'patriarchy'. She states a thesis we might all consider as post-radical-feminism: It is "absurd to blame any class or any sex as a whole" (p.49). Universal fixation of blame or condemnation evidently is not possible. However, being well ahead of the time of post-feminist reflections on gain and loss, she observes: "Anything can happen when womanhood has ceased to be a protected occupation" (p.52). She does not fail to balance this traditional

---

[123] See Virginia Woolf, *A Room of One's Own: Three Guineas*, chapter V, note 117.

"protection of women" against the opportunities of "going it alone."

Nor does Virginia Woolf agree that women have been totally put down or, in currently correct jargon, 'marginalised'. Examining fiction she reports: "If woman had no existence save in fiction written by men, one would imagine her a person of utmost importance" (p.55). Yet she adds: "Imaginatively she is of the highest importance; practically she is completely insignificant" (p.56). It is 'practical importance' that the recent Feminist movement has sought, but we should not fail to recognize the 'imaginative importance' women have held in earlier times. For example, "on the stage woman equals or surpasses men" (footnote, p.56). Education is the key to balancing imaginative importance with practical significance, Woolf concludes. Although she has spoken mostly of 'the privileged classes', she concludes that education must be universal: "For genius like Shakespeare's is not born among laboring, uneducated, people" (p.62).

However, even instituting these changes will not render all equal. "To write a work of genius is almost always a work of prodigious difficulty" (pp.66-67). We cannot expect this from many, only from the strong and the talented. Woolf sees no easy transition to literary prominence for women, even if given the necessary advantages. Why? Because "She is at war with her lot" (p.90). This internal struggle, which Woolf sees as more characteristic of women than of men, can block creativity. She comments: "There will be time for that when I have decided whether she has a pen in her hand or a pick ax" (p.104)...Pick axes have been prominent of late. Yet each sex is hampered in its knowledge of the other, and this inhibits creativity. Both sides are 'terribly hampered' (p.108) in their knowledge of the other sex. Woolf lays the burden of ignorance on both sides.

Given the recent rash of Feminist 'consciousness-raising' and their rewriting of the historical record in order to find a great but unrecorded history for women heretofore neglected, we may smile at Woolf's balance: "To praise one's own sex is often suspect, often silly" (p.111). Since she links the sexes together for creativity, she cannot recommend groups formed exclusively for women. The renewal of creative power, she claims, is a gift "only the opposite sex can bestow" (p.112). We are linked together necessarily. Both should learn to laugh "without bitterness" at the vanities of the other sex" (p.118). It is remarkable to consider this statement, given the rash of attacks on 'patriarchy' and the recent recreation of goddesses for worship. Literature, she says, shows the futility of what is written in the spirit of bitterness and without humor. To think of one sex as distinct from the other interferes with the unity of the mind, she feels sure. It is not natural, she tells us; it requires an effort (p.126).

She looks for the unity of men and women, not for their separation. Such unity makes for the greatest satisfaction, she feels (p.127). This need not exclude lesbian or homosexual relations, since this would "block the mind's unity" only if they excluded the opposite sex. "Perhaps a mind that is purely masculine cannot create, any more than a mind that is purely feminine" (p.128), she says in anticipation of Jung's insistence on the intermingling of images within the two sexes. Already in her time she labels her age as 'stridently sex conscious' (p.129), but the last quarter of the twentieth century certainly has gone beyond hers. And she does not recommend self-focus: "In the shadow of the letter 'I' all is shapeless or mist" (p.130). Union again is her theme: "Poetry ought to have a mother as well as a father" (p.134). She wants to raise the status of women, but not at the expense of setting them in opposition to men.[124]

---

[124] Madonna Kolbenschlag, *Lost in the Land of Oz: The Search for Identity and Community in American Life* (San Francisco, 1988).

The author states, "This is a book about surviving as a spiritual orphan" (p. xi). She wants to give that "inner orphan" the power "to make our lives and our world creative, harmonious, and whole" (*ibid.*). This will happen by examining the myths we live by. Is there an unfolding universal myth? – she asks. This is not a "feminist" book, strictly speaking, except that she states that the world in our contemporary civilization denies "the life-giving 'feminine' experience and values of human society." Yet she speaks more of our

"Thirteen difficult pregnancies" need restrain women no more. But the gain will be a loss in Woolf's eyes—if it sets women in opposition to men. "It is fatal for anyone who writes to think of their sex," she comments (p.136), an idea which might startle recent Feminists. Why does she remove sex from center stage in consciousness? Because "anything written with that conscious bias is doomed to death" (*ibid.*). If in the current phrase "all things are gendered," Virginia Woolf wants the writer to eliminate that conscious focus. This, of course, works counter to the recent popularity of exposing gender bias everywhere in women's past and present. Woolf does not deny that; she can't; she knows what women have lacked and what they need in order to live creatively. It is just that allowing this to shape every perspective can be distorting.

Truth is no simple matter for Woolf, and surely it does not lie along lines of gender division. " . . . for in questions like this, truth is only to be had by laying together many varieties of error" (p.137). "It can lie in no one place, with no one sex." "All of this putting of sex against sex, of quality against quality; all this claiming of superiority and imputing inferiority, belong to the private-school stage of human existence where there are 'sides', and it is necessary for one side to beat another" (p.138). As people mature, she tells us, they should cease to believe in 'sides'.

Writing? "It is much more important to be oneself than anything else" (p.145). And at the end she returns to her earlier theme of the change that will alter women's situation and opens doors: "For most, of course, go on bearing children, but so they say, in twos or threes, not in tens and twelves" (p.148). Writing in 1929, she both voiced the fundamental change needed for women and warned against the focus on blame and accusation which has dominated so much Feminist

---

humanity and of the failure to attend to our wholeness. Our offense is the abuse of the maternity of creation. Still, it is a book written for all.

writing since her time. The question is whether such a focus defeats creativity, as she suggests.

C. The Unhappiest Women

In *Either/Or*[125] Søren Kierkegaard has a short section titled, "The Unhappiest Man" (pp.. 179-188). It is a "take off" on Hegel's "The Unhappiest Consciousness," but Kierkegaard characteristically leaves that connection far behind in developing his own point. He examines the great examples of the 'unhappiest,' people, for example, Job, and asks: Why is he or she the unhappiest of all? Interestingly enough he rejects Job as the champion, because Job had a full life, and also because he struggled with God, which added significance to his life. Søren Kierkegaard's point is that a total emptiness of meaning is the source of ultimate unhappiness, so it is only the 'empty' person, one whose life is 'meaningless', that one can truly label 'unhappy', not simply one who is in conflict. If one has had a significant past, that cannot be taken away; for on the other hand, as long as one has hope for a future, all is not lost. The totally empty person is the only truly unhappy one.

Was Kierkegaard being 'sexist', without being warned of that sin, when he titled his section the unhappiest 'man?' Hardly; what he stated was applicable to both sexes. It marked a human problem: How to find significant content for one's interior life. Typical of Kierkegaard's thought, and the 'existentialism' which developed from it, the focus is on our interior and not our exterior life. Emptiness is a 'spiritual' matter, although this need not be taken in a strictly religious sense, much as Kierkegaard uses that setting himself. If women, and particularly recent feminists, are seeking liberation, are they not also seeking happiness through full and

---

[125] Soren Keirkegaard, *Either/Or*, trans. Lourie, 2 vols. (Oxford, Oxford University Press, 1946).

significant lives? How might Kierkegaard evaluate their goals?

Significantly, if one looks at most feminist agendas, they are connected with external matters. Even the press to remove prejudice from lesbian relationships, or to escape the traditional family structure, all are matters of observable quantities. If lesbian relationships become sanctioned and even consecrated, this tells us nothing about the interior life of any woman. When the women's suffrage movement achieved the vote, why did the movement almost stop? Was it because the exterior goal was achieved and women found that the interior feelings of significance they expected to achieve did not accompany it? Of course, the recent feminist agenda has a whole list of goals, so that it could be argued that universal suffrage did not bring happiness because too much remained undone.

But here one must pause and ask whether any external achievement one can name guarantees happiness or, in Kierkegaard's terms, is it fullness of meaning vs. emptiness. Examining prominent men in the past, many of whom were in the roles women now wish to occupy, we know that public, measurable accomplishment has not always correlated with private happiness. Significance on "the world stage" has not made the famous always personally secure. True, this is no reason women should be artificially barred from any office or success that their talents allow them to achieve. But it does mean that it may involve a cruel deception to think that leaving one role for another, no matter how glamorous, guarantees happiness and significance.

If the failure of the exterior life to mirror itself necessarily in interior happiness is a dilemma which the list of feminist goals faces, one answer is to "let them achieve and find that out for themselves." One usually deals wisely with novices in this way. Acquiring our own individual experience is the only basis upon which one can truly understand. You can speak of dilemmas, but they must be individually explored if they are to be realized. Yet this does raise for us Kierkegaard's question of 'significance'. What is it that makes a life full, and is there any way this can be assured? It also should cause us to look back on the feminist critique of both past and present women's roles. Even if blocked from some offices and roles, were all such women unhappy because the feminist goals which are sought today were then blocked for them?

Reading the history of women, it is clear that they have occupied many roles, although surely many avenues were also closed to them until recently, and even now their 'release' is not universal. In seeking new goals and opportunities, there is an underlying assumption that all who have not had these opportunities in the past vs. those who struggle to attain them in the present, have somehow been 'unhappy'. Kierkegaard's 'unhappiest women' theme tells us we cannot assume that. 'Happiness' is a matter of interior content, of significance which blocks out emptiness, and this cannot easily be detected from an exterior, public examination. Job, that patriarch of grief, is not made out to be unhappy by Søren Kierkegaard, because Job's life was full of significance, even if full of trouble too.

Those women who were restricted to home and family in the past, can we assume that all were 'unhappy' due to their limited opportunities? Of course, "ignorance has always been bliss," so that women whose societies never gave them a hint that other roles were possible could not yearn for unknown options, except of course the rare visionary whose spirit never is restricted by context. Now, when women want and often achieve other often more prominent public roles, there seems to be an assumption that all who do not seek these new goals will find themselves unhappy, while all who do will achieve fulfillment. We need to pause and ask Kierkegaard's question: What really makes a person fully unhappy? And conversely: what offers meaning, significance, content, and thus happiness, to a life?

Blocked as they have been from many public roles, it would seem that women have suffered more than men in history and thus inherit a larger load of negative unhappiness. But can that be true, if we do not equate acquiring external office with the fullness of internal meaning? Somewhat ironically, given feminist rhetoric, could it be that men in the past have subjected themselves to greater unhappiness as a group, just because they have been able to seek a wider range of options in public roles, thus attaching their personal happiness more closely to external achievement than women were once allowed to do? If this is in any sense true, the achievement of 'the feminist agenda' may in fact open at least some women to wider areas of personal disappointment.

One need not become so regressive as to start saying that every mother who gave birth to children and devoted herself to them thereby found herself fulfilled and thus happy. No. That may not have been every individual woman's goal. Furthermore, we know that not every child provides a fulfilled sense of meaning for either mother or father. To be consistent, we have to agree with Kierkegaard that the external success–or failure–of the mother's role in itself does not provide happiness. But neither does the failure in that role dictate unhappiness. That depends on meaning, on fullness, on significance, none of which follows necessarily from public success or failure.

But what Kierkegaard's exploration of 'unhappiness' should teach us is that we must try to discover the interior fullness or emptiness of each person's life, which can only be determined on an individual, not on a class/sex, basis. Thus, each of us must seek what every society offers us as available goals–and then struggle to increase our options, if significance for our lives lies not simply through rebellion. But happiness will still be an interior condition, one often not subject to external appraisal. Of course, occasionally our inner emptiness or fullness spills over into public form. Art and literature and philosophy are often so born. But Søren Kierkegaard teaches us to be cautious of any appraisal based solely on external criteria. Fullness–happiness–emptiness unhappiness–are where you find them. They do not automatically follow from either external success or suffering.

'Happiness' is not a physical fact but a 'spiritual state', of women and of men.

Who, then, deserves the title 'the unhappiest woman'? In fairness, since Kierkegaard awarded a prize in a pre-feminist era, we should award this century's prize to a woman. Unfortunately and ironically, this task is made difficult by the very hiddenness and suppression of women's history which feminists protest. Women who suffered do appear in the record but not in numbers comparable to men. And 'ordinary folk' were seldom recorded. So if it is hard to ferret out the 'significant' roles which women played which were not fully preserved in the record, it is also hard to see the full evidence of their suffering. But oh, you say, their subjugation was their suffering. That assertion is hard to document, since true suffering is internal, often private. It is easier to count public moaning, although if we did that men would be far ahead.

Based on any objective standard, men have suffered more in wars, imprisonment, hard labor. Yet we have agreed with Kierkegaard not to accept the public record but to look for evidence of an internal fullness, significance vs. emptiness. On this score, we've also agreed, since women strove for less public recognition, that they might have been more easily satisfied by what was already at hand. Increased opportunities also mean equally an increased opportunity for failure, as well as for success, as every ambitious man has learned. But if in an earlier era women were often ambitious for their husbands, their happiness was limited to what they could not fully control, as is the case with children. Again, the personal record we need to appraise is only occasionally filled in, largely by women writers or by male accounts when they are sympathetic recorders. Thus, the level of happiness-unhappiness remains impossible to discern as to its division between men and women.

To say that women have 'suffered more' requires a great deal of analysis. We know about the pangs of birth and childrearing. But in spite of the pain and health risks involved, it is hard to say that women as a whole found this to be the source of their unhappiness, any more than of their happiness. That women's political, economic, public roles have been blocked or held back–this we know to be true. Yet again Kierkegaard's thesis is that meaning/significance in life cannot be measured solely by external criteria. Thus, those who are overly restricted have not always been the most unproductive, just as those whose options and ranges are wide have not always, in fact many times seldom, been the world's models of 'happiness and fulfillment'. How is a human life, any life, fulfilled–that is the question we are left with.

Thus, it could be that the unhappiest women we seek, to balance Kierkegaard's male quest, still lies in the future. If past suffering was nevertheless sometimes individually fulfilling, a la Job, we need not recommend it as a goal. But our greatest examples of 'emptiness', Søren Kierkegaard's criteria for ultimate unhappiness, could still lie ahead. Just as we have become culturally disillusioned with the nineteenth-century optimism in 'progress', so we must beware about thinking that the completion of today's feminist agenda means an automatic increase in the level of women's happiness or meaningfulness. That did not happen with the women's suffrage movement. It succeeded, and still women discovered more sources of unhappiness. Let us eradicate them, if possible, so that the real sources of unhappiness, and the unhappiest women, can hopefully be discerned.

D. Women Intellectuals

In a popular book, Paul Johnson has given us a picture of *Intellectuals*[126] which is none too flattering. As feminists would be quick to point out, almost all of those whom Johnson considers are

---

[126] Paul Johnson, *Intellectuals* (San Francisco: Harper & Row, 1988). All page references are to this edition.

"western white privileged males," for example, Rousseau, Tolstoy, etcetera. Many are not 'pure philosophers'; in fact most are not, such as, Ibsen, Hemingway. However, his last investigation is of Lillian Hellman, surely an important novelist and writer. Given his account of the assets and liabilities of the intellectuals who have helped form our outlook in the Modern World, and given feminists hue and cry about being excluded, 'erased' from Western intellectual history, let's examine Johnson's "case against the 'intellectuals'." Then, given Hellman's inclusion and the lively rhetoric about 'feminist ethics' and women's 'other voice' which is different from males, how do male and female come out on this account? Can we find a gender differentiation?

Johnson begins by saying that he wants to examine "the moral and judgmental credentials of certain leading intellectuals to give advice to humanity on how to conduct its affairs" (p.ix). To anyone who has read Johnson's account, we know that we do not need to wait for his clear and almost uniform answer: "Beware! Don't trust them." Of course, we need not take those whom he considers as representative of 'all males', any more than feminists would want to use Lillian Hellman as a model for their cause. Yet we have a question about the 'intellectual's' perspective as such, and it is the case that women are arguing for admission to all ranks today, certainly to be included equally among the ranks of the 'intellectuals'. Thus, as women become intellectuals in increasing numbers, what change can we look for?

Without reviewing his whole fascinating account, what are the charges Johnson levels against 'intellectuals' that we need to be aware of? Why do they come up short in his evaluation? How might the arguments of feminists enter in here and alter our appraisal? (1) Johnson finds 'intellectuals' replacing priests in the Western World, but they go beyond telling us how to conduct our lives. "For the first time in human history... men arose to assert that they could diagnose the ills of society and cure them with their own unaided intellects" (p.1). (2) The Moderns pronounced harsh judgments on church and clergy. In contrast, they believed they "had a unique love of humanity and had been endowed with unprecedented gifts and insights" (p.2) to increase our felicity. Rousseau, his first figure, popularized "the cult of nature" while "delving into the inner self and producing it for public inspection" (p.3). He saw the evil nature of competition and recommended changing human nature.

But in Rousseau's life (3) Johnson finds self-pity and an overpowering egoism (p.10). Next Johnson notes a trait which comes to be his theme about intellectuals: (4) "Loving as he did humanity in general, he developed a strong propensity for quarreling with human beings in particular" (*ibid.*). He "tended to equate hostility to himself with hostility to truth" (p.11). He was vain, egotistical and quarrelsome. Importantly, (5) he was the first intellectual "systematically to exploit the guilt of the privileged" (p.11). Another characteristic appears: (6) "He was a superb self-publicist" (p.11). But (7) the truths Rousseau presents often turn out to be half-truths: his selective honesty is "the most dishonest aspect..." (p.17). On reflection, Johnson concludes: "intellectuals are as unreasonable, illogical and superstitious as anyone else" (p.27).

"Shelley believed that society was totally rotten" (p.98), so (8) feminists are not the first to denounce all that has gone before them (e.g., patriarchy) and to propose total reconstruction. Poetry, in his case, could alone "fill the moral vacuum and give to progress a truly creative force" (p.29). "Poetry lifts the veil from the hidden beauty of the world" (*ibid.*), just as some feminists propose. And (9) "a fundamental criticism of materialism" was to become the central criticism of nineteenth-century society (*ibid.*), as it has been for some feminists. (10) Poetry at its deepest level "is essentially moral and political" (*ibid.*), which tells us that all men have not claimed neutrality and objectivity for their views. The intellectual is to lead humanity to utopia on Earth. Yet again, Shelley "put ideas before people and his life is a testament to how heartless ideas can be" (p.31). (11) He could not see that anyone was "entitled to a viewpoint which differed from his own" (p.48), (now called Politically Correct Thinking). Shelley dearly wanted (12) "a total political transformation of society" (p.49).

For Marx, the evil elements in society were "the bourgeois class as a whole." The new redemptive force was the Proletariat (p.58). So (13) our 'salvation' lies in the ascendancy of a long-suffering, long-quiet (read 'silenced') group. Capitalism was the cause of great moral evil (read 'patriarchy'). Massive works by the intellect do not spring from the abstract workings of the brain; (14) "they are deeply rooted in the personality" (p.69), (read "eliminate the dualism of intellect and emotion"). He was filled with burning desire to create a better world, but (13) it always had an admixture of personal vanity (p.71). His heart is not full of love but of bitterness. Ibsen too concentrated on the problem of personal liberation, but he was more individualistic than Marx. "Liberation consists in securing for individuals the right to free themselves, each according to his particular need" (p.86).

The leading issue: (16) Is personal liberation "at bottom self-centered and heartless" (p.96), as Johnson felt it was for Ibsen. Again, he had an "inability to sympathize with people vs. ideas" (p.99). Yet few equaled him in presenting a woman's feelings; he is a pioneer of feminism. Still "he was a man of words, not deeds" (p.103). In a similar vein, Tolstoy came to believe that "he could effect a moral transformation of society" (p.107). He felt called upon at times to play the Messiah (p.114); but Johnson cautions: (17) "It is the curious delusion of intellectuals... to think that they can solve the perennial difficulties of human education at a stroke, by setting up a new system" (p.113). Hemingway is next; and here we see religion as the intellectuals' common target. He rejected his parents' religion, and he lived "in effect, as a pagan worshiping ideas of his own devising" (p.143).

In contrast, Johnson points out, Kipling was not an 'intellectual'; "he did not believe he could refashion the world by his own unaided intelligence. (18) He did not reject the vast corpus of inherited wisdom" (p.151). In Hemingway Johnson notes attribute no.6 again: "He had a striking talent for self-publicity" (p.153). Yet in spite of his veneration of a 'macho' image, "he shared with Kipling a varying of his habitual masculine approach with an uncomplicated and highly effective presentation of a female viewpoint" (p.161). However, when Johnson concludes by appraising Lillian Hellman, the comments are almost identical: she was one "to whom falsehood came naturally" (p.288). She was the first woman to achieve international status as a playwright. Yet she seems not to have brought any recognizable difference to her art due to her sex.

Johnson ends his exploration of "intellectuals in their Modern incarnation" with his theme, "The flight of reason." This fact is significant because some feminist theorists have heavily criticized their intellectual heritage as being overly rational and have argued for a larger role of emotion. But let us return to Lillian Hellman and an appraisal of how contemporary feminists might "check out" against our list of the 18 characteristics gleaned from Johnson's account. For Hellman, we have to say that she was 'pre-feminist', in contrast to its recently articulated forms, so her similarity to the male intellectuals in Johnson's analysis can be marked off to not "having her consciousness raised." This brings out one important question which we cannot answer: why did so few women prior to recent times seem to espouse feminist goals as they are presented today? Can this be accounted for simply by repression and by being "before their time"?

Certainly the majority of feminist writers: (1) exude a confidence that they have diagnosed society's primary here-to-fore-almost-unrecognized ills and that their intellectual analysis can provide a cure. Aside from the hostility which some (not all) feminists exhibit toward men, most claim (2) a love for all humanity and, more important, feel that their insight is "unprecedented." When it comes to (3) self pity and overpowering egoism, any appraisal of feminism must be uneven. There is self pity, of course; there must be due to the repression, even atrocities, women have suffered and with which the Moderns (although often themselves educated and privileged) identify. 'Egoism' is harder to assess, because many are genuinely "other concerned', but still our question is, "How many might fall into that trap as feminists increasingly follow the life of the intellectual?"

However, (4) is a trait which should give us greater pause. For, loving humanity in general (or at least 50% of it), how many among the swelling ranks of woman intellectuals "quarrel with human beings in particular"? We should stay alert, feminists should stay alert, to watch how those who rise in prominence treat the individuals around them. (5) When it comes to "systematically exploiting the guilt of the privileged," we are close to a core feminist theme. First, men have been the privileged class, they claim; next is white western culture, and so we face a very strong 'guilt trip' about 'silencing' or 'marginalizing' women and minority groups. But, you say, is not this burden of guilt deserved? Yes, of course, the history of dominant groups in their treatment of any minority is filled with enough 'harsh inequalities' to make many feel guilty. But the issue: Is their guilt 'systematically exploited'? That is, is the guilt so dwelt upon that it serves to distort our perspective in any way?

'Feminism' was born in the 'modern age', so its advocates understand the power of publicity; they must be (6) 'self-publicists'. They were often the radical students of the sixties and seventies, who learned about press coverage to their immense advantage. This skill ought not to be censored, you say, but admired, because it shows an awareness to conditions in the contemporary world and how any cause must cooperate with the media to achieve success. Right. But: does the publicity come to center on the individual as much as on the cause, and is it manipulated in any way to distort the opposition? If you reply that this is the world of politics and urge the feminist viewpoint that "the social is the political; no thought is neutral;

objectively is illusion," fine. Yet notice how easily this has and can become a totalitarian form of propaganda that shuts off debate.

A linked question: (7) is there 'selective honesty' or the use of half truths? Yet again, feminists accounts are not unaware of this. Women have been so 'erased' from history, so excluded, that they must rewrite history and over-stress women's unrecognized accomplishments in order to balance the record. That is understandable. But in the process, are the victims fairly presented, for example 'patriarchs', male views about women? Or is there any tendency to 'select the worst' and ignore a balance of views? Perhaps propaganda to promote a cause cannot be balanced, but Johnson has given us a warning in his analysis of how the use of half truths seems to affect the integrity of the user. And if Shelley believed his society was totally rotten, (8) many feminist attacks are not far behind. Of course, maybe this is simply true. But the issue is the dualism, the stark black and white portrayal, which is 'ironic' since philosophical feminists want most of all to overcome an inherited dualism.

Materialism often, although not always, is a villain for feminist attack (9). So we need to ask how much of this comes from feminist exploration of women's viewpoint and how much is at one with earlier points of view, for example, a utopian idealism now carried forward by new banner bearers. Poetry became moral and political for Shelley, (10) which is a perspective many feminists want to spread to all culture, sometimes particularly to education. There is no reason not to expand Shelley's insight (which is also partly Marxist based). But we might ask how much of this is predicated on the assumption that society needs radical transformation and, even more crucial, the claim that it is now feminist theory's time to lead this individual-societal metamorphosis. Of course, politicizing poetry/culture/ education is more questionable if individuals will not necessarily be revolutionized thereby.

After Johnson's list of the 'political vices' of intellectuals, we immediately face the claim of some feminist writers that women speak 'with a different voice'. But perhaps more important: the tirade (it can be called little else) against 'patriarchy' is specifically based on the claim that males have done a 'bad job' on writing/running the intellectual/social history and that a hearing of feminist views can help balance at least some previous inequities. God can be imaged as "mother, lover, friend"; social-individual relations can be based on mutual caring and not on hierarchies; confrontation and competition can be softened with mutuality and non-aggressive cooperation; the exploitation of nature replaced by a feeling of oneness with the world and the animal kingdom. 'Dominance' is linked to 'maleness', 'caring' to the feminine posture. If so, then Johnson's castigation of modern intellectuals plays into the hands of the feminist campaign for change.

However, the problems with this rejoinder are at least two-fold: (A) All women do not accept, or even necessarily represent, such an outline of feminist virtues. And these may be gender roles ingrained by society upon a narrow range of individuals and thus may not at all represent women in general. That is, they are 'stereotypes', that 'no-no' of feminist rhetoric. But more important, (B) feminine theorists are quick to perceive that arguing for women's 'different voice' is a two edged sword; because, (a.) women want to argue for their right and ability to be released from previous gender-assigned roles and so cannot uncritically accept this particular one, even if it is attractive. And, (b.) to admit to any series of gender related characteristics is to be subject to the ancient put-down, "stay in that role," whereas feminist liberation seeks release from women's past roles.

Thus, Johnson's challenge comes back full force: As women move into the intellectual domain in the increased numbers that they press for, will they be subject to the same list of "Achilles heels," as Johnson documents them for their male predecessors? If not, why not, except for appealing to some inherent feminine virtues long underplayed, which if stressed will steel women against, make them immune to, Johnson's list of corruptive practices. Yet, we have just said that not all women will want to be placed on some new pedestal of special virtue, even if constructed by feminist hands. Of course there is always the argument for feminist self-segregation, the withdrawal to male-excluded groups, as some have done. This cannot be an alternative for those who seek equal representation on the world's stage. But, some will say, there is a utopian alternative, a new egalitarian society.

We should not, they argue, simply accept the framework and the ground rules of the essentially male society as we have inherited it. To do so is to "sleep with the enemy." The structure of society and also of our personal relationships must be revolutionized, revisioned, in order to escape old corruptions now well recognized. The irony is that we run right into Johnson's major challenge: Can intellectuals, even a new breed of woman intellectuals, in fact change the world and human nature by the power of their ideas? If the answer given is 'yes', what evidence is there that this has now become possible, where there has been little evidence for it in the past? Christianity and Marxism offer attractive ideals, but there is no clear belief that societies have been formed which gave full embodiment to those ideals.

Most important: we come back to Johnson's underlying uneasiness. Intellectuals, those bent on the change in individuals and in societies in order to achieve greater fulfillment, have not acted in such ideal ways in their own lives. In fact, their record of treatment of those close to them is questionable and forces us to reconsider their stated aims. If Johnson seems to be offering a vast *ad hominem* argument against the person and not the ideal, we have to ask if, in any utopian vision of change, there is a connection between their ideals and their lives which we cannot avoid considering. If modern intellectuals used, even destroyed, other people in the pursuit of their goals, if their egos and personal quest for prominence seemed to come first, what guarantee can be offered that women intellectuals in pursuit of their noble goals will or can stay clear of such destructive pitfalls?

At this point we must consider Lillian Hellman. She achieved the recognition which many feminists now claim as women's right, one which it has been said was often wrongfully denied them by male exclusion. Yet being a woman did not seem to keep Hellman from embodying every unattractive symptom of "the struggle to get to the top." Can feminism so change the condition for achieving fame that future women can avoid Hellman's deceit? That remains to be seen, when statistics allow us to take stock of a generation of women intellectuals and appraise "how they got to the top and what happened to them there." Early "women at the top" are not much admired by today's feminists, for example, Margaret Thatcher, Golda Meir, Indira Gandhi etcetera. How, why, and will the new generation of aspirants be more ideal?

We have skipped over Johnson's characteristic traits of intellectuals outlined in nos. 11-18. But essentially those involve the details of politicizing all thought, fixation on one's own point of view, the suffering group as the instrument of our salvation, utopianism, the constant admixture of personal vanity and self-centeredness; all are based on a rejection of inherited philosophies, or at least projecting their radical transformation. Each of us, male or female, can take Johnson's map of pitfalls on the intellectual's road to ideal transformation and ask our cultural accountants for an audit of our books, once the history of recent feminism has recorded a sufficient track record. However, implicit in Johnson's critique is his conviction that all intellectuals can contract the disease whose symptoms he has diagnosed. Coupled with this is the suggestion that contemporary feminism is not so much 'post Modern' as 'very Modern' in many of its assumptions and tendencies.

Can they, can we, can any intellectual, escape the trap which Modern intellectuals have set for us and for themselves? One reply is that 'feminism' is far from uniform in its theory and in its offered proposals. 'All women' would not argue that they accept any of Johnson's (or my list of) 18 pitfalls, let alone all of them. Perhaps more important, few women, or even all 'feminists', would claim the title 'intellectual', or at least they would want to change its meaning. But we still must ask how many of Johnson's outlined traits do or might characterize today's growing numbers of women intellectuals.

These questions should be studied with both profit and with caution, I suggest. If you opt out of Johnson's description of intellectuals by maintaining your right to dissent and to exhibit 'difference' (both of which are Enlightenment goals), then ultra-democracy removes all possibility of uniformity, or at least it seriously weakens it, whereas united effort and agreement on principle is crucial to achieve reform.

This is the major dilemma of recent feminism: Is there an intellectual unity to be found in the 'sisterhood' of all women?[127] If so, their potential for power is unlimited, once a consciousness of this latent force is raised. But feminists are increasingly aware of diversity within their ranks, based on economics, race, class, etcetra. At the same time that everything 'male' has been castigated in a uniform manner (e.g., 'patriarchy') and western culture and history assumed to be uniform in its outlook due to the prominence of males whether in the church or in society, women are moving to grant increased diversity of perspectives within their ranks.

Yet still they often argue that 'privileged' males have a uniformity in their dominance that excludes both women and 'marginalized' males of many descriptions. The question of a totally egalitarian society arises as an "answer to Johnson's indictment." Will feminist intellectuals, can they, avoid eventually representing 'privilege', just as they claim males have who ascended or emerged

---

[127] See "50 Ways to be a Feminist," chapter I, note 32. Luce Irigaray, *This Sex Which is not One* (Ithaca: Cornell University Press, 1985).

to prominence? Libraries, art galleries, board rooms, even churches, and surely political parties, cannot give equal space to all. As we discover which women will be elected for 'privileged' attention (and surely some are now, e.g., Germaine Greer, Andrea Dworkin), then will these women simply be next century's privileged intellectuals and so become vulnerable to infection by "Johnson's disease"—as all before us, male or female, have been?

E. Post-Feminist Stories

How will novels be written in the future, once feminist proposals have taken hold? All the women characters will be portrayed as talented, virtuous, in rebellion against their suppression, and they will aim to achieve the top spots in every sector. All the men will be either hated patriarchs, torturers, rapists, hard-skinned warriors; or if they have been converted and repented for all their past sins and their guilt in being male, they will be ashamed to let it be known that they possess a penis and be intent upon seeing that all women have their every task shared. And the children, how will post-feminist writers portray them? Most will be unaware of sex differences; or if they are, they will be anxious to play it down. It will not be possible to tell boys from girls in games, and the boys will be particularly careful not to be thought aggressive. Each will, from the cradle on, support the feminist plan to revolutionize society and change individuals. None will feel he or she more talented or beautiful than another, lest hierarchies develop.

In the near future, how will we study all novels written B.F., 'before feminism', and what will tomorrow's children think of all the strange portrayals of the characters they read about? Will they be shocked to find some men portrayed as kind, loving, and forgiving, or will they simply dismiss it as patriarchal propaganda? If they think they detect any individuality among male writers and any failure among the women to speak "with a different voice," how will they explain the fact that the men portrayed seem to be so different from each other, such that it is hard to find any universal quality that unites their thought and disposition, in spite of the fact that each possesses a penis? Will they be shocked to find some women portrayed as selfish, vain, even destructive? But if so, will it be an even greater shock if some of the women portrayed in the romances seem actually to love the knights and to delight in being beautiful and protected and fought over. Worst of all, what will they do if, contrary to all expectations, it seems that some women actually embrace home and motherhood as if they loved it and wanted nothing else?

What happens to the glory, the tragedy, the pathos, the tapestry of incredible variance, when it is all reduced to the war between the sexes, with all the men/evil on one side? Cinderella, of course, does not worry about going to the ball in kitchen rags, because she has read about the 'beauty myth' and will not allow herself to be hoodwinked by the good fairy who thinks she should be 'gorgeous', that is, according to some fabricated standard. The prince will, of course, look for the lost kitchen maid just as eagerly as for the supposed dazzling beauty. He will fit a worn-out leather shoe on her foot, but she will reject him. Cinderella has professional plans and will not be tied down to any prince's castle.

Maidens in towers cannot dream of being rescued by handsome princes, nor princes be turned from frogs back into handsome men by a kiss, for that whole enterprise is 'sexist' and must be denounced. The struggle of the mind seeking truth amidst vast complexity is reduced to a simple opposition: all before feminism's rise is to be dismissed as 'patriarchy'. This relieves us of the mind-boggling problem of trying to fathom the unwieldy diversity and lack of singularity of all that men—and women—have thought or said or written or done. Time now divides into B.F. and A.F. Why? Because women's consciousness was not raised B.F., and they were duped into accepting monolithic male views of themselves. Now Feminist Enlightenment has come, which reveals that the earlier promised 'Enlightenment' was simply the product of patriarchy and the penis.

233

The struggle to know God is revealed to have been hopelessly distorted, even for the memorable women who pursued the divine quest. Except for early periods where the Goddess reigned, or in societies which were matriarchal, the original notions of the world as a female creation were censored out. The entire Judeo-Christian tradition, in spite of its stress on love and compassion and care for the suffering, proves to be entirely a product of a male co-opting of God. That mysterious unifying force, the penis, has controlled men's minds —and women's too until the era A.F. began. It is not that women's presence was not acknowledged B.F. To claim that would be impossible. But it is the fact that women were not prominent, controlling, defining the world in 'women's terms', which so upsets the Post-Feminists. History, therefore, cannot be accepted as received but must be revised.

However, the real test for the Post-Feminist era is to be found in the question with which we began: How will novels be written? Romance, that very popular genre, must be totally revamped. Trollope can no longer present his women as being nearly destroyed by their sometimes unexpressed love for a man. The heterosexuality which has dominated romance must be revised. But then there is the question of whether women or men can find their ultimate meaning in life in their selected partners, or whether no person is to be depicted as controlled by love for another. All literature has portrayed its characters—at least many of them—as searching for love in order to find fulfillment in their lives. But this tragedy of mistaken goals, or of non-fulfillment, will no longer be written.

How will storytellers portray "Camelot today"? Will it still be seen as "one brief shining hour" to be remembered, a time when peace and human harmony were achieved? Or will it be written off as another form of 'patriarchy' and castigated for the role it assigned to women? Can the central love plots be rewritten, or will it all be dismissed as so far in our archaic past that it is no longer even worth considering, let alone revising the plot. Just because men dominated the public scene, whatever the private power role of women, can romance no longer attract us as a human story or be the source of any inspiration? And perhaps more important: What about nursery rhymes and children's stories? Interestingly enough, looking at our inherited classical tales, women feature about as prominently as men. Surely Little Red Riding Hood is the heroine who suffered male harassment (at least I think the wolf was male). So all literature and story B.F., that is, in the Patriarchal Era, does not neglect women entirely. It is not that they are not there; we know that. We object to the role they are given to play.

In fact, once you move away from the political/economic scene, surely our literature, our stories move as much around feminine figures as around male. True, religious literature is slightly different. Because of its cultural role, men have tended to figure more prominently and to be the primary storytellers. But women mystics are legend, and it would be hard to conceive of religious history without the devotion of women. Certainly the history of the Black church would be quite different without its strong women, although the pastor/preacher's role tended to be male. As culturally linked, this was bound to be true, just as Jesus reflects his social situation, even when he preaches love and the equality of all before God. Still, the romance novel will undergo the most severe change, since women can no longer be depicted as love-dependent on men, although I presume men can still be portrayed as love-bound by women. "Goddess forbid" that we should discover that we are still dependent on each other, as Darwin noted in describing our Descent.

CHAPTER VII

The Human Dilemma

A. The Human Situation, The Human Problem, The Human Dilemma

We would, I think, all agree that insight into our personal situation comes in a variety of ways. As we read *Genesis*, many have seen their condition as outlined in that account of creation and the story of the fall. More recently, many read Camus's *The Fall* and use it as a source of insight. Freud gave us new appreciation for an old phenomenon— dreams—and it does not matter whether we "pledge allegiance" to the id, ego, and super ego as factually constituents of our psyche (as Freud wanted us to), or whether we use the unconscious as Jung did to open us to a much wider range of influence, the 'collective unconscious'. One does not need to be English to appreciate Shakespeare or Japanese to realize what Zen has to teach us.

Marx found the industrial revolution as an occasion to develop a new economic theory. His account has proved to be less than factually true, but many have understood human nature and the movement of history in terms of that analysis. It seems ironically necessary to claim the literal, factual truth of one's source of insight in order to accept the portion of truth it opens for us. Christians have burned heretics at the stake, Muslims issued death threats, and Marxists have slaughtered millions in the wake of their claim to insight via Marx. Feminists, we have argued, offer a major current source of insight, if we will but appropriate it. But we are blocked, at least for a time, if some insist that as a sex women offer an exclusive avenue to some forms of understanding.

It need not be factually true, we suggest, that the biological experience of being of the female sex in itself offers insight not otherwise available, or that it can only be appropriated by some particular group. Nor is it necessary, we argue, that only a literal belief in the factual truth of some one 'feminist' theory is the needed condition for appropriating its insight. In almost every case in human history, the would-be prophet witnessed human suffering. Then, in responding to it and illuminating our condition (Jesus, Buddha, Moses, Mohammed), millions have been able to appropriate that insight in a variety of ways. No single orthodoxy has resulted. Marx was distressed by the cry of suffering people, and a theory was born in his response which millions from many races, cultures, and conditions have used as a guide.

Feminism, in its variety of theories and multiple practical goals, offers a contemporary path to insight, provided that, unlike those theories before it, it does not insist either on doctrinal conformity or that its insights belong to only one group (e.g., to one sex). Of course, since that same tendency to orthodox, strident, militant insistence on conformity has gripped every source of religious, philosophical insight we can name, perhaps we must heave a sigh of resignation and allow Feminism to go through its phase of vivid expression by rejecting theories other than its own, for example, insight offered earlier by males. Is there no alternative to beginning with theoretical warfare?

Some insights have at least attempted to be non-exclusive, non-dogmatic, for example, Gandhi and passive resistance, Quakerism. But the irony is that these groups do not seem to have wanted to assume political power, as Roman Catholicism and Marxism did. But some radical feminists do not seem content with anything less than a total change in society's structures, political, educational, religious. The experience of history we cite seems, paradoxically, to suggest that in order to revolutionize society, even in religion and education, one must seek power, even if one does so by non-violent means. An oppressive force is opposed only by an equal and opposite force. But history also seems to report that, except for small ideal communities or individuals who withdraw from the centers of influence, power requires doctrinal unity as a condition for it to gain control.

Let us ignore for the moment the question of whether there is in fact any doctrinal agreement between "all women," or whether there are only groups of related theories. Let us also ignore for the moment the issue of whether power corrupts, so that ironically if women as a sex gain more power, this in itself will instill internal corruption in the movement, a phenomenon we have just seen working itself out in world Communism. To avoid this classical scenario, one must claim to have discovered the origin of sin (e.g., private property, patriarchy) and to know how to prevent its corruptive intrusion (e.g., public ownership of the means of production or the rejection of all patriarchal structures).

The obvious villain in many feminist accounts is male dominance, sometimes symbolized in 'Patriarchy' when it is used as a term of abuse.[128] But most other theories of evil have found corruption's origin in no one sex. Feminists do not like the *Genesis* account of the snake and Eve and Adam's acquiescence in their fall. But Adam's lament, "The woman did give it me and I did eat," has long been accepted as Adam's "cop out" and that both are equally guilty. Adam blames Eve who blames the snake, in our traditional attempt to escape responsibility. Can Feminists truly convince us that male dominance is the sole origin of evil and women the source of good, so that the Feminist, any feminist, revolution will lead to societies without sin?

In order to consider this central, crucial question, we should first "back up" and list what insights we can attribute to recent Feminist interests and their leaders and the rising tide of response. As others

---

[128] Cynthia Cockburn, *Machinery of Dominance Women, Men and Technical Know-How* (Boston: Northeastern University Press, 1988).

Research finds women still filling relatively routine occupations. A misunderstanding of technology is partly at fault. There are processes of tremendous power sustaining the sexual division of labor. Technology is a medium of power, but the author acknowledges women's reluctance to take up technical careers. The book then moves on to outline a detailed study in Britain on the sexual division of labor.

have done before them, how have their theories, arguments, proposals opened human nature to new insight so that they in our era have performed for us what the Darwins and Copernicuses have done before them? Moses found a suffering people in captivity in Egypt and every Jew still celebrates the Exodus. From what bondage has the Women's movement freed those who are female, and is it as equally available to all, just as other revealing insights have been?

Some Feminists borrow a term from Marx/Hegel: "consciousness raising." Whether in every instance these arguments, claims, and reinterpretation of classical texts (e.g., the Bible) have made us see exactly what feminine authors intended, they have our attention, and consciousness has been raised for many, whether pro or con. To that which raises one's consciousness to new levels (which is the traditional role of the study of politics, education, philosophy, and religion), one often testifies and forms a bond that is hard to release. But if in addition to general consciousness-raising, that is, to become aware of women's issues and women's condition, what particular insights can be attributed to Feminism in the way that Freudian analysis opened dreams for our understanding?

First, as I think most Feminists would agree, is the importance of sex. Freud of course pointed this out too, but his theories led to no human liberation movement, only to individual therapy, important as that is. Following hard on the heels of the significance of sex in culture and in theory comes the stress on the distinction between biological sex and gender roles. We have always known that sex is open to certain varieties, but the Gay and Lesbian political/public movements have made this evident. However, even where we note a tendency to stress how much sex roles bind us, the separation of gender from sex makes us see a much greater flexibility in the roles each sex may occupy and a far greater overlap in function than biological sex seemed to allow.

Second, some oppressions are easier to detect, so that if sex or race is used as a tool of subjection, it is more obvious. Of course, as might be expected in the case of both sex and race, elaborate theories have been developed over centuries to justify such obvious discrimination. Interestingly enough, both sex and race have been breaking loose from centuries of discrimination and seeking to establish individual status on the basis of quality and performance. Obviously, incompetence and wide differences in talents and capacities remain. But to break established barriers, one must argue on the basis of the special qualities attributable to sex and/or race, although ironically this reverses the original discrimination by asserting universal compensating privileges.

Oddly, many other forms of discrimination and repression are harder to detect and even more difficult to oppose. Religious preference is sometime known by its exterior signs and so can be controlled by authorities or used for exclusion. Generalized qualities can be attributed to nations, to races, and even to religions, but within any group there are numerous exceptions. Nevertheless, generalizations can be used to exclude the non-conformist. However, when we get to economic, philosophical, theoretical qualities, reigning orthodoxies are harder to combat. Any artist, writer or even worker knows that he/she may face deaf ears if he/she challenges reigning theories or practices. Every new theory or novel cultural form has started with little external support that it can appeal to.

If it is hard to fight prejudice based on theory, in the case of sex we are offered a much more visible, discernible example of prejudice. The irony here is the claim of some Feminists to possess a special quality simply due to their sex.[129] If sex (or race, or religion) is

---

[129] Dorothy E. Smith, *The Conceptual Practices of Power: A Feminist Sociology of Knowledge* (Boston, Northeastern University Press, 1990).

Any evaluation of this work faces two problems: (1) It is so couched in jargon that it is hard to translate into clear sentences; (2) It's major, constant premise is that women's experience, and thus language, are unique, evidently something common to all women that was not allowed expression until recently. Opposed to this is the "man's world" in which women cannot speak correctly and have not been heard. This assumes that the "man's

wrongly used to block out whole classes without evaluating each individual, any claim to group advantage ironically builds upon the same false generalizations used by the oppressive forces. This brings us to "the human situation," which the Women's Movement has made us sensitive to in our era: Since no generalization based on sex, race, etcetera holds universally for all members, how does any individual gain recognition for his or her unique qualities?

Of course, what we must admit is that individuals hide their incompetence or lack of performance behind just such universal classes, for example, "the master race," ethnic or economic superiority. Some groups do perform better than others, at least at certain times (e.g., the Greeks, the Romans, the Egyptians, etc.). Then, instead of arguing on the basis of individual or group quality

---

world" is likewise uniform and universal to all who are male. But there are so many voices in our past that to unify them all as 'male' seems to defy credibility. All new voices have had to find a mode of entry into established ways, and both men and women have searched for not-easy ways to innovate.

Women's voices (intellectually) may have been undernourished (p. 3). Now is the time to assert them. Smith speaks often of "the relations of ruling" (p. 4), but it is hard to give this phrase meaning, except to say that reigning useful categories have always had to be opposed in order to establish any new subtlety of thought. It is hard to see how this differs for men than for women, since the vast majority of men do not speak the uniform intellectual language of all male authors. 'Individual experience' is stereotyped when it is put in bureaucratic language, true enough. Sociology, as a generalizer, does alienate its mode of consciousness "from those of people's lived experience" (p. 7). Could it really be otherwise? There is a disjunction between women's experience and sociology (chapter I), although the issue still is to define this distinctive experience of women in a clear way.

Sociology is itself ideological—that is the theory; but any intellectual enterprise must be, must it not. If sociology needs revolutionizing, as is claimed, then propose it as other innovators have tried to do before. The claim that women's experience is changing—that much is clear. But perhaps it is not so clear that women in different roles have not been understood. But is there any such thing as "women's standpoint" form which sociology can start? What this is has not yet been made out adequately. There is a difference between lived experience for the individual and theoretical explanation, that has always been true, for both men and women. Have social concepts alienated women from their own experience? That charge still needs to be made out.

at a given time, one tries to cling to virtue by claiming group superiority, (e.g., the "ugly American" syndrome). If oppression comes by "universal put-downs" (all women, all Jews are...), and if what we want is individual appraisal, but if one also clings to an outmoded group superiority or claims advantage by possession of some universal quality (e.g., "Black is beautiful"), we face the human dilemma.

The human problem, then, is how to gain attention for individual appraisal, for development of one's potential, for new viewpoints, in the midst of both positive and negative pressures. Any group pressure wants us to conform to some stereotype (all Feminists, all Jews are..., etc.), and so they hem in the individual. The negative pressures are discriminations and prejudices based on race, sex, or even ideological position. The "human problem" is how to escape all universal characterizations in order to be what we each are, he or she, able to be. However, we must admit that the weak and the timid seek to hide behind the protection of groups, those who are afraid to stand alone and to let the individual be.

Women, then, as a sex are in no different situation than any being is who faces the human problem except that, like race, sex can be used as a means to block them and history substantiates this exclusion. However, as blatant sexual prejudice begins to break down, like racial arrogance ("We Germans are good; why shouldn't we admit it?" said a mild-mannered friend of mine) an opposite stress on the advantage, in fact sometimes a claim to exclusive privilege, appears. Although this may set right a former imbalance that has blocked women's advance, it has a side effect of thwarting impartial individual appraisal of performance by appealing to a claimed universal special quality. The human problem is exacerbated as much by over-assertion of special qualities naturally inherent in the group as it is by prejudice that appeals to some supposed universal inferiority.

At this point the human dilemma emerges again. This "dilemma" is that there is no sure way for any human being to avoid prejudice and guarantee the recognition of individual talent, particularly if novel ideas or practices are involved. This is just as much due to "positive prejudice," that is entrenched advantage and claimed privilege which pushes to preserve its own advantage, as it is to a prejudice based on supposed human inferiority due to some universal "negative quality," for example, sex, race and religion. Thus, every human being is in the dilemma of having advantages pressed against him or her not based on individual talent and accomplishment (e.g., "The boss's son" syndrome; the family connection). We all face denials not based on any quality appraisal but which are simply used to keep some group back from individual achievement.

The Feminist movement has made it crystal clear, as any movement must at its inception, that women have been unnecessarily discriminated against due only to their sex. But this is not the same as to say that all women can now claim recognition for unusual qualities that their group specially possess. Of course, any sex or any race or any religious group has certain qualities which make them distinctive, such as, bearing children, athletic prowess, intelligence, or a special religious sensitivity. But these qualities may be a "drag" as well as an advantage. We need to ask if any physical function or group character in itself can assure success.

If the Feminist movement has succeeded, that is succeeded in proving to us that we all face the human dilemma, have women suffered no more than any other members of a class or group? The answer, as Feminists have loudly announced, is "yes," they have. Why, then, if we are all trapped in the same dilemma, have women been held back more than others? Because their sex has subjected them to special handicaps by being obvious, which only now are being partially redressed. As has been stressed—menstruation, pregnancy, birthing, nursing, and the trials of hysterectomies, the special restrictions of child caring and rearing—until relief recently became available, all these special factors put women at a disadvantage in the general competition.

Members of subjugated races or peoples have also been held back, so that even the most child-restricted women in an "advanced society" may have an enviable position compared to women in the more poverty afflicted areas of say Africa or Asia.[130] What has happened is that birth control and safe abortion, for women in societies offering these choices have given those women an advantage of some release from "natural" burdens. Although some prejudiced remarks have depreciated women's intelligence and

---

[130]Lois Beck and Nikki Keddie, ed. *Women in the Muslim World* (Cambridge, MA and London: Harvard University Press, 1978).

As the women's movement has developed in its more recent incarnation, few books could be more important to explore than this one. All feminists agree that in the United States the movement began with the middle-class. There are good reasons for this, but the point is the use of 'women' must be expanded worldwide. And the Islamic world is both considered "backward" on women's rights and little known directly in the West. As we learn about Middle Eastern women, our perspective increases. We learn that, for example, in the Middle Eastern traditional family, which plays a crucial role, there is a preference for a bride's virginity. Often women are involved in heavy labor, which is not considered so common in the West. They work longer hours and receive lower wages. Marriage is social, not individual, and the family's strength is still equated with large numbers of sons. A mother gains status through her sons.

Nomadic tribes still exist and nomadic women work very hard. Sometimes women do nearly all the physical labor. Boys and girls do not play together; men and women do not really mix. Contacts between women and unrelated men are quite limited. As most of us do not understand, veiling and the seclusion of women began as a sign that a man could afford servants, although these practices have spread to the lower and middle classes. Women in urban jobs are increasing, but it is still a low number. 'Work' does not mean 'liberation either. Women's schooling and equal rights are not seen as serving a useful function in such societies. For all that women in the industrial West still lack, reading this heavy volume makes us see how far there still is to go for so many.

See also: Virginia Fabella and Mercy Amba Oduyoye ed., *We Dare to Dream* (Hong Kong: Asian Women's Resource Centre for Culture and Theology and the EATWOT Women's Commission in Asia, 1989).

Thomas P. Fenton and Mary J. Heffron, ed., *Women in the Third World* (Maryknoll, NY: Orbis Books, 1987).

Ada Maria Isasi-Diaz and Yolanda Tarango, *Hispanic Women, Prophetic Voice in the Church* (San Francisco: Harper and Row, 1988).

professional competence, where education and opportunity are available, any such insensitive "put down" can be nullified. Still, women may require further release from the burden of childbearing and confinement to home care. The average wife in an Indian village does not have such options, where large families are the norm and educational opportunities still restricted.

Because all of us are born into a world of both prejudice and privilege, it is difficult to easily detect the obstacles and the advantages we face. Those born to advantages take them for granted. Those born to prejudice often take them as insurmountable obstacles; they seem too much for any man or woman to oppose. Marx raised the consciousness of the working class in order for them to see their potential power. Christianity told its followers they were the children of a God who loves them. The Buddha preached that release from suffering could be achieved. Lincoln wanted to free the slaves, and Martin Luther King, Jr. preached about a dream for the Black oppressed. The Women's movement takes its place in the line of these "liberators," telling its people they can be free—if they try.

However, all such assertions come with their price. The Marxist revolution; belief that God loves you in spite of suffering; confidence that inner oppositions are not insurmountable; the claim that a subjugated race can move to realize its potential—in each case some factors still operate to hold us back, as those who have pursued any avenue for release know. Thus, how to overcome that "restraining drag" is our first question. In women's case, the release from restriction to childbearing is a first answer. But just as all slaves did not want to be free, or just as all Christians do not follow their master's instructions, so all women may not want to compromise their "child centeredness" in order to realize achievements in other areas.

We encounter "the final dilemma," then, when we discover that some, perhaps many, are either not willing to pay the price for their release or do not realize what is required of them in order to do so. It is not possible to distribute information equally or to rouse everyone, no matter for what group or cause. Individual gain always stands as a more obvious alternative to any abstract promise of group release. Every Black who makes it to the top does not seek the release of all Blacks. In the case of Marxism, the success of the cause may be connected to the use of violence. But if it takes force to break restraining bonds, the Feminist movement is restricted from this by having vocally opposed what they term the male tendency to violence and aggression. Are peaceful, non-violent revolutions possible? Individually, perhaps. For the masses involving half the human race, this is hard to envisage.

Thus, Feminists by their call to sisterhood,[131] by their accusations of Patriarchy, by their stress on Women's History, have made vivid for us the obstacles to release they have faced. But as the movement develops diversity and fails to unite all women to a single program (see Preface) we begin to realize, once again, the difficulty of the human situation and the dilemmas which confront us. As women are forced to make choices about children and motherhood versus professional/artistic roles, they raise for us all an awareness that freedom and fulfillment always come at a price. Violence, if it is rejected as a means, always gives repressive forces an advantage, against which we must either struggle or resign ourselves to a lesser role.

---

[131]Marcia Cohen, *The Sisterhood: The Inside Story of the Women's Movement and the Leaders Who Made it Happen* (New York, Fawcett Columbine, 1988).

It is edifying, for anyone studying current Feminist literature, to read the history of the Movement. This large volume (445 pp.) does a detailed and yet easily readable account, focusing around the biographies of its leaders, e.g. Betty Friedan. Cohen is a writer and editor, so the account is both lively and complete. However, she does a careful job of outlining the tensions and "squabbles" of leaders, the various directions the movement should take, and of how it moved ahead in spite of its division.

B. Popular Culture and Human Fulfillment

Susan Faludi's *Backlash*[132] rests on two major assumptions, and these could undermine her thesis in spite of massive documentation: (1) She takes the media, popular culture, and political intrigue as the main evidence for "the undeclared war against women." But how reliable have the media ever been as a key to our understanding? Movies, popular culture—we are surrounded by trash. All but the discerning must pick their way carefully through a vast outpouring, all the while looking for a grain of truth and an honest reporter. (2) Sensationalism sells. Authors seek fame, film makers seek a fortune, politicians an office; each must catch public attention, and that is seldom done by careful appraisal and calm analysis.

If a woman was spared all this adversity in the privacy of her home, the public arena subjects her to the same distortions that all who aspire are open to. To seek public power and attention is to invite distortion. Purity of motive is not common among power seekers. And Faludi herself seems to fall prey to the "vast conspiracy" theory, when all that may be happening is that women are being welcomed to "the way the race is run"—and won. (3) Moreover, she clings to a universalism about women which can be used against women too. What may actually be happening is the surfacing of the diversity that exists among all peoples, the cracking apart of a universalism for 'women' that some originally claimed—or hoped for.

Popular culture is, I believe, no place to assess the possibility for human fulfillment. The pressures which our culture places upon us need to be questioned if we are to ask where fulfillment lies and from whence it comes. Just as the assertion of "human rights" first came from male political reconstructionists, so as women press for, and hopefully gain, their rights for themselves, it pays us to look back on

---

[132]See Susan Faludi, *Backlash*, chapter II, note 55.

our cultural and religious history. We ask: Where have men claimed to find fulfillment so that women can "follow suit" in seeking it for themselves, once they have become co-workers on the public scene? All men have not thought alike; all men have not held similar ambitions. Childbirth and public restrictions long held women off the center stage of politics and economics. But all men who are operative there have not proclaimed prominence and power to be an automatic good. We need to re-examine all the world's religions, philosophies, study St. Francis, Florence Nightingale, the Buddha, the Shaker communities, and the monastics.

Those who do not merit public envy or public adulation often imagine the 'stars' they admire to be happy. Money, office, and leadership roles offer acknowledged attractions. But biographers would have no popular audience if a careful study of the immortals of culture and finance did not often reveal a dark side. As German folk stories often depict, and as Jung argues, each personality has a "shadow," a Mr. Hyde to its Dr. Jeckel, a Judas among the disciples. If the lack of public spotlights have made women seem immune from this fault and men the sole possessors, the individual struggle we must constantly wage to control self-corruption now appears as the shadow on the Women's Movement's legitimate agenda.

The "have nots" always imagine "the haves" to be happy. But that justly famous novel, Theodore Dreiser's *The American Tragedy*,[133] exposes the illusion of this supposition. So if women claim for themselves all the powers and the offices which men have dominated as their exclusive road to happiness, we may be rewriting *The American Tragedy* free of sexual bias. Women can become disillusioned, subject to unintended corruptions, too. This may help explain the aversion of most feminists to focus on women who have

---

[133]Theodore Dreiser, *The American Tragedy* (New York: Signet Classic, New American Library, 1964).

been politically powerful in the past as role models, the powerful Queens, the Prime Ministers. From their weak estate, they project carrying private virtue into public office. Except that they give birth and men do not, why should women be any less subject to a distortion of their motives and to a blindness in their perceptions than men have been? True enough, once released to compete, women can duplicate men's powers. But are they immune to the blunders which many men have made? Probably not, once they stop rocking the cradle.

Underdogs join together more easily. Is Faludi's main lament over the splintering of a projected unity of purpose as women rise and also over an already transient splintering of universally held goals? Men have faced adversaries waiting to cut them down for centuries. Political intrigue was rife in universities, board rooms, and political parties before women demanded entry. Once the door is at least partially opened, did women feel they would not be subject to the same demeaning blasts men have fought against, in art and in literature as well as in politics, for centuries? What Faludi documents as 'backlash' is the same attempt to get the better of one's competitors, now generously extended to include women in the distortions they employ.

"Good news is no news," a successful reporter snapped at me when I asked why stories seemed to focus on the negative rather than the positive side of a new religious movement I was researching. A *New York Times* editor, in reading the text of his story to me for comment replied, when I commended him on the fairness of his presentation, "but I can't guarantee what the editors upstairs will do to it before it is printed." Sure enough, his calm text was there in print, but it was "spiced up" with a series of 'sensational' bits added by the editors. These actually did not fit the context of the story, as others later commented to me, but what of accuracy must we sacrifice to get attention in the media race? Popular culture runs on sensationalism, else tabloids and "yellow journal" publications would not do so well financially.

Faludi documents the sensationalism, thus the distortion, of the gains by the Women's Movement. Only a few writers have the time or even care to be precisely accurate. Women, by the pressure they have mounted and which Faludi ends by urging them to continue, open themselves to popular distortion, exposé treatment and sweeping universal claims which probably couldn't be true, given human diversity. Socrates was not elected to public office for urging young Athenians to challenge reigning views. But in point of fact, few care to seek out the truth and even fewer struggle to express it. The Sophists were far more popular in Socrates' day. "How long, Oh Lord, how long?" When can we hope to appraise the Women's Movement fairly?

The accurate history, the 'truth' about feminism cannot be written for some time. Certainly we should expect to find final truth neither in the media, ingenious as they are in their contrivances, nor in the popular culture. Plato's *Dialogues* would be a box office bust if cinematized. Politicians, artists, writers all must wait for the passing of time before their place in, or their absence from, "the court of the immortals" can be agreed upon. True, we have a rash of "women's histories" which are intended to right the asserted "imbalance" in the historical record. Many of these are admittedly polemical in their intent, not 'impartial' history but rather designed to further women's present agenda. Thus, we cannot claim 'truth' for these specially selected accounts until they are set in the context of the whole human story of the era as it is reported in our received accounts. 'Truth' is a prize not easily attained and has always been rare in its appearance.

Had Faludi studied Hegel at Harvard, she would have learned that he thought backlash, the negative side to his 'dialectic' of history, the antithesis to any thesis, absolutely essential to the eventual production of truth and to promoting advance. We may no longer share Hegel's basic optimism that, in spite of its destruction (and he stresses this), negative reaction is the essential fuel to progress—and Faludi uses it in just that way in her conclusion. Still, the spotlight on women, one

251

which is necessary at this stage of their advancement, must be broadened to set women within the general human story. How many men in the past were also denied the rights and privileges which women found themselves excluded from? How much of women's, or any individual's, advancement shared the fate of our common human condition in its time?

When slavery was accepted, women were not the only slaves, and they perhaps even received fairer treatment in some instances, in spite of "the rape of the Sabine women." When there were serfs, peasants, common people, and when kings or generals or dictators hold all power, how did the majority fair when both sexes were under repression? In general servitude, were men and women more united then than they now are when the individual's rights can be asserted? Does liberty exact its price by working against human unity? When someone like Virginia Woolf uses words expressively, powerfully, we catch a glimmer of the hard fought insight which attaining truth requires and then provides. But we should not expect to find this, except rarely, in popular culture or in the commercial media. The television camera seldom focuses on truth-as-such, although it adds immensely to available information.

"Eternal vigilance is the price of freedom" or cultural advance—else empires, whether political or economic, would not rise and fall. Envy dogs the steps of any who succeed; backlash was not invented for women; it is sexually non-discriminatory; it attacks all those whose prominence we wish were ours. Marilyn Monroe, Judy Garland, Virginia Woolf were not forced to suicide by male backlash against their powerful presence. They felt the instability, the unrelenting pressure to perform for applause; they shuddered under the terrors that afflict most creative talent, the weakness of the human spirit to withstand constant pressure to perform.

Success breeds division, whether among the Beatles or in a creative partnership. General Motors feels a backlash against its power just as the Women's Movement does. Japan rises from the ashes; American power, whether military or cultural, often breeds dislike. Women are not immune to the barely hidden glee those on the rise feel when their competitors are thought to fail or to collapse under negative pressure. The war between the sexes is an ancient enterprise, but it is rarely the most destructive threat we face. Welcome to "Darwin's World."

C. The Significance of Life, the Simple Things in Life

If the Women's Movement offers us a fresh perspective on many, if not all, of the important questions in human existence, one of them certainly is: What gives a human life meaning? In an earlier time, the right to vote, to hold property, to be considered a full 'citizen', to have equal access to education—these were clear goals for women that paralleled the pressure for "the rights of man." True, all men had not always possessed these rights, and millions still are blocked from them. But as we rose up to press for 'equality' for all men, it was logical that women, as they gained freedom from childbirth and uncontrolled pregnancy, should follow their own quest for an equal share of democracy, of equal opportunity. However, once any goal one seeks is achieved, the unexpected question comes with success: Does that in itself give life the desired significance?

We know of course that slavery of any kind, whether political, sexual, alcohol or drug-related, does not allow us "a room of one's own," the room to fulfill ourselves. But once opportunity is opened up, oddly, we find that such release in itself is seldom fulfilling. In perhaps realizing this unconsciously, the Women's Movement, even in the lands of the greatest existing individual opportunity, has wanted an equal share in all the offices of power and privilege and leadership. There is nothing wrong with this in itself, except that millions of women in more deprived circumstances would settle for much less. "The power game" should be open for all to play, except we know that only a very few can win and that it always has involved a struggle which demands a single-minded concentration and acquired skill in manipulating "the rules for access." Not all can be presidents of a country or of a bank, and we know that the ambitious climber often uses any means available to block an opponent of any race or sex.

"Welcome to the land of multiple personal disappointments." Although like every teenager who explores social relationships, we cannot expect women to abandon social, economic, political, or church "mountain climbing" until they have tried it for themselves. Of course, as with their male competitors in this high-stakes game, a few—unfortunately a very few of either sex or of any race—will emerge as historical figures, as heroes and heroines in our memory, as fathers and mothers of our country or of their bank. Only a few will give themselves for a higher cause or for others as much as for themselves. Such objects of our appreciation and adulation are not many. What of "the teaming masses yearning to be free"? Can anyone expect life to be fulfilled except by receiving the gold medal at the power Olympics? Is it even to be considered, as women press for "equality of prominence," that significance could lie in the little things in life, not in the big, and so lie within everyone's reach?

Par Lagerkvist won a Nobel prize in literature, but not for writing about Swedish nobility or film makers. His novel, *Barabas* is most widely-known, and much of what he wrote has a religious tone or undercurrent, although he was far from conventional in his approach. He writes of simple folk as he knew them in rural, southern Sweden. Although presented as a novel, *Guest of Reality*[134] is admittedly semi-autobiographical. All of his writing centers around the search for human meaning, the problems of love and destructiveness, the enigma of the human soul. However, it is interesting to consider the conditions of his own life and, in this case, the way in which he

---

[134]Par Lagerkvist, *Guest of Reality* (London, Quartet Books, 1989). All page references are to this edition.

portrays women in his writing. Of course, in his *The Sybil* the main figure is a woman at the center of religious ecstasy and destruction. But in *Guest of Reality* his women are simple country folk, very simple.

The surroundings in which he grew up were non-literary, non-intellectual. Despite the fact that he became estranged from this background and lived abroad for years, he does not paint his fictionalized characters as lacking because they were neither literary nor 'cultivated'. They had no need of it. Their existence was so rich that they required nothing over and beyond. Poverty was combined with spiritual certainty. For all this, and for all of Lagerkvist's inability to live that way himself, he portrays his mother in masterful tones. "There was nothing unreal or remarkable about her," he reports, "she was always seeing to things in the kitchen or in one of the rooms, chatting with the children..." (p. 7). There were six. He paints himself as "a loner," unable to join in. Yet he reports: "There was an intimacy between all in the family which held them together and separated them from the outer world" (p. 16). We know, or we can learn, where the seats of power and prominence lie. But is it so simple as that life's only significance is to be found in our success there?

The family Lagerkvist portrays is not 'happy' in the "Left Bank," "Greenwich Village" sense of that word. Anders, the youngest (taken to be the author) says of his father: "He always went about serious and at times as if oppressed...the melancholy part of his being held him back" (p. 18). Certainly he did not seek "full sexual satisfaction," in the modern sense, as his goal in life. Cultural roles were defined rigidly for him, but this did not spark rebellion. And grandmother: "She could never rest, always must have had something to do and so her work was never finished" (p. 31). "And while with her one seemed to see everything very clearly, and that gave one a special secure feeling" (p. 33). Of grandfather: "His aim in life had been to fear God...He had a tranquillity that nothing could disturb" (p. 37).

Of course, it would be hopelessly romantic to think that every person confined to "the simple things" as a result finds his or her life full of significance. Still, the reality is that those few who rise to prominence and influence, culturally, economically, or politically, are not necessarily personally satisfied. We know this to be so by reading "exposure" biographies and by our glimpses into the inner lives of the rich and famous. Thus, those who wish to seek prominence should certainly do so and have their "consciousness raised" to realize both the potential in their lives and to seek removal of all social prejudice and legal blocks to their progress. However, no one should "go for it" on the assumption that goal-achievement in the public sense will automatically make his or her life seem full of significance. Neither, of course, will being restricted to "simple things" ensure it. 'Significance' seems to lie in how one deals with simple things and people, or prayer and beautiful people, not in the external situation.

The basic decision for each individual, male or female of any race, is whether the pursuit of the top offices, political, economic, artistic, is to be one's aim. Or is your focus to be on the small, on the unpublicized aspects of life and people? "All things great and small"—one must decide which is the focus. Of course, one may argue for balance and seek to combine public eminence with private virtue. It is not that this cannot be done; it is just that it is both difficult and rare. The public domain tempts one to unethical behavior in order to compete successfully. It also forces one necessarily to concentrate on himself or herself, since eminence cannot be achieved in any sector without intense awareness of one's personal role, combined with a calculated stress and an exhibition of one's talents—or even an exaggeration of them. Hubris is often the result, and then "the simple things" are trampled upon.

Does any of this indicate that the gods of the recent Women's Movement are somehow "wrong"? Should they not press for equality in every public sphere? Should Feminists abandon the attempt to find significance "in the fast lane," in the acquisition of power and influence? Not at all. If fixed social roles once held them back, if the role of "mother" need not limit them as it did before, if economic and legal bars have in many cases been lowered, there is no reason for any person not to seek what she or he finds attractive.

But one might consider what can add significance to life, and it may well be that this will vary from individual to individual. However, we should admit that the non-prominent might easily find their lives still significant, even if they are invisible within the masses, 'marginalized' to use the current catch phrase. Of course, the "insignificant" people are not guaranteed a feeling of significance simply by living unnoticed. It surely is the case that 'success' does guarantee visibility—just not necessarily a feeling of personal 'significance'. If women did not write many chapters of our history heretofore, it does not mean that they were 'insignificant', except to the power press.

Unfortunately, what adds significance to our lives often can only be seen in retrospect, and many times this was not directly and necessarily sought. In fact, the record is such that we know that many gain what they want but then, looking back from the heights, find it has not meant to them quite what they assumed it would in their ascent. One can do both, of course, but that may involve luck as well as care. Perhaps there was a hint in recent feminist agendas that achievement of certain goals would somehow improve life for many, if not for all. But practical goals should be detached from personal significance, since somewhat ironically, in retrospect, what proves to add this meaning often has not been consciously aimed for. However, aiming, having goals may—or may not—produce this as a gift, as an unexpected by-product.

"Yes, the world was...however it wanted to be," comments Anders in *Guest of Reality* (p.46). Here we have the opposite of the Modern notion of 'Progress' or of Hegel's dialectical view of history's unfolding. Reality? We are its guests. "One way or the other, it wasn't to be counted upon. It pleased itself" (ibid). Here is

THE DESCENT OF WOMEN

the core concept of 'significance' and of 'simple' things. If the world in which we live is a gigantic stage for Wagnerian opera on a mass scale, 'significance' can come from engaging in large projects, in striving to be, as Hegel put it, a "world historical figure," or at least in trying to gain your life's meaning by participating in the on-stage chorus. But if 'reality' does not bend to our wishes, does not create Utopias on demand, then life's meaning may not necessarily be found in large external projects. They are what they are and come out as they do. But significance for us, for human beings, may not be found there.

God re-enters the human drama, not as its controller and designer as was oft imagined, but as the reference point which gives "the little things" their significance for us, since God does not need large events from which to derive divine significance. That comes simply from his or her being, and once again in our religious history the divine can become the standard for human significance too. One need not cling to life in the face of the threat of death, since death is "inimical to life itself" (p. 59). "Life is mercifully jumbled and inconsistent" (p. 78). That is sufficient—and it is perhaps better than significance intently sought for in some "grand design." Of course, life's routines can become "an empty convention" (p. 89) too. But that comes from demanding more from them than they can give, rather than from accepting them as significant in themselves, "just the simple things in life."

D. Human Fulfillment: Past, Present, Future

Every age has its patent medicines, its new religious movements, its political orators, and its "buzz words" which come to stand for all that is good – or all that is bad. If we had to single out one word that symbolizes this for our time, a leading candidate would be 'liberation'. Another day would have had 'democracy' for its good word, 'Communist' or 'heretic' or 'counterrevolutionary' for its bad. Revolutions and the hope to institute a utopia in society or radical transformations in human nature—these goals are our inheritance from the Modern World. So it is not surprising that, as liberation theologies were born and the Feminist movement sprang to life from the ashes of the drive for Women's Rights, 'liberation' would seem like a natural hallmark term, whether its meaning was analyzed or not.

Human beings have always suffered discrimination based on outer characteristics, race having been first among these in our history. Religious beliefs and nationality are close seconds as contenders for the object of persecution. Yet sex stands in a special class, since it has always been there, always been a negative (as well as positive) factor, but one we have only recently come to think might be eliminated or at least lessened. Thus, we are now more acutely aware than we once were of sex as a basis for discrimination. As a consequence of this new realization, we are often more vociferous, if not hostile, in our protest for women's release. But the issue is whether it is really 'liberation' that women, and all of us, seek. Perhaps it is really an older notion of 'fulfillment'.

Liberation tends to be associated with release from restricting bonds, everything from literal slavery to political or economic repression. Human beings need some degree of freedom (how much is the issue) in order to achieve their life's satisfaction, and totalitarian political regimes or economic exploitation often block our access. We must say 'almost', for some individuals have done amazing things under political/economic repression. But they are the extraordinary ones; the majority are simply crushed. Prison literature is famous, whether St. Paul, Martin Luther King, or Nelson Mandela. The magnificent survival of these heroes does not justify their imprisonment, but it does indicate that the human spirit is sometimes capable of resilience in the face of restraint, and it is not necessary that all collapse under repression.

Would the Women's Movement today be better off to refocus on a goal of human fulfillment and sidetrack the notion of liberation from central attention? What do we need in order to feel fulfilled in life, and how can our social, political, educational, and economic structures enable us to achieve this? We need "user friendly" schools and communities and governments, ones that equip us with the tools we need for self-expression and allow us the development of our skills, whatever these may be. For women, this means to have political weight ("one woman, one vote"), an openness in every situation to be considered on the basis of merit and not sex, which Blacks and Asians may say about 'race'. But why were external features ever used to oppress peoples?

First among the reasons for oppression has to be the protection of "one's own turf." We want to save our race, religion and the positive factors we connect with this, and so we block intrusions from outside that specified group. Family protection functions the same way on a smaller scale. But underlying all this is the difficulty of evaluating quality by any standard. Since so much of human value is unseen, unless one is an athlete (which may be why Olympic games have been less subject to racial prejudice, although often interfered with by politics). One will make a sweeping judgment based on perceptible universal qualities, rather than to go through the difficult and uncertain course of individual evaluation, which puts the burden back on the evaluator. Women at last saw their need for evaluation based on individual quality, as we all do, although women perhaps more so. However, liberation from all external restraints may not be what women require most for their fulfillment.

Of course, there are special circumstances where women have major concerns as they are aware: for example, childbearing, childrearing, and home care. But what sometimes is forgotten today is that women's release from these physiologically imposed burdens became possible only relatively recently. Until that release women were free to compete with men only under special circumstances. Multiple pregnancies were common, even necessary, if one wanted children to survive into adulthood. Poor health care took its toll.

Added to this was the fact that the woman confined by a series of pregnancies, was also burdened with home care which took her full-time until the advent of household appliances and labor-saving devices (household help offered release only for those who could afford it).

Once released from washing clothes in a river and finding fuel for fires three times a day, plus gathering the food, more worlds are open to women today than earlier generations could have dreamed of. (Well-to-do, powerful women have always been an envied exception.) Pregnancy was uncontrollable except by sexual abstinence; and abortion, so much an issue today, certainly was either unknown or dangerous until medicine progressed to that stage of easy possibility. Thus we know many, if not most, of the options women press for today were impossible and even inconceivable centuries before us. We really should not need to try to explain why generations before us did not protest as we do or why they could not even envisage what we now do as women's full potential.

How, then, did human beings achieve fulfillment in "early times," or how can they today in the vast areas of the globe which still seriously restrict human potential physically and politically? Is it impossible for any human being to feel fulfilled except in the utopian, fully liberated, conditions envisaged by radical social theories? "How ya' gonna keep 'em down on the farm once they've seen the executive suite?" Can no woman today find fulfillment in her home, in her children, in her husband (in spite of what they teach at Wellesley), in her domestic effort? Is it not allowed for any woman today to find fulfillment in this way, once new opportunities and alternatives are open? Is no nun allowed to seek the cloister, if she openly chooses to be "Christ's bride?"

By asking this we come across what is perhaps the chief requirement for human fulfillment: the ability to find an outlet for our talents, be that cooking or occupying presidencies, so that we are not arbitrarily blocked. Of course, behind this lies the problem of finding the "one best outlet for our individuality," and that is not easy. We cannot desire what we do not know about or dream of becoming. For everyone who yearns for and finally achieves success in Hollywood thousands are disappointed, as they are in teaching, in the art world, or even in marriage. On a candid day, we would have to admit that we are often our own worst enemies, that we are not always failures due solely to discriminatory restraint ("The fault, dear Brutus,...").

We also face the problem of the unknown. Anyone who would argue for some new idea, some new product, some new behavior, faces the same difficulty any writer does to have a first screen play accepted in Hollywood or a first novel published in New York. Our history is full of stories of innovators who were rejected in their own time, prophets without honor in their own country or field. If so, we must make the chase be its own reward, to feel fulfilled simply because one has made the attempt to change the course of art, science, education, economics, or politics. Women are not alone in finding it hard to get their innovative products attended to publicly. The novice who must struggle up the ladder is an ancient story of trying to pass a dangerous obstacle course. Many try and should do so; few alone succeed.

Thus, how could a woman, any woman, feel fulfilled in the past when their roles were of necessity publicly restricted? Few could have yearned for what they did not even know was available, or what they did not know would become possible. Many dealt in human relations and found family and friends fulfilling. Hear the stories of quilt making, the way women told about their lives in the quilts they created by hand. We have forgotten how much satisfaction the human race has found in small things. Our liberation tendencies make us think in grand terms, whereas the majority will always have to find satisfaction in small things, especially where life's horizons are not bright.

The religions of the world, of course, have always met this need, whether Christianity, Islam, Buddhism, Confucianism, or some new equivalent. They do not all agree about the course we should follow or the goal to be sought. But almost all agree that there is an inner path, a spiritual discipline which is primary, although this may be connected to outer activity in a variety of ways. Thus, we cannot look to religion as the instigator of some new external reform program, although it is true that human beings often live in intolerable situations from which they need at least an inner release. Religions can support social change, and perhaps they can do so more effectively if the individual has found inner fulfillment and the spiritual strength to work against the forces destructive to humanity.

If past ages could not have imagined the physical release that is available to some, if not to all, women today, how is fulfillment to be found now and in the future? First, we can list the external circumstances which need to be instituted: physical abuse abolished, equal pay, voting and economic rights for those deprived, release from physical hard labor, etcetera. At the same time we know from the past that liberation from these will not necessarily lead to personal fulfillment, for all women or for all men. Many have found fulfillment in small ways and in restricted circumstances. To imagine that we must all be publicly successful if we are to find fulfillment is to doom vast numbers to frustration.

Today's women look back in horror to the lives of those of the Victorian era, or to the concubine in the harems of Egypt or the Chinese aristocrat's wife with the bound feet. They come near rage in thinking about how these women suffered. But in examining historical records there is no reason to suppose that more felt unfulfilled then than do today, granted their consciousness level was different. Some even liked a Victorian lifestyle;[135] some were well

[135]David Deirdre, *Intellectual Women and Victorian Patriarchy* (Ithaca. Cornell University Press, 1983).

"This book is about three Victorian women who did not become exiles from Victorian culture and society and yet denied the patriarchal injunctions against female authorship" (p. VIII):

treated in luxurious harems (just as not all women disenjoy the life of a prostitute). The Chinese women whose feet were bound had everything done for her. It was a sign of her husband's wealth and position. We must be careful to see that the definition of 'fulfillment' is subject to individual context and is also dependent on the inner state of the individual, which may or may not be directly connected to outer circumstances.

If one counts numbers, probably far more men have suffered persecution, imprisonment, torture, suppression and died in wars than women. And the ratio might be the same today. The miners who protest hideous conditions and pay in Soviet mines are mostly men. Amnesty International, who renders us a service by monitoring conditions of political repression around the world, should break their statistics down and tell us how many men are political prisoners vs. women. This has nothing to do with the wrongness of some conditions or prejudices which women face. These need redress. But it might indicate that more men are physically or politically restricted from seeking fulfillment than women.

What, then, of the future? Will our search for fulfillment be any different as today's women seek what their foremothers could never have thought of? In an odd sense, today's women have few historical role models, in spite of recent research into women's history, since the physical or cultural situation that a woman faced before the mid-twentieth-century was entirely different. It set severe limits on what most women could seek. Fulfillment had to take different forms and in most cases had to involve "family first." Frequent pregnancy allowed little else. But we must not be provincial in our outlook and think that every woman in the before-birth-control-health-care era

---

Martincau, Browning, and Eliot. Because they received recognition as working intellectuals, their careers implicitly refute the myth that autonomous womanhood was impossible in Victorian society.

somehow felt unfulfilled. Many probably did find fulfillment in their situation, but some certainly didn't.

Kierkegaard has advised us not to take how one feels at a later time and use it to interpret an earlier situation as if all felt that way then, either romanticizing or rejecting one's own childish days or history's early eras. In rewriting women's past we must be careful to see that most women did not feel as most leaders and writers in the movement do today. They could not do so for many reasons, most particularly due to the burden of pregnancy, child care and home care, from which they have (or rather, some have) only recently been released. The point is that 'fulfillment' for human beings is not an absolute matter, else the rich and famous would automatically feel fulfilled, which we know is not true.

Thus, our feeling about ourselves and our lives stems primarily from inside ourselves, although there is nothing wrong with luxuries. They simply do not in themselves constitute fulfillment for most. Terror, torture, poverty and imprisonment make life difficult; they should always be fought against. Only the exceptional person can feel fulfilled under such circumstances. However, the religions of the world would not be so powerful if the inner person did not need sustenance, as is true of art, music, drama, and literature. They would be quite different fields if what we possessed physically alone could satisfy all fully. This being so, what of the recent women's liberation movement?

To respond to this question we need Kierkegaard's distinction between objective and subjective. Objectively there are issues to be dealt with on that level: whom to elect, how to govern financial affairs, how to train for the Olympics, how to prepare tonight's family meal. To each his own daily life problems. For women, some of the objective issues are abortion, birth control, pre-and postnatal care, equal pay, open opportunities not based on sex discrimination, rape and physical abuse. These are major issues and probably always will remain serious factors as long as human beings know how to disagree and as long as some are stronger. Progress has been made on some fronts, but the world offers us many backward areas which we can work to improve.

However, our subjective problem is quite different. Given the objective situation, favorable or unfavorable, desirable or undesirable, our problem is how to relate to it, and how to appraise it for ourselves. We know that persons in situations we envy feel unfulfilled and demonstrate this from time to time, e.g., suicide. We know that people in obscure situations would not willingly trade their place and that they feel fulfilled and satisfied with life. All women will never pick the fast track. Some will find fulfillment in home and motherhood. Others will compromise, forgo the family and move into a public scene. But we should never mistake objective achievement for personal fulfillment.

No matter how much is accomplished on the objective level, and the women's movement may and can do much, subjectively we all have to make choices and cannot live out all options simultaneously. Ironically, given the special qualities of their sex, this is more difficult for women than for men, and it is hard to foresee any radical change, although some (e.g., Shulamith Firestone)[136] have argued for it, for example, by giving up childbirth. Certainly Communism did not in itself effect any radical change in women's situation. There, of course, is the lesbian lifestyle option, now officially less discriminated against. But societies will not be reproduced in this manner, and it is likely that the majority of women will remain heterosexual.

However, even as the bearers of the human race, women today can restrict and control their family size and select the time for children far more than their foremothers—an immense improvement. But always and always, the mother must choose to stress either home

---

[136]See Shulamith Firestone, *The Dialectic of Sex*, chapter I, note 10.

or career, in the sense that both cannot be done fulltime simultaneously. Or she may delay career advancement until her children are on their own. But in any case choices must be made and priorities assigned. Personal fulfillment would not be so difficult if we: (1) really understood all the options open to us in advance; and (2) could find a way to ensure the outcome for all fully and at the same time. We have our options, and we are fulfilled when we feel we have made the right choices.

Simone de Beauvoir has labeled women as the "second sex."[137] This is true in the sense that she feels women are defined, and have defined themselves, primarily against men. But this could be changed as women assert greater independence. Of course, many men define themselves by others around them and by their social context, so that the problem de Beauvoir outlines as special for women actually applies to many of us. Only the strong of either sex achieve fully self-definition, although de Beauvoir is right that women start the race slightly behind.

But as bearers of the womb, women will always be "the second sex" in another and perhaps more basic sense: They must always choose between marriage and family as a priority or compromise that for other goals. One can say that men can or should or do compromise career goals for their family and assist the women close to them in theirs. This can and does happen in "advanced industrial societies." But as the only one who gives birth, women face a harder choice, adequate daycare not withstanding. The affluent have always had an easier time achieving physical release. But we will never get beyond the situation where choices are forced upon us, and where our sense of fulfillment will come from the wisdom of our choices—something we may only be able to discern in retrospect.

---

[137]See Simone de Beauvoir, *The Second Sex*, chapter I, note 7.

Although it is not by any means urged by all Feminists, so much stress is placed on sex versus gender that there is bound to be a tendency to think that fulfillment is found in sex itself, although certainly some relief can come that way. Of course, if sex is a complicated relationship, then in spite of its satisfactions or even exaltations, the accompanying problems will dim the prospects of sex as an avenue of fulfillment. Of course, the ideal of 'liberation' from prohibitions presents itself to us, since most feminists argue for freedom from restraint where sex is concerned.[138] So that in fact the notion of sexual relations as the avenue to fulfillment depends upon the absence of restraints blocking us on the road to human fulfillment, which is quite doubtful as a premise.

However, fulfillment in the past had to be different for women, since women only recently "crossed the Rubicon" of gaining the ability to control childbirth and some freedom from the total burden of caring for the family as a full-time occupation. And even if we know that achieving human fulfillment in the present is always precarious for the majority, will the future, can the future, be totally different? Much recent postulated theory has had a utopian overtone, hinting that fulfillment depends on the constitution of radically different social structures and societies, which some assume to be an achievable goal.

Considering the future of feminism and human fulfillment, let us list some of the problems we face in envisaging "a new future for us all": (1) Corruption seems to have destroyed some of Communism's valuable goals. Self-seeking crept in rather than the good of the people as the only aim. Much in Communist proposals for the improvement of human suffering involved laudable goals. Now, as its corruptions become evident, we tend to forget how much human good Communism projected. The problem is that, unless women can be

---

[138]See Andrea Dworkin, *Intercourse*, chapter III, note 63.

guaranteed immunity from corruption as they gain release and stature and power, we may find ourselves again facing pockets of corruption. Then as we focus on abuse we may forget all that was laudable that women have accomplished.

Considering the future, we tend to think that once gains are instituted they will increase in momentum and so move ahead, thus changing basic structures. We do not need Hegel's notion of negativity and the antithesis in order to realize that goals instituted are often lost or blocked as history moves along. When we achieve a partial agenda, we often stop there rather than moving on. How else can we explain the vacuum in the women's movement after the Women's Rights effort achieved the vote? Losses occur. Women in Iran are probably less free under Muslim Fundamentalism than under the sometimes brutal Shah. Athens and Rome and London fell into decline after being beacons of progress. But beware the conspiracy theory of 'backlash'.

However, more fundamental to the whole question of the future is the structure of human values which we seek to institute in order to achieve human fulfillment. Focusing on ignored or repressed or unrecognized values, as Feminist theory often has, we feel elated at the prospect of bringing these to fruition, and we see this as a possibility. Birth control and abortion gives women freedom from total absorption in giving birth to and caring for children. But other values are downgraded in importance as women move more into the public scene. The family comes under fire, as it has by radical feminist critics, and heterosexuality is downplayed in the attempt to free women from unwanted relationships.

But the theme of our "Feminist Dilemma" is that every major social movement, which the press for women's liberation is, encounters dilemmas which make choices a necessity among the competing values we always face. We cannot achieve one new order without quickly being reminded of what is being lost in the gain (e.g., mother centered families, which most families always have been in spite of supposed 'patriarchies'). Then "counter revolutions" set in and lost values make their claim to recovery, which is bound to happen unless one buys the extremist picture that all past history was bad and that every woman past and present, once enlightened, will seek total release from all former values.

Yet any study of history (unless it is ideologically biased) reveals to us many fine and valuable aspects of past societies (e.g., the close community of the Middle Ages) as well as what we seek to free ourselves from (e.g., The Inquisition). Thus, unless all women suffered in all past societies and none knew fulfillment, then as proposed new social relations are instituted someone will later on rewrite the history of the women's liberation movement. They will highlight the values we have lost in our "progress," and the forms of human fulfillment which earlier were achieved without "advanced theory." Human fulfillment is no easier now than it was then or ever will be.

Postscript

In our "critical" (meaning, 'evaluative') reflection on the recent feminist agenda for women's future, we should note the importance of 'criticism'. Marx thought that in his time the criticism of religion was the beginning of all criticism. And so it was in many senses, since God was under challenge. The churches in Marx's time were not rising to face the problems of the industrial age and its sometimes devastating human consequences. The 'criticism' of religion was thus crucial and important to Marx in appraising his age and in plotting an improved future.

As the twentieth century draws to a close, is 'feminism' of necessity "the beginning of all criticism" for us? A good case can be made that 'feminism' is the crucial focus if we want to understand how our century has failed, or at least why it has not come out as favorably as many predicted and expected. "The women question" has always been with us, but in this century it has taken on dramatically new forms. It is important for us to understand this, and to do so may speed the general appraisal of our century.

However, if heretofore the accounts of our situation given by men have had a "male bias," is there any point in worrying about the burst of feminist accounts which seek to rewrite history? Are we in danger of focusing too much on women singly and thus either ignoring or distorting crucial issues which both sexes should face together? Is there a possibility that women's powerful prose and inflamed indictments will argue too much "to the women" and so deflect us from solving issues by distorting our perspective? If 'man' has been too prominent in our past, can there be a danger that 'women' will be raised to obscuring proportion and not simply into balance? Granted that we must always pay attention to sex and attempt to achieve balance anew in each age, is it possible for 'women' to become too much the object of attention? How much of our insight depends on seeing both sexes together and neither separately? Can "the human" embrace both sexes equally? As we know by observing ourselves, and perhaps particularly among adolescents, 'sex' can become an obsession. Ironically, it can equally be ignored which, as Freud pointed out, causes both distortion and agony.

How, then, can we use the impetus of the Feminist Movement to put sex "in its right place?" We know that at least since Freud we have not been blind to sex's hidden powers. Freud showed us the damage that results when sex is not dealt with consciously if its powers are neither admitted nor brought into open acknowledgment. Feminism has made us aware of how both sex and gender often function as a restriction on individual fulfillment, due to the incitement of prejudice in fixing rigid gender rules and then claiming a biological inevitability for them. Freud gives us evidence of the damage which our sex drive can do to us when not acknowledged. What the Feminist challenge to existing gender rule stereotypes has done is to argue to remove biological sex as a social determinant. Ironically, one must raise sex to prominence and make it the focal point of discussion in order to argue for its removal.

Thus, if we want individual roles to be determined by individual choice and not by sexual division, we have to try to eliminate sex from social consideration. Oddly, we have recently increased our awareness of how sex is used restrictively, which can work to accentuate sexual division if not counterbalanced. And Darwin may have an important word of advice for us as we move through this period in "Woman's Descent."

Do not think that you can ignore biological inheritance, he might say, agreeing to this extent with Freud. But if you see how humans have descended and how intellectual control finally allows certain freedoms of self-determination in the later stages of our development, be aware of the role of, and the necessity for, struggle; and also recognize the interdependence of both sexes. Women are not alone;

men are not alone.[139] Only cooperation and mutual dependence can create desired change. Antagonism cannot do it, whether sexual, or cultural, or economic.

If, then, the next needed state for Woman's Descent is to keep sex from becoming an obsession and thus looming so large in every consideration that it blocks, even distorts, other issues—we must remain alert as to how sex is also used as a blanket cover for discrimination which is not related to sex. Then, we must seek to reduce any sex-based antagonism while allowing a freer choice of gender rules.

---

[139]Franklin Abbott, ed., *New Men, New Minds* (Freedom, CA: The Crossing Press, 1987).

The editor gathers essays of men in the Movement for Human Liberation, thus adding male support to the feminist quest. The pro-feminist men's movement rests on his perception of changing roles for males. "The father archetype can change and so can the son and so can the journey" (p. 2). If this involves the way of compassion and forgiveness, as the editor suggests, they must be avenues open to all human beings, ones not restricted to any sex. In any case, the editor suggests that men are questioning the role of masculinity too. To one writer "sexism" does not seem accurately to describe "the disabilities and growing concerns of many men" (p. 104). Thus, the theme is that the problem of male gender roles is as serious for women and may lie behind some of the oppression between the sexes. Male issues are not as much centered on political and economic discrimination, but they are no less real.

Barbara Ehrenreich, *The Hearts of Men: American Dreams and the Flight From Commitment* (Garden City, NY: Anchor Books, 1983).

The author begins with a traditional premise: "women need men much more than men need women" (p. 1). We have accepted the assumption of a male bread-winner society. This leads to the notion that a woman doesn't earn enough to support even herself. Thus, men do not have the same necessity "to cleave unto just one woman."

But this ideology has collapsed in the last 30 years, the author concludes. Our expectations of adult womanhood have changed dramatically, just as men are no longer burdened with the automatic expectations of marriage and breadwinning. She recognizes that men were just as restricted in earlier social expectations as women were. There is a male revolt against the breadwinning ethic too. The question is: Do "we rebels of both sexes have enough in common to work together toward a more generous, dignified and caring society" (p. 3)?

Letty M. Russell, *Growth in Partnership* (Philadelphia: The Westminster, 1981).

Mary Vetterling-Braggin, ed., *Femininity, Masculinity and Androgyny* (Totowa, NJ: Rowman and Allanheld, 1982).

Some feminists have highlighted 'connectedness' as a particular difference in women's approach vs. a male tendency to confrontation. Once we become aware that any stress on women's 'difference' can actually be used to block the open options in approach that we seek, can this still be taken as a certain part of one important if culturally constructed gender role? If so, we must put it on its own, urge nonconfrontation for male and female alike, promote 'connectedness' as an approach. This is particularly important if we know that to create cooperative effort between the sexes is crucial to our further 'descent', for example, our human advance.

Simply due to their sex, all women do not share the virtue of promoting connectedness, although it might appear more frequently in an oppressed group as one of their instruments for survival, a technique useful to the nonpowerful. Now, at this stage of advance it is crucial that such 'difference' be seen as a tool to moderate the increased hostility between the sexes, whether individually or in groups.

Thus, one adaptive technique developed by women in their descent to the present stage can now be consciously employed, by both male and female intelligence, in order to direct their further evolution toward new characteristics, just as instinct and the struggle to survive brought us to this point. Yet as we use our emerging intelligence to control and to modify our future development, this should always be set against the larger background of *The Descent of Man* to the present – and the *Descent of Woman* into the future.

Epilogue

Forty-seven, plus three, ways to be a Feminist

Ms. magazine celebrated its twenty-second anniversary by featuring a cover story, "50 Ways To Be A Feminist."[141] It offered a graphic illustration of the rapid diversity occurring within 'feminism' and the resulting dramatic shifts in direction. A majority now celebrates divergence, rather than pressing for an intellectual conformity and a unity on all goals, if we examine the projects and activities of the women highlighted in this article (actually 47, not 50). Of course, there are concerns which apply to "women only" (just as there are for men too). But perhaps the amazing thing is that almost every activity *Ms.* featured could apply to any sex, race, or society and could be advocated or led by any race or group—or by men as well as by women. Is a universalization of feminism underway—a spreading out beyond the confines of any one group?

Some hostility was still focused on the male of the species, such as spousal abuse. Nevertheless, the majority emphasis was on "social problems," with an amazing lack of blame or criticism focused on any group or sex. By loose count, 14 of the women featured have concerns for minority or racial groups and their plight and special needs. Seven could be called organizers of social action projects. Interestingly, most (12) are involved in some artistic activity, writing, music, art, performance. Certainly some do express anger over the conditions they struggle to correct. But this tends to be directed toward the conditions they seek to change and the situations which cause them, not necessarily against males as such. There is no

---

[141] Vol.V, no.1, pp.33-64. Special Issue.

suggestion that simply possessing a penis makes any group act or think alike.

Some are professors/teachers, but these are only a few. Most are not academics but rather are on the front lines of active social change. Two are concerned about medical issues of special concern to women, two are in politics, and only two stress "lesbian rights." Still, other than those injustices which can be connected to physiology, their concerns—and their activities—could just as well be global. Abortion rights have a closer personal connection to women, but certainly the issue affects men equally. Some do focus on environmental issues, but surely that involves the Earth's whole population. Most important: There is rarely a claim that "only women" have these concerns. The only claim is that these are the agendas in which recent 'feminists' have elected to involve themselves.

One might go so far as to say that 'feminists' have openly moved toward universal human causes. There is an underlying theme of 'activism'; they all praise the way in which each woman who is featured has pioneered or led groups devoted to change. On reflection, perhaps the most amazing thing about the survey is the number of women leaders who are from minority groups, thus putting a new twist to the claim that 'feminism' has been primarily a white, middle-class movement. Of course, those featured represent the *Ms.* editor's choice, and it seems obvious that the magazine wanted to feature minority activists. Still, in doing so they illustrate both the movement's diversity and its dedication to what we might loosely call "social justice" causes. This is avowedly not a group of 'intellectuals', at least in the usual sense of that term. These are people who are out on the front lines of pressing social concerns.

Of course, all the way through this focus on what Darwin would call women's 'descent' we have been appraising a broad spread of the recent massive writings by women; we have stressed the theme that the need is for all of us to join together, if lasting improvement is to be achieved, and to heed Darwin's warning of how difficult (although possible) basic change is and how easily any advancement can be lost. Moreover, change based on hostility to any person or group is questionable, due to the corroding effects of hate, in spite of the fury and the power that anger can unleash. Some of the women featured by *Ms.* express their anger, but often this tends to be against social injustices and not so much against any sex or class. Yet the majority of the causes featured could easily invite us all to join in the effort without exclusivity. There is no suggestion there is a pressure for a "women only" group, although in fact most of them are still primarily women who have joined together.

The Grey Panthers have "a vision of peace and justice for all" (p. 35). Some issues they focus on are not led by members of one race only but are multiracial. Many are 'economically' focused, which means trying to help groups raise their economic level or make themselves self-sustaining. There still is an echo of the earlier 'revolutionary' fervor. But it is interesting that this argument comes from a retired senior congresswoman who proclaims that "the challenge of the women's movement is to transform the power structure" (p. 46). True, the now common term 'empowerment' appears frequently. Yet instead of offering political revolutions, it tends to mean enabling individuals and groups to take a greater degree of control over their destiny within a given society. A sense of humor also appears joined with a cartoonist's use of irony.

I do not at all mean to suggest that feminism has lost its militant drive. I simply mean to observe that the chosen examples indicate a broadening of both the base and the areas of concern, as well as a lessening attack on 'patriarchy' as a whipping boy (whipping man?), and that this offers an openness to all who might support the cause, while not lessening the fact that the leadership in each case has come primarily from women thus far. One person *Ms.* featured denies that a concern about feminism means that you can't be concerned about other issues. "On the contrary," she reports (p. 52), "it's so important to see the connections." Her commitment to building bridges remains. In almost every instance those featured have emphasized a "common cause," rather than a separation into exclusive compounds.

"We have to move into the general society," (p. 34) one reports. Of course, she adds, this is in order "to get women to identify as feminists." But given the way 'feminism' is specified on these pages, it almost means to become identified with, and to work for, some cause that alleviates human suffering. One expresses the concern as being focused on "people who are underserved" (p. 58). True, she means primarily women in these situations. But given this agenda, the interesting thing is that nothing prevents these activities from being extended to the whole human race. At no time are the problems which these women seek to correct said to be due to the evil intentions of men as a sex. Their "...vision of what a women's world might be" (p. 62) could easily be extended to both sexes, to all races.

"Women learn from talking openly to each other" (p. 64), the Boston Women's Health Collective reports. But surely this is true of both sexes. Still, in these instances, it is women who have pioneered the activities, although there is no claim that women alone can accomplish these virtues or achieve these human goals. They are not sex-linked and somehow women's special possession. But the examples given do come from *active* women. Oddly, this has similarities to the way in which women went into volunteerism in an earlier age and in fact pioneered many social causes, for example, nursing, League of Women Voters and Hull House. However, today these "social causes" are more women-directed, and the leaders are aggressively seeking to change the root social causes of the problems. One says that she seeks to aid "all who are on public assistance or among the working poor" (p. 63).

Is our claim that the women's movement has lost all distinctiveness? Hardly. But do remember that birth control and abortion rights now allow many more women to enter into these causes full-time, whereas in an earlier day women activists often could work only part-time and from their homes as a base. But if the aim is to aid "all of the working poor," then surely there is a new universal aim and also a universalism of those who could join the cause. 'Feminism' need not direct itself solely to women as a sex or involve only women in the effort, although in some cases some problems that need correcting may fall disproportionately on women and so raise the attention of women more specifically.

Of course, if you take society by and large—any society—the accounts of these activities featured are "off beat"; they are not the average; they are not on the society page of every city newspaper. To say this is not a "put down," since most innovative, socially oriented activities are not "standard." But the era's "famous names" are not included on the pages of *Ms.*, "the rich and famous" women, the elite of the social structure. The point is not that "real feminists" need to or should seek such prominence, but that, again, if "contemporary feminism" began in a narrow strata of the women of the world, this new advocated pluralism is equally not in the mainstream, nor is it Aristotle's Golden Mean of activity. Many special and constructive causes may not be, but neither can we claim that these 50 feminists (actually 47) are somehow representative of "all women."

If these women are to be offered as our "new model feminists," to serve as Plato's model "Philosopher-King" did for men in *The Republic* as the standard for which we should strive, are these models really exclusively women's models? Or are they simply examples of ideals which we wish more human beings would emulate, models of virtuous activities such as monks and nuns often exemplified in the Middle Ages? We do need models. Virtue is often a minority and even a lonely activity, not a majority phenomenon (Kant notwithstanding). So women who are today released, as Virginia Woolf said, from that burden of "thirteen difficult pregnancies" could become our minority models of virtue, just as men tended to serve this role in pre-birth-control times. Not all women will serve these "good purposes," of course, only the memorable few. And men need not be excluded from "the circle of virtue," provided that a few can qualify themselves.

Feminist Bibliography*

1. Abbott, Franklin, editor. *New Men, New Minds*. Freedom, California: The Crossing Press, 1987.
2. Achterberg, Jeanne. *Woman as Healer*. London: Rider, 1991.
3. Alic, Margaret. *Hypatia's Heritage*. London: The Women's Press Limited, 1986.
4. Allen, Anita L. *Uneasy Access*. Totowa, New Jersey: Rowman and Littlefield, 1988.
5. Allen, Jennifer and Iris M. Young, editors. *The Thinking Muse*. Bloomington, Indiana: Indiana University Press, 1989.
6. Amanecida Collective. *Revolutionary Forgiveness*. Maryknoll, New York: Orbis Books, 1987.
7. Anderson, Bonnie S. and Judith P. Zinsser. *A History of Their Own*, Volumes I and II. New York: Harper and Row, 1988.
8. Andolsen, Barbara Hilkert; Christine E. Gudorf; Mary D. Pellauer, editors. *Women's Consciousness, Women's Conscience*. San Francisco: Harper and Row, 1987.
9. Andrews, Lynn V. *Star woman*. New York: Warner Books, 1986.
10. Angelou, Maya. *Gather Together In My Name*. New York: Bantam Books, 1974.
11. ———. *The Heart of a Woman*. New York: Bantam Books, 1982.
12. ———. *I Know Why the Caged Bird Sings*. New York: Bantam Books, 1970.
13. ———. *Singin' and Swingin' and Getting Merry Like Christmas*. New York: Bantam Books, 1976.
14. ———. *Wouldn't Take Nothing for My Journey Now*. New York: Random House, 1993.
15. Armstrong, Karen. *The Gospel According to Women*. Garden City, New York: Anchor Press/Doubleday, 1987.
16. Armstrong, Nancy and Leonard Tennenhouse, editors. *The Ideology of Conduct*. New York and London: Metheun, 1987.
17. Bacon, Margaret Hope. *Mothers of Feminism*. San Francisco: Harper and Row, 1986.
18. Ballaster, Ros; Margaret Beethan; Elizabeth Frazier; Sandra Hebron, editors. *Women's World*. London: Macmillan Education Limited, 1991.
19. Banks, Olive. *Facts of Feminism*. Oxford: Basil Blackwell Limited, 1981.
20. Barrett, Michele. *Women's Oppression Today*. London: Verso, 1986.
21. Battersby, Christine. *Gender and Genius: Towards a Feminist Aesthetics*. Bloomington and Indianapolis: Indiana University Press, 1989.
22. Beall, Anne E. and Robert J. Sternberg, editors. *The Psychology of Gender*. New York and London: Guilford Press, 1993.

---

* This bibliography is not complete, of course. It almost could not be. Through library computer connections, I have located over four thousand volumes which are roughly "feminist," and I am sure there are more. In fact, this list is simply those books which I own and have read through as background to writing this volume and also the draft of various essays which preceded it. In that sense, it is "the fairest" bibliography to offer to the reader, since it is in fact my own library and thus the basis on which this essay is written.

23. Beauvoir, Simone de. *The Ethics of Ambiguity*. Secaucus, New Jersey: Citadel Press, 1980.

24. ———. *Memoirs of a Dutiful Daughter*. New York: Harper and Row, 1959.

25. ———. *The Second Sex*. London: Pan Books, 1988.

26. Beck, Lois and Nikki Keddie, editors. *Women in the Muslim World*. Cambridge, Massachusetts and London: Harvard University Press, 1978.

27. Beer, Gillian. *Darwin's Plots*. London: Ark Paperbacks, 1983.

28. Belenky, Mary Field; Blyth McVicker Clinchy; Nancy Rule Goldberger; Jill Mattuck Tarule. *Women's Ways of Knowing*. New York: Basic Books, 1986.

29. Bell, Linda A. *Rethinking Ethics in the Midst of Violence*. Lanham, Maryland: Rowman and Littlefield Publishers Inc., 1993.

30. Belsey, Catherine and Jane Moore. *The Feminist Reader*. London: Macmillan Education Limited, 1989.

31. Bender, Sue. *Plain and Simple*. NewYork: HarperCollins, 1989.

32. Bennett, Anne McGrew. *From Woman-Pain to Woman-Vision*. Minneapolis: Fortress Press, 1989.

33. Bennington, Geoffrey and Jacques Derrida. *Jacques Derrida*. Chicago and London: University of Chicago Press, 1993.

34. Benstock, Shari. *Textualizing the Feminine*. Norman: University of Oklahoma Press, 1991.

35. Berger, Pamela. *The Goddess Obscured*. Boston: Beacon Press, 1985.

36. Bernard, Jessie. *The Female World from a Global Perspective*. Bloomington and Indianapolis: Indiana University Press, 1987.

37. Birkett, Jennifer and Elizabeth Harvey, editors. *Determined Women*. London: Macmillan Press Limited, 1991.

38. Black, Naomi. *Social Feminism*. Ithaca and London: Cornell University Press, 1989.

39. Bly, Robert. *Iron John*. New York: Addison Wesley, 1990.

40. Boff, Leonardo. *The Maternal Face of God*. San Francisco: Harper and Row, 1987.

41. Bokenham, Osbern. *A Legend of Holy Women*. Notre Dame and London: University of Notre Dame Press, 1992.

42. Bolen, Jean Shinoda. *Goddesses in Every Woman*. New York: Harper and Row, 1984.

43. Boneparth, Ellen and Emily Stoper, editors. *Women, Power and Policy: Toward the Year 2000*, second edition. New York: Pergamon Press, 1988.

44. Boucher, Sandy. *Turning the Wheel*. San Francisco: Harper and Row, 1988.

45. Braidotti, Rosi. *Patterns of Dissonance*. Cambridge: Polity Press, 1991.

46. Brock, Rita Nakashima. *Journeys by Heart*. New York: Crossroad, 1988.

47. Brodzki, Bella and Celeste Schenck, editors. *Life/Lines*. Ithaca and London: Cornell University Press, 1988.

48. Brown, Wendy. *Manhood and Politics*. Totowa, New Jersey: Rowman and Littlefield, 1988.

49. Brownmiller, Susan. *Femininity*. New York: Fawcett Columbine, 1984.

50. Buck, Claire, editor. *The Bloomsbury Guide to Women's Literature*. New York: Prentice Hall, 1992.

51. Butler, Judith. *Gender Trouble*. New York: Routledge, 1990.

52. —— and Joan W., Scott, editors. *Feminists Theorize the Political*. New York: Routledge, 1992.
53. Bynum, Caroline Walker; Stevan Harrell; Paula Richman, editors. *Gender and Religion*. Boston: Beacon Press, 1986.
54. Cady, Susan; Marian Ronan; Hal Taussig. *Wisdom's Feast*. San Francisco: Harper and Row, 1989.
55. Cahill, Lisa Sowle. *Between the Sexes*. Philadelphia: Fortress Press, 1985.
56. Candelaria, Michael R. *Popular Religion and Liberation*. New York: State University of New York Press, 1990.
57. Carabillo, Tony and Judith Meuli. *The Feminization of Power*. Los Angeles: Fund for the Feminist Majority, 1988.
58. Carmody, Denise åÉk and Mahwah, New Jersey: Paulist Press, 1987.
80. Collins, Patricia Hill. *Black Feminist Thought*. London: Harper Collins Academic, 1990.
81. Condren, Mary. *The Serpent and the Goddess*. San Francisco: Harper and Row, 1989.
82. Conn, Joann Wolski, editor. *Women's Spirituality*. New York and Malwah, New Jersey: Paulist Press, 1986.
83. Conway, Jill Ker, editor. *Written By Herself*. New York: Vintage, 1992.
84. ——; Susan C. Bourque; Joan W. Scott, editors. *Learning About Women*. Ann Arbor: University of Michigan Press, 1989.
85. Cooey, Paula; Sharon A. Farmer; Mary Ellen Ross, editors. *Embodied Love*. San Francisco: Harper and Row, 1987.
86. Cott, Nancy F., editor. *Root of Bitterness*. Boston: Northeastern University Press, 1986.
87. Daly, Mary. *Beyond God the Father*. Boston: Beacon Press, 1973.
88. ——. *The Church and the Second Sex*. New York: Harper and Row, 1975.
89. ——. *Gyn/Ecology*. Boston: Beacon Press: , 1978.
90. ——. *Outercourse*. San Francisco: Harper and Row, 1992.
91. ——. *Pure Lust*. Boston: Beacon Press, 1984.
92. —— with Jane Caputi. *Webster's First New Intergalactic Wickedary of the English Language*.   Boston: Beacon Press, 1987.
93. David, Dierdre. *Intellectual Women and Victorian Patriarchy*. Ithaca and London: Cornell University Press, 1989.
94. David-Ménard, Monique. *Hysteria from Freud to Lacan*. Ithaca and London: Cornell University Press, 1989.
95. Davis, Angela. *Women, Race and Class*. New York: Vintage Books, 1983.
96. Day, Peggy, editor. *Gender and Difference in Ancient Israel*. Minneapolis: Fortress Press, 1989.
97. DeBerg, Betty A. *Ungodly Women*. Minneapolis: Fortress Press, 1990.
98. Deckard, Barbara Sinclair. *The Women's Movement*. New York: Harper and Row, 1983.
99. Delany, Sheila. *A Legend of Holy Women*. Notre Dame, Indiana: University of Notre Dame Press, 1992.

100. Deleuze, Gilles and Leopold von Sacher-Masoch. *Masochism*. New York: Zone Books, 1991.
101. Derrida, Jacques. *Limited Inc*. Evanston, Illinois: Northwestern University Press: 1988.
102. ———. *Margins of Philosophy*. Chicago: University of Chicago Press, 1982.
103. ———. *Positions*. Chicago: University of Chicago Press, 1981.
104. ———. *The Post Card*. Chicago: University of Chicago Press, 1987.
105. ———. *The Truth in Painting*. Chicago: University of Chicago Press and London, 1987.
106. Diamond, Irene and Lee Quinby, editors. *Feminism and Foucault*. Boston: Northeastern University Press, 1988.
107. Dillard, Annie. *An American Childhood*. New York: Harper and Row, 1987.
108. ———. *Pilgrim at Tinker Creek*. London: Picador, 1976.
109. Doane, Janice and Devon Hodges. *Nostalgia and Sexual Difference*. New York: Methuen, 1987.
110. Donnelly, Doris, editor. *Mary, Woman of Nazareth*. New York and Mahwah, New Jersey: Paulist Press, 1989.
111. Donovan, Josephine. *Feminist Theory*. New York: Continuum Publishing Company, 1990.
112. Douglass, Jane Dempsey. *Women, Freedom and Calvin*. Philadelphia: Westminster Press, 1985.
113. Downing, Christine. *Goddess*. : Crossroad, 1988.
114. ———. *Journey Through Menopause*. New York: Crossroad, 1987.
115. ———. *Psyche's Sisters*. San Francisco: Harper and Row, 1988.
116. Downs, Donald Alexander. *The New Politics of Pornography*. Chicago and London: The University of Chicago Press, 1989.
117. Dreyer, Elizabeth. *Passionate Women*. New York and Mahwah, New Jersey: Paulist Press, 1989.
118. DuBois, Ellen Carol. *Feminism and Suffrage*. Ithaca: Cornell University Press, 1978.
119. Duchen, Claire. *Feminism in France*. London: Routledge and Kegan Paul, 1986.
120. Dupré, Louis. *The Philosophical Foundations of Marxism*. New York: Harcourt, Brace and World, 1966.
121. Dworkin, Andrea. *Intercourse*. New York: The Free Press, 1987.
122. ———. *Woman Hating*. New York: E.P. Dutton, 1974.
123. Echols, Alice. *Daring to be Bad*. Minneapolis: University of Minnesota Press, 1989.
124. Ehrenreich, Barbara. *The Hearts of Men*. Garden City, New York: Anchor Books, 1983.
125. Eisenstein, Zillah R. *The Radical Future of Liberal Feminism*. Boston: Northeastern University Press, 1986.
126. Eisler, Riane. *The Chalice and the Blade*. San Francisco: Harper and Row, 1987.
127. Elwes, Teresa. *Women's Voices*. London: Harper Collins, 1992.
128. Engelsman, Joan Chamberlain. *The Feminine Dimension of the Divine*. Wilmette, Illinois: Chiron Publications, 1987.

129. Epstein, Cynthia Fuchs. *Deceptive Distinctions*. New Haven and London: Yale University Press, 1988.

130. Ettinger, Elizabeth. *Rosa Luxemburg*. Boston: Beacon Press, 1986.

131. Evans, Sara M. *Born for Liberty*. New York: The Free Press, 1989.

132. Fabella, Virginia and Mercy Amba Oduyoye, editors. *With Passion and Compassion*. Maryknoll, New York: Orbis Books, 1988.

133. Fabella, Virginia and Sun Ai Lee Park, editors. *We Dare to Dream*. Hong Kong: Asian Women's Resource Centre for Culture and Theology and the EATWOT Women's Commission in Asia, 1989.

134. Faludi, Susan. *Backlash*. London: Chatto and Windus, 1991.

135. Farganis, Sondra. *The Social Reconstruction of the Feminine Character*. Totowa, New Jersey: Rowman and Littlefield, 1986.

136. Fausto-Sterling, Anne. *Myths of Gender*. New York: Basic Books, 1985.

137. Feldstein, Richard and Judith Roof. *Feminism and Psychoanalysis*. Ithaca and London: Cornell University Press, 1989.

138. Fenton, Thomas P. and Mary J. Heffron, editors. *Women in the Third World*. Maryknoll, New Jersey: Orbis Books, 1987.

139. Ferguson, Kathy E. *The Man Question*. Berkeley: University of California Press, 1993.

140. Fiorenza, Elizabeth Schussler. *Bread Not Stone*. Boston: Beacon Press, 1984.

141. ———. *In Memory of Her*. New York: Crossroad, 1988.

142. Fiorenza, Francis Schussler. *Foundational Theology*. New York: Crossroad, 1988.

143. Firestone, Shulamith. *The Dialectic of Sex*. New York: Bantam Books, 1970.

144. Fischer, Kathleen. *Women at the Well*. New York and Mahwah, New Jersey: Paulist Press, 1988.

145. Flinders, Carol Lee. *Enduring Grace*. San Francisco: Harper and Row, 1993.

146. Fowler, Robert Booth. *Carrie Catt: Feminist Politician*. Boston: Northeastern University Press, 1986.

147. Fraser, Antonia. *The Warrior Queens*. New York: Alfred A. Knopf, 1989.

148. Fraser, Nancy and Sandra Lee Bartky. *Revaluing French Feminism*. Bloomington: Indiana University Press, 1992.

149. French, Marilyn. *The War Against Women*. London: Hamish Hamilton, 1992.

150. Friedan, Betty. *The Feminine Mystique*. New York: Dell Publishing, 1983.

151. ———. *The Second Stage*. New York: Summit Books, 1986.

152. Friedl, Bettina. *On to Victory*. Boston: Northeastern University Press, 1987.

153. Friedman, Marilyn. *What Are Friends For?: Feminist Perspectives on personal relationships and moral theory*. Ithaca: Cornell, 1994.

154. Frye, Marilyn. *The Politics of Reality*. Freedom, California: The Crossing Press, 1983.

155. Fuss, Diana. *Essentially Speaking*. London and New York: Routledge, 1989.

156. Gadon, Elinor W. *The Once and Future Goddess*. San Francisco: Harper and Row, 1989.

157. Galland, China. *Longing for Darkness*. New York: Viking, 1990.

158. Gallop, Jane. *Around 1981*. New York: Routledge, 1992.

159. ———. *The Daughter's Seduction*. Ithaca and London: Cornell University Press, 1982.

160. ———. *Reading Lacan*. Ithaca and London: Cornell University Press, 1985.

161. Garner, Shirley Nelson; Claire Kahane; Madelon Sprengnether, editors. *The (M)other Tongue*. Ithaca and London: Cornell University Press, 1985.

162. Garry, Ann and Marilyn Pearsall, editors. *Women, Knowledge, and Reality*. Boston: Unwin Hyman, 1989.

163. Gatens, Moira. *Feminism and Philosophy*. Cambridge: Polity, 1991.

164. Gebara, Ivone and Maria Clara Bingemer. *Mary Mother of God, Mother of the Poor*. Maryknoll, New York: Orbis Books, 1989.

165. Giles, Mary E. *The Feminine Mystic*. New York: Crossroad, 1982.

166. Gilligan, Carol. *In a Different Voice*. Cambridge, Massachusetts and London: Harvard University Press, 1982.

167. Gimbutas, Marija. *The Language of the Goddess*. San Francisco: Harper and Row, 1989.

168. Goldenberg, Naomi R. *Changing of the Gods*. Boston: Beacon Press, 1979.

169. Goodrich, Nolana Lorre. *Heroines*. New York: Harper Collins, 1993.

170. Gould, Carol C., editor. *Beyond Domination*. Totowa, New Jersey: Rowman and Littlefield, 1983.

171. Grant, Judith. *Fundamental Feminism: Contesting the Core Concepts of Feminist Theory*. London: Routledge, 1993.

172. Greene, Gayle and Coppélia Kahn, editors. *Changing Subjects*. London: Routledge, 1993.

173. Greer, Germaine. *The Female Eunuch*. London: Paladin, 1970.

174. ———. *The Mad Woman's Underclothes*. London: Picador, 1986.

175. Griffiths, Morwenna and Margaret Griffiths. *Feminist Perspectives in Philosophy*. London: Macmillan, 1988.

176. Grimshaw, Jean. *Feminist Philosophers*. London: Harvester Wheatsheaf, 1986.

177. ———. *Philosophy and Feminist Thinking*. Minneapolis: University of Minnesota Press, 1986.

178. Guettel, Charnie. *Marxism and Feminism*. Toronto: The Women's Press, 1974.

179. Gundry, Patricia. *Neither Slave Nor Free*. San Francisco: Harper and Row, 1987.

180. Gurko, Miriam. *The Ladies of Seneca Falls*. New York: Schocken Books, 1974.

181. Haddad, Yvonne Yazbeck and Ellison Banks Findley, editors. *Women, Religion and Social Change*. Albany: State University of New York Press, 1985.

182. Haddon, Pauli. *Body Metaphors*. New York: Crossroad, 1988.

183. Hall, Nor. *The Moon and the Virgin*. New York: Harper and Row, 1980.

184. Hamilton, Alice. *Exploring the Dangerous Trades*. Boston: Northeastern University Press, 1985.

185. Hampson, Daphne. *Theology and Feminism*. Oxford: Basil Blackwell, 1990.

186. Hamscombe, Gillian and Virginia L. Smyers. *Writing for Their Lives*. Boston: Northeastern University Press, 1987.

187. Harding, M. Esther. *Woman's Mysteries*. New York: Harper and Row, 1971.

188. Harding, Sandra, editor. *The "Racial" Economy of Science: Toward a Democratic Future*. Bloomington and Indianapolis: Indiana University Press, 1993.
189. ———. *The Science Question in Feminism*. Ithaca and London: Cornell University Press, 1986.
190. ———. *Whose Science? Whose Knowledge? Thinking from Women's Lives*. Ithaca: Cornell University Press, 1991.
191. Hare-Mustin, Rachel T. and Jeanne Marecek, editors. *Making a Difference*. New Haven and London: Yale University Press, 1990.
192. Harris, Maria. *Women and Teaching*. New York and Mahwah, New Jersey: Paulist Press, 1988.
193. Harrison, Beverly Wildung. *Making the Connections*. Edited by Carol S. Robb. Boston: Beacon Press, 1985.
194. Harstock, Nancy C.M. *Money, Sex, and Power*. Boston: Northeastern Unoversity Press, 1985.
195. Haughton, Rosemary. *The Re-Creation of Eve*. Springfield, Illinois: Templegate Publishers, 1985.
196. Hawley, John Stratton and Donna Marie Wulff, editors. *The Divine Consort*. Boston: Beacon Press, 1986.
197. Hebblethwaite, Margaret. *Motherhood and God*. London: Geoffrey Chapman, 1984.
198. Heine, Susanne. *Matriarchs, Goddesses and Images of God*. Minneapolis: Augsburg, 1988.
199. ———. *Women and Early Christianity*. Minneapolis: Augsburg, 1988.
200. Hellwig, Mouika K. *Christian Women in a Troubled World*. New York and Mahwah, New Jersey: Paulist Press, 1985.
201. Henley, Nancy M. *Body Politics*. New York: Simon and Schuster, 1977.
202. Hewitt, Nancy A. *Women's Activism and Social Change*. Ithaca: Cornell University Press, 1984.
203. Heyward, Carter. *Touching Our Strength*. San Francisco: Harper and Row, 1989.
204. Saint Hildegaard of Bingen. *Symphonia*. Edited by Barbara Newman. Ithaca: Cornell University Press, 1985.
205. Hinchman, Lewis P. and Sandra K. Hinchman, editors. *Hannah Arendt: Critical Essays*. Albany: State University of New York Press, 1994.
206. Hirsch, Marianne and Evelyn Fox Keller, editors. *Conflicts in Feminism*. New York: Routledge, 1990.
207. Hole, Judith and Ellen Levine. *Rebirths of Feminism*. New York: Quadrangle, 1971.
208. Hooks, Bell. *Ain't I a Woman: Black Women and Feminism*. Boston: South End Press, 1981.
209. Hardy, Sarah B. *The Woman that Never Evolved*. Cambridge, Massachusetts: Harvard Press, 1981.
210. Hurcombe, Linda, editor. *Sex and God*. New York and London: Routledge and Kegan Paul, 1987.
211. Hurston, Zora Neale. *Their Eyes Were Watching God*. Urbana and Chicago: University of Illinois Press, 1978.
212. *Hypatia*. (Three volumes.) Bloomington, Indiana, 1991.

213. Ianello, Kathleen P. *Decisions Without Hierarchy*. New York: Routledge, 1992.
214. Ide, Arthur Frederick. *Woman as Priest, Bishop and Laity*. Mesquite, Texas: Ide House, 1984.
215. Ireland, Mardy S. *Reconceiving Women: Separating Motherhood from Female Identity*. New York and London: The Guilford Press, 1993.
216. Irigaray, Luce. *Elemental Passions*. New York: Routledge, 1982.
217. ———. *An Ethics of Sexual Difference*. Ithaca: Cornell University Press, 1984.
218. ———. *Je, Tu, Nous*. New York: Routledge, 1993.
219. ———. *Speculum of the Other Woman*. Ithaca: Cornell University Press, 1985.
220. ———. *This Sex which is not One*. Ithaca: Cornell University Press, 1985.
221. Isazi-Diaz, Ada Maria and Yolanda Tarango. *Hispanic Women, Prophetic Voice in the Church*. San Francisco: Harper and Row, 1988.
222. Jacobus, Mary; Evelyn Fox Keller; Salley Shuttlesworth, editors. *Body/Politics*. London and New York: Routledge, 1990.
223. Jaggar, Alison M. *Feminist Politics and Human Nature*. Totowa, New Jersey and Sussex: Rowman and Littlefield and Harvester Press, 1983.
224. ——— and Paula S. Rothberg. *Feminist Frameworks*, Third Edition. New York: McGraw Hill, 1993.
225. Jardine, Alice A. *Gynesis*. Ithaca and London: Cornell University Press, 1985.
226. Johnson, Buffie. *Lady of the Beasts*. New York: Harper and Row, 1981.
227. Jones, Kathleen B. *Compassionate Authority*. New York: Routledge, 1993.
228. Kaplan, Cora. *Sea Changes*. London: Verso, 1986.
229. Kaschak, Ellyn. *Engendered Lives*. New York: Basic Books, 1992.
230. Katoppo, Marianne. *Compassionate and Free*. Maryknoll, New York: Orbis Books, 1981.
231. Kauffman, Linda. *Discourses of Desire*. Ithaca and London: Cornell University Press, 1986.
232. ———, editor. *Gender and Theory*. Oxford and New York: Basil Blackwell, 1989.
233. Keller, Catherine. *From a Broken Web*. Boston: Beacon Press, 1986.
234. Keller, Evelyn Fox. *Reflections on Gender and Science*. New Haven and London: Yale University Press, 1985.
235. Kelly, Carde Marie. *Symbols of Inner Truth*. New York: Paulist Press, 1988.
236. Kent, David A. *The Achievement of Christina Rossetti*. Ithaca and London: Cornell University Press, 1987.
237. Keohane, Naunell O.; Michelle Z. Rosaldo; Barbara C. Gelpi, editors. *Feminist Theory*. Chicago: University of Chicago Press, 1981.
238. Kerber, Linda K and Jane Sherron De Hart. *Women's America: Refocusing the Past*, Third Edition. New York and Oxford: Oxford University Press, 1991.
239. King, Karen L. *Images of the Feminine in Gnosticism*. Philadelphia: Fortress Press, 1988.
240. King, Ursula. *Women and Spirituality*. London: Macmillan Education, 1989.
241. Kittay, Eva Feder and Diana T. Meyers, editors. *Women and Moral Theory*. Totowa, New Jersey: Rowman and Littlefield, 1987.

242. Kofman, Sarah. *The Enigma of Woman*. Ithaca and London: Cornell University Press, 1985.
243. Kolbenschlag, Madonna. *Lost in the Land of Oz*. San Francisco: Harper and Row, 1988.
244. Kraemer, Ross S., editor. *Maenads, Martyrs, Matrons, Monastics*. Philadelphia: Fortress Press, 1988.
245. Kramarae, Cheris and Paula Triechler. *A Feminist Dictionary*. London: Pandora Press, 1985.
246. Labarge, Margaret Wade. *A Small Sound of the Trumpet*. Boston: Beacon Press, 1986.
247. LaCugna, Catherine Mowry, editor. *Freeing Theology: The Essentials of Theology in Feminist Perspective*. New York: Harper Collins, 1993.
248. Laffey, Alice L. *An Introduction to the Old Testament: A Feminist Perspective*. Philadelphia: Fortress Press, 1988.
249. Lagerquist, L. DeAne. *From Our Mothers' Arms*. Minneapolis: Augsburg, 1987.
250. Landes, Joan B. *Women and the Public Sphere in the Age of the French Revolution*. Ithaca and London: Cornell University Press, 1988.
251. Lane, Ann. Mary Ritter Beard: *A Sourcebook*. Boston: Northeastern University Press, 1988.
252. Larcom, Lucy. *A New England Girlhood*. Boston: Northeastern University Press, 1986.
253. Lasky, Melvin S. *Utopia and Revolution*. Chicago: University of Chicago Press, 1976.
254. LeDoeuf, Michèle. *Hipparchia's Choice*. Oxford: Blackwell, 1989.
255. Lee, Carol. *The Blind Side of Eden*. London: Bloomsbury, 1989.
256. Lemaire, Anika. *Jacques Lacan*. London and New York: Routledge and Kegan Paul, 1977.
257. Lerner, Gerda, editor. *Black Women in White America*. New York: Vintage Books, 1973.
258. ———. *The Creation of Feminist Conscioiusness: From the Middle Ages to Eighteen-seventy*. New York and Oxford: Oxford University Press, 1993.
259. ———. *The Creation of Patriarchy*. New York and Oxford: Oxford University Press, 1986.
260. Levesque-Lopman, Louise. *Claiming Reality*. Totowa, New Jersey: Rowman and Littlefield, 1988.
261. Loades, Ann, editor. *Feminist Theology*. London: SPCK, 1990.
262. Lorde, Audre. *Sister Outsider*. Freedom, California: The Crossing Press, 1984.
263. Lovell, Terry, editor. *British Feminist Thought*. London: Basil Blackwell, 1990.
264. Luke, Helen. *Woman: Earth and Spirit*. New York: Crossroad, 1989.
265. MacHaffie, Barbara J. *Her Story*. Philadelphia: Fortress Press, 1986.
266. Mahowald, Mary Briody, editor. *Philosophy of Woman*. Indianapolis: Hackett Publishing Company, 1983
267. Malcolm, Kari Torjesen. *Women at the Crossroads*. Downers Grove, Illinois: Inter Varsity Press, 1982.

268. Malson, Micheline R.; Jean F. O'Barr; Sarah Westphal-Whil; Mary Wyer, editors. *Feminist Theory in Practice and Process*. Chicago and London: University of Chicago Press, 1989.
269. Manning, Rita C. *Speaking from the Heart*. Lanham, Maryland: Rowman and Littlefield, 1992.
270. Marks, Elaine and Isabelle de Courtiuran. *New French Feminisms*. London: Harvester Wheatsheafs, 1980.
271. Martin, Jane Roland. *Reclaiming a Conversation*. New Haven and London: Yale University Press, 1985.
272. Martin, M. Kay and Barbara Voorhies. *Female of the Species*. New York: Columbia University Press, 1975.
273. Massey, Marilyn Chapin. *Feminine Soul: The Fate of an Ideal*. Boston: Beacon Press, 1985.
274. McFague, Sallie. *The Body of God*: An Ecological Theology. Minneapolis: Fortress Press, 1993.
275. ———. *Metaphorical Theology*. London: SCM Press Ltd. , 1983.
276. ———. *Models of God*. Philadelphia: Fortress Press, 1987.
277. ———. *Speaking in Parables*. Philadelphia: Fortress Press, 1975.
278. Merchant, Carolyn. *The Death of Nature*. San Francisco: Harper and Row, 1983.
279. Messerschmidt, James W. *Capitalism, Patriarchy, and Crime*. Totowa, New Jersey: Rowman and Littlefield, 1986.
280. Mies, Maria. *Patriarchy and Accumulation on a World Scale*. London: Zed Books, 1986.
281. Miles, Rosalind. *The Rites of Man*. London: Graften, 1991.
282. ———. *The Women's History of the World*. London: Paladin Press, 1988.
283. Mills, Patricia Jagentowicz. *Woman, Nature, and Psyche*. New Haven and London: Yale University Press, 1987.
284. Mitchell, Juliet. *Psycho-analysis and Feminism*. New York: Vintage, 1974.
285. ———. *Woman's Estate*. New York: Vintage Books, 1983.
286. ——— and Ann Oakley, editors. *What is Feminism?* New York: Pantheon Books, 1986.
287. Moi, Toril. *Feminist Theory and Simone de Beauvoir*. Oxford: Blackwell, 1990.
288. Mollenkott, Virginia Ramey. *The Divine Feminine*. New York: Crossroad, 1988.
289. ———. *Godding*. New York: Crossroad, 1988.
290. Moltmann-Wendel, Elisabeth. *A Land Flowing with Milk and Honey*. New York: Crossroad, 1989.
291. ———. *The Women around Jesus*. New York: Crossroad, 1988.
292. ——— and Jürgen Moltmann. *God: His and Hers*. London: SCM Press, 1991.
293. Moore, Henrietta L. *Feminism and Anthropology*. Cambridge: Polity Press, 1988.
294. Moraga, Chernie and Gloria Anzaldau, editors. *This Bridge Called My Back*. New York: Kitchen Table and Women of Color Press, 1983.
295. Morgan, Elaine. *The Descent of Woman*. New York: Bantam Books, 1972.
296. Morgan, Robin, editor. *Sisterhood is Global*. New York: Anchor Press/Doubleday, 1984.

297. Morton, Nelle. *The Journey is Home*. Boston: Beacon Press, 1985.
298. Naylor, Gloria. *Linden Hills*. New York: Penguin Books, 1986.
299. ———. *Mama Day*. New York: Vintage Contemporaries, 1989.
300. ———. *The Women of Brewster Place*. New York: Penguin Books, 1983.
301. Nicholson, Linda J., editor. *Feminism/Postmodernism*. London and New York: Routledge, 1990.
302. Nies, Judith. *Seven Women*. New York: Penguin Books, 1978.
303. Noddings, Nel. *Women and Evil*. Berkeley: University of California Press, 1989.
304. Nord, Deborah Epstein. *The Apprenticeship of Beatrice Webb*. Ithaca: Cornell University Press, 1985.
305. Nussbaum, Martha K. *Love's Knowledge: Essays on Philosophy and Literature*. New York and Oxford: Oxford University Press, 1990.
306. Nye, Andrea. *Feminist Theory and the Philosophies of Man*. London and New York: Routledge, 1989.
307. ———. *Words of Power*. New York and London: Routledge, 1990.
308. Ochs, Carol. *Women and Spirituality*. Totowa, New Jersey: Rowman and Littlefield, 1983.
309. O'Connor, Flannery. *Three* (Wise Blood; A Good Man is Hard to Find; The Violent Bear it Away). New York: Signet Books, 1949, 1953, 1955, respectively.
310. Oduyoye, Mercy Amba. *Hearing and Knowing*. Maryknoll, New York: Orbis, 1986.
311. O'Faolain, Julia and Lauro Martines, editors. *Not in God's Image*. New York: Harper Torchbooks, 1973.
312. Okin, Susan Moller. *Women in Western Political Thought*. Princeton, New Jersey: Princeton University Press, 1979.
313. Olson, Carl, editor. *The Book of the Goddess*. New York: Crossroad, 1988.
314. Osbourne, Martha Lee. *Genuine Risk*. Indianapolis: Hackett Publishing Company, 1981.
315. Paglia, Camille. *Sexual Personae*. New Haven and London: Yale University Press, 1990.
316. Pateman, Carol and Elizabeth Gross, editors. *Feminist Challenges*. Boston: Northeastern University Press, 1986.
317. Pearsall, Marilyn. *Women and Values*. Belmont, California: Wadsworth Publishing Company, 1986.
318. Petchesky, Rosalind Pollack. *Abortion and Women's Choice*. Boston: Northeastern University Press, 1984.
319. Phelps, Stanlee and Nancy Austin. *The Assertive Woman*. San Luis Obispo, California: Impact Publishers, 1987.
320. Plaskow, Judith. *Standing Again at Sinai*. San Francisco: Harper and Row, 1990.
321. ——— and Carol P. Christ, editors. *Weaving the Visions*. San Francisco: Harper and Row, 1989.
322. du Plessix Gray, Francine. *Soviet Women Walking the Tightrope*. London: Virago, 1989.
323. Pollak, Vivan R. *Dickinson*. Ithaca and London: Cornell University Press, 1984.
324. Pollock, Griselda. *Vision and Difference*. London and New York: Routledge, 1988.

325. Pomeroy, Sarah B. *Goddesses, Whores, Wives, and Slaves*. New York: Schocken Books, 1975.
326. Powers, Marla N. *Oglala Women*. Chicago and London: University of Chicago Press, 1986.
327. Rabuzzi, Kathryn Allen. *The Sacred and the Feminine*. New York: The Seabury Press, 1982.
328. Rafter, Nicole Hahn and Elizabeth A. Stanko. *Judge, Lawyer, Victim, Thief*. Boston: Northeastern University Press, 1982.
329. Reed, Evelyn. *Women's Evolution*. Pathfinder Press: New York, 1975.
330. Reinharz, Shulamit, with the assistance of Lynn Davidman. *Feminist Methods in Social Research*. New York and Oxford: Oxford University Press, 1992.
331. Rhode, Deborah L. *Theoretical Perspectives on Sexual Difference*. New Haven and London: Yale University Press, 1990.
332. Rhodes, Lynn N. *Co-Creating*. Philadelphia: Westminster Press, 1987.
333. Richards, Janet Radcliffe. *The Sceptical Feminist*. London: Penguin Books, 1980.
334. Riley, Denise. *Am I that Name?* Minneapolis: University of Minnesota, 1988.
335. Rittner, Carol and John K. Roth. *Different Voices*. New York: Paragon House, 1993.
336. Robinson, Lillian. *Sex, Class, and Culture*. New York and London: Methuen, 1986.
337. Ross, Maggie. *Pillars of Flame*. San Francisco: Harper and Row, 1988.
338. Rossi, Alice S., editor. *The Feminist Papers*. Boston: Northeastern University Press, 1988.
339. Rowbotham, Sheila. *The Past is Before Us*. London: Penguin Books, 1989.
340. Ruether, Rosemary Radford. *To Change the World*. New York: Crossroad, 1981.
341. ———. Disputed Questions: *On Being a Christian*. Nashville: Abingdon, 1982.
342. ———. *Faith and Fraticide*. New York: The Seabury Press, 1974.
343. ———. *Gaia and God*. San Francisco: Harper Collins, 1982.
344. ———. *Liberation Theology*. New York: Paulist Press, 1972.
345. ———. *Mary: The Feminine Face of the Church*. Philadelphia: Westminster Press, 1977.
346. ———. *New Woman/New Earth*. New York: The Seabury Press, 1975.
347. ———. *The Radical Kingdom*. New York: Harper and Row, 1970.
348. ———. *Sexism and God-Talk*. Boston: Beacon Press, 1983.
349. ———. *Women-Church*. San Francisco: Harper and Row, 1985.
350. ———. *Womenguides*. Boston: Beacon Press, 1985.
351. ——— and Rosemary Skinner Radford, editors. *Women and Religion in America*, Volumes 1-3. San Francisco: Harper and Row, 1981, 1983, 1986, respectively.
352. Russell, Letty M. *Church in the Round*. Louisville, Kentucky: Westminster/John Knox Press, 1993.
353. ———, editor. *Feminist Interpretation of the Bible*. Philadelphia: Westminster Press, 1985.
354. ———. *The Future of Partnership*. Philadelphia: Westminster Press, 1979.
355. ———. *Growth in Partnership*. Philadelphia: Westminster Press, 1981.
356. ———. *Household of Freedom*. Philadelphia: Westminster Press, 1987.

357. ———. *Human Liberation in a Feminist Perspective: A Theology*. Philadelphia: Westminster Press, 1974.

358. ———, editor. *The Liberating Word*. Philadelphia: Westminster Press, 1976.

359. ———; Kwok Pui-lan; Ada Maria Isasi-Diaz; Katie Geneva Cannon, editors. *Inheriting Our Mothers' Gardens*. Philadelphia: Westminster Press, 1988.

360. Sawicki, Marianne. *Faith and Sexism*. New York: The Seabury Press, 1979.

361. Sayers, Dorothy L. *Mind of the Maker*. San Francisco: Harper and Row, 1941.

362. Schaef, Anne Wilson. *Co-Dependence*. San Francisco: Harper and Row, 1986.

363. ———. *Women's Reality*. San Francisco: Harper and Row, 1985.

364. Scharf, Lois and Joan M. Jensen, editors. *Decades of Discontent*. Boston: Northeastern University Press, 1987.

365. Scheffler, Judith A., editor. *Wall Tappings*. Boston: Northeastern University Press, 1986.

366. Scheman, Naomi. *Engenderings*. New York: Routledge, 1993.

367. Schottroff, Luise. *Let the Oppressed Go Free*. Louisville: Westminster/John Knox Press, 1991.

368. Schneiders, Sandra M. *Women and the Word*. New York and Mahwah, New Jersey: Paulist Press, 1986.

369. Sewell, Marilyn, editor. *Cries of the Spirit*. Boston: Beacon Press, 1991.

370. Shaw, Peter. *The War Against the Intellect*. Iowa City: University of Iowa Press, 1989.

371. Sidel, Ruth. *On Her Own*. New York: Viking Press, 1990.

372. Simmel, Georg. *On Women, Sexuality and Love*. New Haven: Yale University Press, 1984.

373. Smith, Christine M. *Weaving the Sermon*. Louisville: Westminster/John Knox Press, 1989.

374. Smith, Dorothy E. *The Conceptual Practices of Power*. Boston: Northeastern University Press, 1990.

375. ———. *The Everyday World as Problematic*. Boston: Northeastern University Press, 1987.

376. Smith, Jackie M. *Women, Faith, and Economic Justice*. Philadelphia: Westminster Press, 1985.

377. Smith, Joan. *Misogynies*. London: Faber and Faber, 1989.

378. Soble, Alan, editor. *Philosophy of Sex*. Totowa, New Jersey: Rowman and Allanheld, 1980.

379. ———. *Pornography*. New Haven and London: Yale University Press, 1986.

380. ———. *The Strength of the Weak*. Philadelphia: Westminster Press, 1984.

381. Soelle (Sölle), Dorothee. *Of War and Love*. Maryknoll, New York: Orbis Books, 1983.

382. ———. *The Window of Vulnerablilty*. Minneapolis: Fortress Press, 1990.

383. Sommers, Christine Hoff. *Who Stole Feminism? How Women have Betrayed Women*. New York: Simon and Schuster, 1994.

384. Soskice, Janet Martin. *After Eve*. London: Marshall Pickering, 1990.

385. Spackman, Barbara. *Decadent Genealogies*. Ithaca and London: Cornell University Press, 1989.
386. Spelman, Elizabeth V. *Inessential Woman*. Boston: Beacon Press, 1988.
387. Spender, Dale, editor. *Feminist Theorists*. New York: Pantheon Books, 1983.
388. ———. *There's Always Been a Women's Movement in This Country*. London: Pandora Press, 1983.
389. Spretnak, Charlene. *Lost Goddesses of Early Greece*. Boston: Beacon Press, 1978.
390. ———, editor. *The Politics of Women's Spirituality*. Garden City, New York: Anchor Press/Doubleday, 1982.
391. Stagg, Evelyn and Frank Stagg. *Woman in the World of Jesus*. Philadelphia: Westminster Press, 1978.
392. Stalney, Liz and Sue Wise. *Breaking Out Again*. New York: Routledge, 1983.
393. Starhawk (pseudonym of Miriam Simos). *The Spiral Dance*. San Francisco: Harper and Row, 1979.
394. Stein, Edith. *Woman*, Volume II. Washington, D.C.: ICS Publications, 1987.
395. Steinem, Gloria. *Moving Beyond Words*. New York: Simon and Schuster, 1994.
396. ———. *Outrageous Acts and Everyday Rebellions*. New York: Signet Books, 1986.
397. ———. *Revolution from Within*. Boston: Little, Brown and Company, 1992.
398. Stevens, Maryanne, editor. *Reconstructing the Christ Symbol: Essays in Feminist Christology*. New York and Mahwah, New Jersey: Paulist Press, 1993.
399. Stratton, Joanna. *Pioneer Woman*. New York: Simon and Schuster, 1981.
400. Suchocki, Marjorie Hewitt. *God-Christ-Church*. New York: Crossroad, 1988.
401. Swidler, Leonard. *Biblical Affirmations of Woman*. Philadelphia: Westminster Press, 1979.
402. Tamez, Elsa. *Bible of the Oppressed*. Maryknoll, New York: Orbis Books, 1982.
403. ———, editor. *Through Her Eyes*. Maryknoll, New York: Orbis Books, 1989.
404. Tavris, Carol and Carole Wade. *The Longest War*. San Diego: Harcourt Brace Jovanovich, 1984.
405. Taylor, Barbara. *Eve and the New Jerusalem*. London: Virago Press, 1983.
406. Teish, Luisah. *Jambalaya*. San Francisco: Harper and Row, 1985.
407. Tennis, Diane. *Is God the Only Reliable Father?* Philadelphia: Westminster Press, 1985.
408. Teresa of Avila. *The Interior Castle*. New York, Ramsey, New Jersey, and Toronto: Paulist Press, 1979.
409. Terrien, Samuel. *Till the Heart Sings*. Philadelphia: Fortress Press, 1985.
410. Teubal, Savina J. *Hagar the Egyptian*. San Francisco: Harper and Row, 1990.
411. Thompson, Dorothy. *Queen Victoria*. London: Virago Press, 1990.
412. Thurston, Bonnie Bowman. *The Widows*. Minneapolis: Fortress Press, 1989.
413. Toor, Djohariah. *The Road by the River*. San Francisco: Harper and Row, 1987.
414. Trebilcot, Joyce. *Mothering*. Savage, Maryland: Rowman and Littlefield, 1983.
415. Trible, Phyllis. *God and the Rhetoric of Sexuality*. Philadelphia: Fortress Press, 1978.
416. ———. *Texts of Terror*. Philadelphia: Fortress Press, 1984.
417. Trollope, Anthony. *Nina Balatica, Linda Tressely*. Oxford: Oxford University Press, 1991.

418. Tuana, Nancy. *The Less Noble Sex: Scientific, Religious, and Philosophical Copnceptions of Woman's Nature*. Bloomington and Indianapolis: Indiana University Press, 1993.
419. Ulanov, Ann Bedford. *Receiving Woman*. Philadelphia: Westminster Press, 1981.
420. Vetterling-Braggin, Mary, editor. *Femininity, Masculinity, and Androgyny*. Totowa, New Jersey: Rowman and Allanheld, 1982.
421. ———. *Sexist Language*. Totowa, New Jersey: Littlefield, Adams, and Co., 1981.
422. ———; Frederick A. Elliston; Jane English, editors. *Feminism and Philosophy*. Totowa, New Jersey: Rowman and Littlefield, 1977.
423. Walker, Barbara G. *The Skeptical Feminist*. San Francisco: Harper and Row, 1987.
424. ———. *The Woman's Dictionary of Symbols and Sacred Objects*. San Francisco: Harper and Row, 1988.
425. ———. *The Woman's Encyclopedia of Myths and Secrets*. San Francisco: Harper Collins, 1983.
426. Warren, Mary Anne. *Gendercide*. Totowa, New Jersey: Rowman and Allanheld, 1985.
427. Weaver, Mary Jo. *New Catholic Women*. San Francisco: Harper and Row, 1986.
428. Weber, Alison. *Teresa of Avila*. Princeton, New Jersey: Princeton University Press, 1990.
429. Weber, Christin Lore. *Blessings*. San Francisco: Harper and Row, 1989.
430. ———. *WomanChrist*. San Francisco: Harper and Row, 1987.
431. Webster, John C.B. and Ellen Low Webster, editors. *The Church and Women in the Third World*. Philadelphia: Westminster Press, 1985.
432. Wehr, Demaris S. *Jung and Feminism*. Boston: Beacon Press, 1987.
433. Welch, Sharon D. *A Feminist Ethic of Risk*. Minneapolis: Fortress Press, 1990.
434. ———. *Communities of Resistance and Solidarity*. Maryknoll, New York: Orbis Books, 1985.
435. Whitmont, Edward C. *Return of the Goddess*. New York: Crossroad, 1982.
436. Wiethaus, Ulrike, editor. *Maps of Flesh and Light: The Religious Experience of Medieval Women Mystics*. Syracuse: Syracuse University Press, 1993.
437. Williams, Juanita H. *Psychology of Women*. New York and London: W.W. Norton and Company, 1987.
438. Winter, Miriam Therese. *WomanPrayer WomanSong*. Oak Park, Illinois: Meyer Stone Books, 1987.
439. Wire, Antoinette Clark. *The Corinthian Woman Prophets*. Minneapolis: Fortress Press, 1990.
440. Wolf, Naomi. *The Beauty Myth*. London: Vintage Press, 1990.
441. Wollstonecraft, Mary. *Political Writings*. Toronto: University of Toronto Press, 1993.
442. ———. *A Vindication of the Rights of Women*. Buffalo, New York: Prometheus Books, 1989.
443. Woolf, Virginia. *Orlando*. Oxford: Oxford University Press, 1992.
444. ———. *A Room of One's Own; Three Guineas*. Oxford: Oxford University Press, 1992.
445. Wynne, Patrice. *The Womanspirit Sourcebook*. San Francisco: Harper and Row, 1988.

446. Yorburg, Betty. *Sexual Identity*. Huntington, New York: Robert E. Kreiger, 1981.
447. Young, Iris Marion. *Throwing Like a Girl and Other Essays in Feminist Philosophy and Social Theory*. Bloomington, Indiana: Indiana University Press, 1990.
448. Young, Pamela Dickey. *Feminist Theology/Christian Theology*. Minneapolis: Fortress Press, 1990.

INDEX